ROUTLEDGE LIBRARY EDITIONS: 18TH CENTURY PHILOSOPHY

Volume 12

PHILOSOPHICAL COMMENTARIES BY GEORGE BERKELEY

PHILOSOPHICAL COMMENTARIES
BY GEORGE BERKELEY

EDITED AND WITH AN INTRODUCTION
BY GEORGE H. THOMAS

LONDON AND NEW YORK

First published in 1989 by Garland Publishing, Inc.

This edition first published in 2019
by Routledge
2 Park Square, Milton Park, Abingdon, Oxon OX14 4RN

and by Routledge
52 Vanderbilt Avenue, New York, NY 10017

Routledge is an imprint of the Taylor & Francis Group, an informa business

© 1989 garland Publishing, Inc.

All rights reserved. No part of this book may be reprinted or reproduced or utilised in any form or by any electronic, mechanical, or other means, now known or hereafter invented, including photocopying and recording, or in any information storage or retrieval system, without permission in writing from the publishers.

Trademark notice: Product or corporate names may be trademarks or registered trademarks, and are used only for identification and explanation without intent to infringe.

British Library Cataloguing in Publication Data
A catalogue record for this book is available from the British Library

ISBN: 978-0-367-13518-8 (Set)
ISBN: 978-0-429-02691-1 (Set) (ebk)
ISBN: 978-0-367-13797-7 (Volume 12) (hbk)
ISBN: 978-0-367-13798-4 (Volume 12) (pbk)
ISBN: 978-0-429-02862-5 (Volume 12) (ebk)

Publisher's Note
The publisher has gone to great lengths to ensure the quality of this reprint but points out that some imperfections in the original copies may be apparent.

Disclaimer
The publisher has made every effort to trace copyright holders and would welcome correspondence from those they have been unable to trace.

Philosophical Commentaries by George Berkeley

TRANSCRIBED FROM THE MANUSCRIPT AND EDITED WITH AN INTRODUCTION AND INDEX BY GEORGE H. THOMAS, EXPLANATORY NOTES BY A. A. LUCE

GARLAND PUBLISHING, INC.
NEW YORK & LONDON 1989.

For a complete list of the titles in this series,
see the final pages of this volume.

Library of Congress Cataloging-in-Publication Data

Berkeley, George, 1685–1753.
 [Commonplace book]
  Philosophical commentaries/ George Berkeley; transcribed from
 the manuscript and edited with an introduction and index by
 George H. Thomas; explanatory notes by A. A. Luce.
  p. cm. — (The Philosophy of George Berkeley)
  Reprint. Originally published: Alliance, Ohio: Mount Union
 College, c 1976.   Includes Index.
  ISBN 0-8240-2440-0
  1. Philosophy—Early works to 1800. I. Thomas, George H.
 (George Hasson), 1928– . II. Luce, A. A. (Arthur Aston, 1882– . III.
 Title. IV. Series.
   [B1341.T47]   1989   192—dc19   89-30831

Printed on acid-free, 250-year-life paper.
Printed on United States of America

Acknowledgements

I wish to thank those person who had a part in the making of my edition of Berkeley's _Philosophical Commentaries_. Professor A. A. Luce, of Trinity College, Dublin, introduced me to the fascinating manuscript of the _Commentaries_ through his 1944 edition, revised his excellent notes from that edition and permitted me to print them with my edition, discussed my work with me during a year that I spent at Trinity College and afterward engaged in an extensive correspondence with me on specific entries and general problems with my edition. Professor E. J. Furlong frequently and helpfully discussed my project with me, and together with the officials of Trinity College gave me a year's position as "research associate" on their staff with all their facilities at my disposal. Dr. David Berman, also of Trinity College, gave freely of his time, knowledge, and advice. He proofread my "Introduction" and gave me several beneficial comments. To my own college, Mount Union College, I owe a debt for the sabbatical leave and many other aids that enabled me to begin and complete this work. Dr. Bertil Belfrage, of the University of Lund, Sweden, worked closely with me in my research. He corrected many of my readings of the manuscript, confirmed others, and reassured me even when we disagreed. He painstakingly proofread my entire transcription, and generously shared his time and scholarship with me. Professor C. M. Turbayne, of the University of Rochester, strengthened me in my endeavor by giving me helpful advice. Mr. T. C. Skeat, Keeper of Manuscripts, and the British Museum were most gracious on several occasions. Professor Frederick Oppermann, of Mount Union College, proofread my "Introduction" and gave me many helpful suggestions. My wife Rebecca, my daughter Catherine, and Mrs. Mary Lou Snyder spent many hours proofreading my typescript with me. To all these persons I am deeply grateful.

TABLE OF CONTENTS

Editor's Introduction
    The Nature and Purpose of the
        Philosophical Commentaries i
    The Two Notebooks and Their Order v
    The Dating of the Manuscript. ix
    The Marginal Letters and Signs xv
    The Manuscript
        Description xviii
        Catalogue of Contents. xix
        Specimen of the Manuscript xxiii
    A History of the Editions xxv

Philosophical Commentaries: the Text
    Notebook B. 1
    Notebook A 49

Luce's Notes
    A General Note 117
    Table of Key Doctrinal Notes 118
    Notes on the Entries. 119

Index 330

EDITOR'S INTRODUCTION

In this new edition of George Berkeley's Philosophical Commentaries I have tried to satisfy existing needs for (1) an accurate transcription of Berkeley's manuscript, (2) an introduction to set it in perspective, (3) extensive notes to aid in interpreting it, and (4) a full index to facilitate the use of it. My transcription I made first, striving to avoid problems of perspective and interpretation that might bias my editorial work. Interpretation I have left to Professor Luce's excellent notes. The perspective I must try to provide in the following introduction.

The Nature and Purpose of the Commentaries

The present title of the Philosophical Commentaries provides a clue to its nature and purpose. Luce is convinced that Berkeley began the Commentaries as commentaries on his own earlier writings on immaterialism. So in his 1944 edition of the notebooks Luce changed the name to fit his view.

Before Luce's 1944 edition the notebooks were called the Commonplace Book. This earlier title, as well as the new one, reveals a view of their nature and purpose. Fraser, who gave this title to his 1871 edition, saw the notebooks as "random speculations" and "stray thoughts," and referred to the "chaos" of Berkeley's remarks.[1] In his 1901 edition he spoke of the ". . . random entries or provisional memoranda, meant only for private use."[2] So he

---

[1] Alexander Campbell Fraser (ed.), The Works of George Berkeley (Oxford: Clarendon Press, 1871), IV xii, 27-35, 419n. For the same text see: Alexander Campbell Fraser, Life and Letters of George Berkeley (Oxford: Clarendon Press, 1871), pp. xii, 27-35, 419n.

[2] Alexander Campbell Fraser (ed.), The Works of George Berkeley (Oxford: Clarendon Press, 1901), I 4-5.

called it the Commonplace Book.

Fraser'd view and his title set the pattern for the interpreters who followed him. Even R. I. Aaron, who understood a great deal about the Commentaries, spoke of it as Berkeley's "private jottings."[1]

It was not until 1932 that another view entered the literature. Then Luce came out in opposition to the scrapbook-diary-jottings interpretation, and presented a view of the notebooks as Berkeley's "storehouse and workshop." He insisted that the notebooks (the Commentaries proper as distinguished from the peripheral parts of the manuscript) are "a book, that is a purposeful composition."[2] As evidence of the purposeful, orderly, and bookish character of the Commentaries, Luce cited: the form of the notebooks with their carefully observed margins and system of marginal signs; the regular spacing between the entries; Berkeley's reference to the entries as "sections"; his reference to his literary plans and strategy; his self-given advice on style and language; the blank verso pages with occasionally added corrections, criticism, and interpretation; and his use of many of the entries, often verbatim, in his published works.[3] Luce argued that Berkeley used the notebooks to prepare his materials for publication. They were the "storehouse and workshop" out of which Berkeley produced the New Theory of Vision, the "Draft Introduction" to the Principles, the Principles as published, and Part II of the Principles (which he lost and never re-wrote). Therefore, Luce held that ". . . the sole and adequate purpose. . . was authorship."[4]

---

[1] R. I. Aaron, "Locke and Berkeley's Commonplace Book," Mind, XL (October, 1931), p. 445.
[2] A. A. Luce, "Berkeley's Commonplace Book -- Its Date, Purpose, Structure, and Marginal Signs," Hermathena, XXII (1932), p. 99.
[3] I have taken some of this list of evidence from Luce's expansion of his argument in his later articles.
[4] Luce, "Berkeley's Commonplace Book," p. 101.

In 1943 Luce advanced his "commentaries" theory.[1] He held that the "storehouse and workshop" explanation is correct as it explains why Berkeley wrote and how he used what he wrote. But it is inadequate for it does not explain why he wrote in the particular form in which he did. It is the latter question that Luce sought to answer in his theory.

Luce raised what he referred to as the question of the original purpose of Berkeley's writing. This original purpose, he insisted, was Berkeley's commentary on his own early draft on immaterialism, written in 1705 or 1706 shortly after Berkeley's graduation and now lost. Therefore, the Commentaries is a "half-way house," an intermediate stage rather than the initial stage in Berkeley's literary career.

Luce drew his arguments mainly from internal evidence. He argued that "ye immaterial hypothesis" (entry 19) appears in entries 17-24, on the second page of the Commentaries, "fully fledged, and thought out into its remoter consequences, with objections to it stated and answered."[2] This maturity of thought and form shows Berkeley examining, criticizing, sifting, and rewriting an earlier draft, not asserting his thesis for the first time.

Even the earlier entries (1-16) on time and eternity, which are so brief and cryptic in themselves, fall into place when viewed as comments on an earlier draft on these themes. Luce pointed out that Berkeley actually mentioned such an early draft on time in a letter written in 1730 to Samuel Johnson.[3]

---

[1] A. A. Luce, "The Purpose and the Date of Berkeley's Commonplace Book," Proceedings of the Royal Irish Academy, XLVIII (February, 1943), pp. 273-279. See also A. A. Luce, "Editor's Introduction," Philosophical Commentaries generally called the Commonplace Book -- George Berkeley (London: Thomas Nelson and Sons, Ltd., 1944), pp. xxxii-xxxix.
[2] Luce, "Purpose and Date," p. 275.
[3] A. A. Luce and T. E. Jessop (eds.), The Works of George Berkeley (London: Thomas Nelson, 1949), II 293.

Luce also called attention to Berkeley's extensive remarks on vision in the Commentaries.[1] Most of the references are in notebook B, the earliest written notebook. There his theory of vision appears in full development with all the problems of the New Theory of Vision thought out in detail. Luce insisted that some of these entries, e.g., 224-227, cannot stand on their own feet. The best example is entry 224 ("Query whether the sensations of sight arising from a man's head be liker the sensations of touch proceeding from thence or from his legs?") which is almost nonsense when taken alone. Taken as a comment on an early draft of the New Theory of Vision, sections 101ff. (on the inverted retinal image), it is quite intelligible. Therefore, these entries appear to be "comments, not compositions."

Luce maintained that in two specific entries in the Commentaries Berkeley actually referred to an earlier draft, and may have done so in two additional ones.[2] Berkeley's advice to himself concerning his language in 209 and 300 may well have referred to what he had already written, especially 209 in which he said he had to "correct" his language. In entry 858, marked with the marginal "I" for "Introduction," Berkeley said he had to cancel all passages of a certain type. This Luce took as a reference to a draft of the "Draft Introduction" to the Principles, making 858 a comment on a written document. In entry 265 Berkeley referred to "my first arguings" in a categorical parallel to Locke's arguings (the Essay) which were, of course, written. This latter passage Luce saw as an "almost certain" indication that Berkeley was commenting on a written draft of his own.

Luce did not claim to have established his theory beyond the possibility of doubt, but he did insist that the case for the commentary character of the notebooks was very strong. It was strong enough for him to change its title from the Commonplace Book to the Philosophical Commentaries.

---

[1] Luce, "Purpose and Date," pp. 276-277.
[2] Ibid., pp. 277-278. See also Luce, "Editor's Introduction," pp. xxxvii-xxxix.

One other interesting view of the purpose of the Commentaries is that of John Wild, originally published in 1932.[1] Wild's conjecture partly agrees with Luce's theory and partly disagrees. He held that the original purpose of the notebooks was as commentaries, but he suggested that Berkeley may have begun them as comments on Locke's Essay (which Berkeley was reading at that time). Wild did not fully substantiate his view, but he did offer enough parallels between the early entries in the Commentaries and Locke's Essay to make his view deserving of further study.

We may sum up by saying that the nature and purpose of the Commentaries is not one but several. Some of the entries are random jottings, "'out of his [Berkeley's] head,' as we say, straight into the notebooks;"[2] Others and the way they were used show the Commentaries to be Berkeley's "storehouse and workshop," out of which he wrote his earlier published works. However, in its original purpose, the Commentaries may well have been intended as just that -- commentaries on an already written text, Berkeley's own earlier writings on immaterialism or at least on Locke's Essay.

The Two Notebooks and Their Order

The manuscript of the Commentaries consists of two notebooks bound in the reverse order. Theodor Lorenz was the first to discover this important fact.[3] He noticed that there were marks of an earlier binding on the back of folio 95 (in the middle of the manuscript as bound), and that the pages of the manuscript were of two different sizes. Having determined that there were two notebooks, he went

---

[1] John Wild, George Berkeley (New York: Russell & Russell, Inc., 1962), pp. 22-24, 53.
[2] Luce, "Purpose and Date," p. 274.
[3] Theodor Lorenz, "Weitere Beiträge zur Lebensgeschichte George Berkeleys (IV)," Archiv für Geschichte der Philosophie, XVIII (1905), pp. 553-554.

on to suggest that they had been bound in the wrong order.

G. A. Johnston labeled the notebooks, as bound, "A" and "B"; and, following Lorenz's suggestion, printed them in his edition of the Commentaries in the reverse order, B-A.[1] He also acted on another conjecture of Lorenz -- which was mistaken -- and transposed entries 377-399 to the end of the notebooks.

In his edition Luce accepted Lorenz's theory of the two notebooks and the reversed binding, but he correctly restored entries 377-399 to their proper place at the end of notebook A.[2]

We need not dwell on the division of the two notebooks. Lorenz's observations of the original binding marks and the different sized pages are obvious to anyone who examines the manuscript.

However, any rearrangement of the manuscript demands justification. So we must examine closely the arguments for reversing the order of the notebooks from A-B to B-A. Three types of arguments have been advanced in this case, arguments from dates, doctrines, and style. My judgment is that arguments from style are quite convincing, while those from dates and doctrines are inconclusive.

The argument from the dates in the notebooks points us in the right direction. In notebook A we find the date August 28, 1708; in notebook B, January 10, 1705 (1706, New Style) and December 7, 1706. This would incline us to put notebook B before notebook A. However, since the dates are outside the Commentaries proper, refer to specific events (the signing of the statutes of societies and "the Adventure of the Shirt"), and could possibly have been writ-

---

[1] G. A. Johnston (ed.), Berkeley's Commonplace Book (London: Faber & Faber, 1930).
[2] A. A. Luce (ed.), Philosophical Commentaries generally called the Commonplace Book -- George Berkeley (London: Thomas Nelson and Sons, Ltd., 1944).

ten into the notebooks at later times -- all three dates could have been written on the same day --, the dates do not bind us to a reversal of the notebooks' order.

The doctrinal arguments are very important in interpreting the Commentaries, but there is reason to hold them in suspense. It is too easy to become engrossed in problems of interpretation and questions of whether and when Berkeley changed his mind on certain points. There is also a danger of circularity here. We may indeed use a development in Berkeley's thought to justify reversing the order of the notebooks; but that very pattern of development derives from our reversal of the notebooks.

While the arguments from the dates and doctrinal development are suggestive, it is the stylistic arguments that are most conclusive. Here we have objective and unambiguous evidence. Perhaps the most imaginative argument comes from Luce's study of the orthography of the word "idea" in Berkeley's early writings.[1] In a copy of the Of Infinites, which Berkeley read publically November 19, 1707, "idea" is always written with lower case "i's"; and so it is in the "Sermon on Life and Immortality," dated January 11, 1708. In the early part of notebook B of the Commentaries, "idea" is also written with lower case "i's." Toward the end of notebook B and in the beginning of notebook A, we find a mixture of lower case and capital "i's." However, toward the end of notebook A, "idea" is written exclusively with the capital "I." And in the "Draft Introduction" to the Principles, dated November 15-December 18, 1708, and in the manuscript of the Principles 85-145, we find "idea" written always with a capital "I." On this basis alone the only reasonable conclusion is that Berkeley wrote the notebooks in the order of B-A.

There is also the argument from the use of the word "Nihilarians." In entry 633, in notebook A, Berkeley reminded himself to treat the mathematicians with respect

---

[1] Luce, "Berkeley's Commonplace Book," pp. 117-122.

and not to call them "Nihilarians" ("Mem: . . . to Confute the Mathematicians with the utmost civility & respect and not to call them Nihilarians. &c:"). He followed that advice to the end of notebook A. But the question arises, where did he call them "Nihilarians"? -- At the end of notebook B! In entries 372 and 399, in notebook B, Berkeley sarcastically referred to the "Nihilarians"; and he continued with this phrase in the beginning of notebook A, e.g., entry 471. Furthermore, toward the end of notebook B he frequently referred to the "nothings" of the mathematicians (e.g., 319, 338, 345, 384, 394), a practice that he continued in the early part of notebook A (e.g., 439, 448, 449, 464, 466, 488, 492). Therefore, Berkeley treated the mathematicians with a complete lack of "civility & respect" at the end of notebook B[1] and the beginning of A, even calling them "nihilarians." In entry 633 he determined to discontinue this practice in his writing, and did so for the rest of notebook A -- the second written notebook!

Another stylistic argument centers around Berkeley's use of the term "powers." In entry 802, in notebook A, he reminded himself not to speak of sensible objects as powers or combinations of such ("Not to mention the Combinations of Powers but to say the things the effects themselves to really exist even w^n not actually ~~seen~~ perceiv'd but still with relation to perception."). He discussed sensible objects as "powers" in the beginning of notebook B (e.g., 41, 52, 80), and even referred to them as "combinations of powers" (293). In the latter sections of notebook B and in A he never spoke of sensible objects as "powers." He used "power" simply to refer to an "occasion,"

---

[1] It is this section which Lorenz and Johnston transposed to the end of notebook A, making it the concluding section of the <u>Commentaries</u>. The fact that it includes the uncivil treatment of mathematicians and the reference to them as "Nihilarians," as well as a mixture of small and capital "i's" on "ideas" is enough to refute the conjecture upon which the transposition of entries 377-399 to the end was based.

the observable relation of cause and effect (e.g., 461, 493), or else he used it for the causal power of God (e.g., 298, 433, 856). Therefore, his rejection of "powers" in entry 802 must be later than his use of the term in notebook B -- the first written notebook!

Lastly, Berkeley's notebooks reveal a similar stylistic change with the term "person." In entry 713, in notebook A, he stated his decision to use the term "mind" where he had formerly used "person," and reminded himself to try to avoid using "person" ("The Concrete of the Will & understanding I must Call the Mind not person, lest offense be given, there being but one volition acknowleged to be God. Mem: Carefully to omit defining of Person, or making much mention of it."). Berkeley used "person" as a technical term only in the beginning of notebook B (e.g., 14, 25, 142, 185, 192, 200)[1] -- therefore, the order B-A.

We have no information about when and by whom the notebooks were bound as they now are; but there can be no doubt that they were bound in the wrong order. Read them as A-B, and they yield only confusion and error. Read them in the corrected order, B-A, and the Commentaries become of utmost value in tracing Berkeley's early doctrinal development.

The Dating

Before we try to date Berkeley's Philosophical Commentaries, we must specify exactly what we are trying to date. Our task is to date the Commentaries proper, not the peripheral parts of the manuscript. The manuscript in which the Commentaries is found contains many additional sections: statutes of college societies, queries on Locke's philosophy, sermon notes, mathematical equations, a copy of Berkeley's A Description of the Cave of Dunmore, etc.

---

[1] I am ignoring Berkeley's ordinary, non-technical use of the word in entries such as 36, 285, 859, and 860.

These sections lie outside our present investigation. We must date the series of entries, now numbered 1-888, that constitute the Commentaries proper.

In addition to the main stream of continuous entries (1-888) Berkeley made a great many changes and additions. He struck out words and phrases. He changed others. And he added entire entries on some of the verso pages. These cancellations, changes, and additions are impossible to date precisely. In fact, we cannot even be sure whether many of these revisions were made with the original entries or later. Therefore, what we are to date are the first and last entries of the series, entry 1 on folio 104 and entry 888 on folio 94.

There are several types of arguments that can be, and have been used to date the Commentaries. I shall concentrate on three: arguments from the peripheral sections of the manuscript, an approach from biographical coherence, and arguments from particular entries. First, many scholars have argued from dates recorded in the peripheral parts of the manuscript. On folio 96, verso, opposite the beginning of the statutes of the Friday Society, Berkeley wrote, "Mem. the following statutes were agreed to & sign'd by the Society consisting of eight person, Jan: 10. A.D. 1705 [1706, New Style]." And on folio 103, recto, he wrote the statutes of the Thursday Society adding that they were signed on "December the Seventh in the year one thousand seven hundred and Six." These two dates have been used in dating the Commentaries. January 10, 1706, has been taken as the beginning of the entire manuscript and December 7, 1706, as the beginning of the Commentaries proper. On folio 95, recto, Berkeley wrote, "August 28th. 1708 wit the Adventure of the Shirt." This latter date has been taken as the closing date of the Commentaries.

However, there seems to be no way in which temporal connections can be established with any certainty between the peripheral sections of the manuscript and the Commentaries proper. Berkeley sometimes left pages of his manuscripts blank and filled them later, and he did not enter the different sections of the "Commentaries manuscript" in a regular order.¹ So he could have written these passages with the dates into the manuscript at much later times. We can even conceive of Berkeley's entering all three dated passages into the manuscript on the same day. Therefore, argument from the dates in the manuscript are inconclusive.

Another argument from the peripheries is the public-private notebook argument. Some scholars have maintained that since the first notebook began with the statutes of the college society (or societies), it was originally the minute book of the society.² Then the notebook would have remained public property (or at least have been restricted to public use -- some have suggested that Berkeley was the

---

¹The only extant manuscript of Berkeley's Principles (British Museum, Add. MS. 39304) contains only sections 85-145. Berkeley left blank a large number of pages at the beginning of the manuscript before writing section 85 on folio 35. In the "Commentaries manuscript" (British Musuem, Add. MS. 39305) he probably wrote the long demonstration on folios 161-162 before the surrounding folios on mathematics and originally left the surrounding folios blank [See A. A. Luce, "Another Look at Berkeley's Notebooks," Hermathena, CX (1970) p. 11.] . Berkeley wrote the mathematical equations on folios 168, verso, and 169, recto and verso, before A Description of the Cave of Dunmore. After he had written the equations, he inverted the notebook and, starting from the back, copied the cave essay onto the blank pages up to the equations, finishing it on the folio following the equations. The fact that Berkeley wrote the queries on Locke's philosophy on folio 102, verso as well as recto, indicates that he filled folio 103 before 102. And he probably filled folio 95 before 94, since the last entries of the Commentaries (880-888) were written small and crowded into the bottom half of folio 95.

²Aaron, "Locke and Berkeley's Commonplace Book," pp. 443-445. Luce, "Berkeley's Commonplace Book," p. 100. Luce, "Purpose and Date," pp. 281-283. Luce, "Editor's Introduction," pp. xxix-xxx. Luce, "Another Look," p. 16.

secretary of the society[1]) until some time after December 7, 1706. Only after that date would Berkeley have been free to convert the notebook to his own private use -- for his own Commentaries.

Besides the objection already raised concerning the peripheral dates, there is another difficulty for this view. The statutes explicitly state that they were signed. Yet as they stand in the notebook there are no signatures. This lack implies that this was not the official minute book of the society.[2] Therefore, there is no reason to think that this was ever a public notebook. It was probably Berkeley's own private notebook from the beginning.

There are other arguments from the peripheral sections of the manuscript which I shall not discuss. They are all based on a supposed connection between the peripheral dates and the Commentaries. If we take away the support of the peripheral dates, we take away the cogency of the arguments. Therefore, we have reason to doubt all of this type of argument.

The approach from biographical coherence is a much more significant type of argument. Luce's dating of the Commentaries rests in large measure upon its consistency with relevant biographical data. To understand this approach we must survey the relevant events of Berkeley's life from his graduation to his publication of the Principles.[3]

Berkeley received his B.A. degree from Trinity Col-

---

[1]Luce, "Purpose and Date," p. 281; "Editor's Introduction," p. xxx; "Another Look," p. 16.
[2]See Bertil Belfrage, "George Berkeley's 'Philosophical Commentaries': a Review of Prof. A. A. Luce's Editions," Logik Rätt och Moral: filosofiska studier tillägnade Manfred Moritz, S. Halldén et al. (ed.) (Lund: Studentlitterature, 1969), p. 26.
[3]A. A. Luce, The Life of George Berkeley (London: Thomas Nelson and Sons, Ltd., 1949), pp. 36-51.

lege, Dublin, in the spring of 1704. Hoping for a fellowship, he stayed on "in College" with plenty of leisure to study and to write. During this period Berkeley wrote the Arithmetica and Miscellanea Mathematica (both published later, in 1707), Of Infinites (published only posthumously), and a draft on immaterialism (postulated by Luce). He also participated in the Friday Society, organized January 10, 1706, as a natural history society. In fact, Berkeley read his A Description of the Cave of Dunmore at the opening meeting of the Friday Society.

On September 24, 1706, the anticipated fellowship vacancy occurred. William Mullart vacated his fellowship and accepted the "college living" of Clinish. Berkeley then devoted his time to study and preparation for the fellowship examination, to be held at the end of eight months. During this period of concentrated study he published his Arithmetica and Miscellanea Mathematica and participated in the Thursday Society which was organized December 7, 1706, for the study of the "new philosophy."

Berkeley excelled on the examination and was appointed Fellow of the College, June 9, 1707. It is in this period of the summer vacation of 1707 (beginning in July) that Luce located the beginning of the Philosophical Commentaries. During this period of only minor responsibilities as a Junior Fellow, Berkeley worked continuously and systematically on the Commentaries, read Of Infinites before the Dublin Society on November 19, 1707, wrote a draft of the "Draft Introduction" to the Principles (postulated by Luce), and finished the series of entries in the Commentaries in August, 1708. From November 15, 1708 to December 18, 1708, Berkeley revised his earlier draft to form the "Draft Introduction" to the Principles. He then published the New Theory of Vision in May or June, 1709, and the Principles in May, 1710.

Apart from supporting arguments, which we shall examine next, the approach from biographical coherence is only an hypothesis yet to be substantiated. However, even to this extent it is quite important in that it sets the general context in which we must consider the dating of the Commentaries.

The supporting arguments are those from the particular entries within the Commentaries. We have a specific date for Berkeley's Of Infinites (read November 19, 1707). Scholars have tried to connect certain entries with that work and, therefore, with that date. Luce connected Of Infinites with entries 351-358 of the Commentaries.[1] He noted that these entries (duplicated in 415-425) correspond "point after point, page after page" to Of Infinites. Moreover, the authorities quoted in Of Infinites are those referred to in this section (the 300's) of the Commentaries. The no-words-without-ideas doctrine of Of Infinites appears at the head of the demonstration in entry 378. And the reference to Newton in entry 374 -- that his theory of fluxions does not necessitate infinite divisibility -- is directly related to the theme of Of Infinites. Therefore, Luce connected Of Infinites and its November 19, 1707 date with entries in the 300's.

In entry 709 of the Commentaries Berkeley quoted from Some Familiar Letters between Mr. Locke and Several of His Friends. This work was published in May or June, 1708. Judging from Locke's popularity at Trinity College, Dublin, and Berkeley's interest in him, Berkeley would probably have read the work shortly after its publication. So entry 709 was written after (probably shortly after) May/June, 1708.

In entry 858 Berkeley again gave himself stylistic advice -- to cancel all passages that promised demonstration of his principles. Furthermore, he marked the entry with a marginal "I" for "Introduction." Luce connected that entry with his postulated early draft of the "Draft Introduction."[2] In entry 586 Berkeley said that he would set forth the nature of demonstration in the "Introduction." Luce claimed that "no doubt he [Berkeley] did so write at that

---

[1] Luce, "Another Look," pp. 20-22.
[2] Luce's reason for postulating an earlier draft of the "Draft Introduction" to the Principles is that the "Draft Introduction" appears to be a very advanced form, almost ready for the press, with quotations from Locke written out in italics.

time in the Introduction of that time;"[1] So the written and cancelled passages, Luce insisted, were not in the "Draft Introduction" but in the postulated earlier draft of the "Draft Introduction." Therefore, since Berkeley began the "Draft Introduction" on November 15, 1708, he must have written entry 858 some time before November, 1708.[2]

If we take the arguments from particular entries as reasonably compelling we can draw the following conclusion: entry 858 was written before November, 1708; 709 after June, 1708; and the 300's around November, 1707. These dates correlate well with Luce's hypothesis based on biographical coherence.[3] Therefore, we can say with probability that Berkeley began the <u>Commentaries</u> (entry 1) in the summer of 1707 and made the last entry (entry 888) in the fall of 1708.

Marginal Letters and Signs

One of the distinctive aspects of the <u>Philosophical Commentaries</u> is the system of marginal letters and signs that Berkeley employed. In fact, it is this marginalia that marks off the <u>Commentaries</u> proper from the other contents of the notebooks. Only the central part of the manuscript, the con-

---

[1] Luce, "Another Look," p. 21.
[2] There are other entries in the <u>Commentaries</u> that can be dated relative to external events, but they admit such an inclusive time span that they are of little significance. In entry 374 Berkeley refers to Newton as "Sir Isaac." Since Newton was knighted April 16, 1705, entry 374 must have been written after that date. Berkeley used entry 748 in a section of the "Draft Introduction" dated December 2, 1708. Therefore, entry 748 must have been written before that date. However, little is gained by placing entry 374 after April 16, 1705, and entry 748 before December 2, 1708.
[3] This view is based upon an assumption that we should make explicit, that Berkeley wrote the <u>Commentaries</u> at a fairly constant rate.

secutive series of individual entries, has these distinguishing symbols.

Nearly every entry in the Commentaries has at least one of these symbols affixed to it. Some have none; but exclusive of entry 378 (which is a special case -- six parts having marginal signs and thirteen not having them) and the entries that are comments on recto entries (which are covered by the same marginal sign as the recto entries), there are only thirteen entries out of the 946 that have no marginal symbols. Furthermore, some entries have more than one marginal symbol. Many have three; quite a few have four; and a couple have five -- all different.

In the case of these multiple letters and signs it is often possible to tell when one was written relative to others from their position in the text. Berkeley wrote single marginal symbols with a regular spacing in the margin. Later ones he wrote irregularly spaced and often crowded into the small space remaining.

This system of marginal letters and signs was not part of the original Commentaries. It is, in Luce's words, "an afterthought." One indication of their being an addition to the original is that some marginal letters duplicate a note already written in the entries. In many of the entries Berkeley added at the end, "Introd:" or "Exord:" or "Preface." With entry 717 he wrote "Introd:" in the margin. However, as they now stand these entries have an "I" (for Introduction) written in the margin, as do the other marginal "I" entries. Therefore, Berkeley first wrote out "Introd:" in some entries before he introduced the marginal symbols; but once he invented the system of marginalia which included the "I," he appended the "I" to them. Also, the fact that Berkeley's index to the marginal letters is in the second written notebook, rather than the first, points to the system's being "an afterthought."

Berkeley's index to the marginali is quite helpful, though incomplete.[1] Only the letters are indexed; but

---

[1]See folio 3.

these letters indicate several things to us. Often the marginal letter is a key to the content of the entry, as "M" may point to a discussion of matter. However, in many cases the letter does not specify content but rather the context in which an entry is to be taken. An entry on spirit may have a "G" before it, indicating that it is specifically a comment on the spirit of God.

What is not included in Berkeley's index are the mathematical symbols ("+," "X," "X" with "1," "2," "3," or "3a"), the "ob:," and the asterisk. The "ob:" occurs only beside entry 36 and is written so small that previous editors have overlooked it. Its meaning or use remains to be determined. Berkeley frequently used a marginal asterisk, usually beside entries written on the verso pages. It is quite clear from asterisks written <u>within</u> the opposite recto entries that it was a sign used to correlate two entries (e.g., 383 and 383a). For a detailed treatment of the mathematical symbols I refer the reader to Luce's discussion in his note on folio 3 (in his notes accompanying this edition).

Some marginal symbols have been stroked out. Berkeley stroked out all of the following symbols: "I," "M," "E," "S," "N," "+," "X," and "1." The only ones that he never stroked out were "T," "G," and "Mo." He sometimes stroked out two letters together (M̶S̶) and sometimes separately (M̶S̶). The stroke seems to have been Berkeley's way of shifting an entry from one context to another, or of "ticking off" an entry already settled in his mind or already used as intended in another manuscript being prepared for publication.

Another peculiarity that demands attention is the circling of marginal signs. Berkeley sometimes circled the "+" (⊕) and the "1" (①). Luce suggested that this convention may have indicated an entry once rejected or "ticked off" but taken up again or reconsidered.

The entire marginalia of the <u>Commentaries</u> must be considered in terms of (1) its use to Berkeley and (2) its value to us. No doubt it had several functions for Berkeley. He used some symbols to mark entries for further attention -- or for no further attention. He also used the symbols for grouping entries according to content or context. And he used them in organizing entries for inclusion in his published works.

Just as the marginal symbols had several uses for Berkeley they serve us in many ways. They function in a limited way as an index, enabling us to group entries according to topic. They help us to follow the development of his earlier published works. And, as the most important aid in our interpretation of Berkeley's thought, they are of great value for us in knowing the context in which to place or interpret an entry. So it is clear that the marginal letters and signs are not to be ignored; they are an integral part of the <u>Commentaries</u>.

The Manuscript

Berkeley's <u>Philosophical Commentaries</u> is in a manuscript that includes other material as well. Before I record the contents of the manuscript let me describe its general appearance, and survey what is known of the history of the manuscript from the time it left Berkeley's hands until it found its way into the British Museum in London.

<u>Description</u>. The manuscript in which the <u>Commentaries</u> is found is amont the "Berkeley Papers" in the British Museum and is numbered Add. MS. 39305. It is 180 folios, or as we number pages, 360 pages. It is actually two notebooks bound together (approximately 200 mm. x 158 mm.) so that one notebook shows slightly larger than the other. The pages are unlined paper upon which Berkeley wrote entirely in ink (The pencil markings are not his.). In the <u>Commentaries</u> portion of the manuscript the writing is, with very few exceptions, on the recto pages with the verso pages either blank or with only a few lines. Its paragraph-like entries are separated by deliberate spacing between them. The margin is carefully observed, with a system of marginal signs marking almost every entry.

<u>History</u>. At Berkeley's death the manuscript passed

into the hands of his son George, and then on to Berkeley's grandson George Monck Berkeley. It then left the Berkeley family, passed through the Grimston family and on to the Rose family in whose possession it remained until coming to rest in the British Museum. Rev. Hugh James Rose lent the manuscript to J. S. M. Anderson, who used it in preparing his History of the Church of England in the Colonies (first edition, 1845-55; second edition, 1856). Archdeacon Henry John Rose made the manuscript available to A. C. Fraser who prepared an edition of it in 1871. In 1916 Mrs. W. F. Rose presented the manuscript to the British Museum, where it has remained.

Catalogue of Contents. The following is a listing of the contents of the manuscript in which the Commentaries is found:

Notebook A

Folio

1-2	Two pages added by the binder -- different texture, thicker and heavier paper, numbered (three pages if we count the page glued to the front cover). Folio 1 contains the British Museum's number of the manuscript -- 39,305 -- along with a list of Johnston's and Luce's (1944) editions, my proposed edition, and Luce's 1932 Hermathena article. Opposite folio 1 someone has penciled in an abbreviated index to the manuscript.
3r.	Berkeley's index to the marginal signs. Also "G: B: Coll: Trin: Dub. Alum:" and "George Berkeley A. B. ex aed. Xti" (not by Berkeley).
3v.	Blank.
4r.-94r.	Entries 400-888 of Philosophical Commentaries.

Verso pages mostly blank, though many have entries added.
Marginal signs before nearly every entry.
Lines across folios 3r. and 78r.
Seal of the British Museum on about every twelfth verso page.
Folio numbers penciled in, upper right of recto pages.
Numbers "1754, 1755, 1755" on upper right of folio 7r. (not by Berkeley).
Some pencil marks in the text -- parentheses, X marks, transcribed words, underlining (not by Berkeley).
Bottom of each page badly water-stained.

94v.   Blank.

95r.   "August 28th. 1708 ~~wit~~ the Adventure of the Shirt."
Quotation from "Clov. B. 7."
Inverted sums.

95v.   Blank.

Notebook B

Folio

96r.   Blank.
Shows blottings (two cancellations and three words blotted) from an opposite verso page other than 95v. Therefore, there must have been some written page(s) which are no longer included.

96v.   "Mem. the following statutes were agreed to & sign'd by the Society consisting of eight persons, Jan: 10. A. D. 1705" (written in a careless and hurried hand).

97r.-101r.   Statutes of the Friday Society (written in a careful and beautiful hand, but growing progressively worse, with erasures and blot-

	tings toward the end).
	Verso pages blank.
101v.	Blank.
102r. &v.	Queries on Locke's philosophy.
103r.	Statutes of the Thursday Society with date, "December the Seventh in the year one thousand seven hundred and Six."
103v.	Quotation from Cicero and the note "13 c. Math. v. 22 & 30."
104r.-164r.	Entries 1-399 of <u>Philosophical Commentaries</u>. Most verso pages blank, some with entries added (159v. and 163v. completely filled with entries). Smears and blots. Marginal signs. Line across top of folio 161r. Seal of British Museum about every twelfth verso page. Folio numbers penciled in, upper right of recto pages. Pencil marks (not by Berkeley). Not water-stained.
164v.	Notes and queries on Locke -- inverted.
165r.	Blank.
165v.	Brief notes for a sermon -- inverted.
166r. &v.	Propositions and mathematical problems entitled "De Motu" -- inverted.
————	Page cut out between folios 166 and 167.
167r.	End of <u>A Description of the Cave of Dunmore</u> -- not inverted.

167v.	Blank.
———	Unnumbered folio, left blank.
———	Page cut out between unnumbered folio and folio 168.
168r.	Blank.
168v.-169v.	Equations.
———	Page torn out between folios 168 and 169.
170r.	Blank.
170v.-179v.	<u>A Description of the Cave of Dunmore</u> -- inverted. On verso pages only; recto pages blank. Lacking last page of the text (last page on 167r., not inverted). Prominent marks from original binding on last page.
180r.	Penciled in: "(EFD)179ff. Exam' by E.S. 4/10/18." (Not by Berkeley.)
———	Two blank pages added by the binder -- different weight and texture of paper, not numbered (three pages if we count the page glued to back cover).

I agree in Nothing w:t the Socinians as to ye nature of ye Deity & ye duty

The House it self the Church it self is no [illegible] tjou? invisible tjsd chorg

or uisible is a god

+ Berkeley's &c arguments do not seem to prove against space, but only against bodies.

+ Aristotle as good a man as Euclid & Newton, much to not even misspoken.

× Lines not proper for demonstration

⊕ We see the house it self, the church it self [struck through] a being an Idea & nothing more.

× Instead of inquiring our Doctrine much how its Geometry.

E Rules of writing or preserving the ideas of in the table the books, as is the ind of before.

n In Algebra &c know — vast view of ring could really out and not dif.

n Hyps & such like unaccountable things confuse my I think.

A History of the Editions

<u>Fraser's Editions</u>. A. C. Fraser was the first scholar to discover the manuscript of Berkeley's <u>Philosophical Commentaries</u>. It was he who published the first edition of it. In 1871 Fraser published the manuscript in two different collections, but both with the same text -- his edition in volume IV of his <u>The Works of George Berkeley</u> (Oxford: Clarendon Press, 1871) and in his <u>Life and Letters of George Berkeley</u> (Oxford: Clarendon Press, 1871). He published a second edition in 1901.

The only distinguishing mark of Fraser's first edition is simply that it was the first, for its accuracy cannot be trusted. It does give us some idea of the genesis of Berkeley's philosophy and its early development, but its flaws are myriad.

Some of the weaknesses of Fraser's first edition are quite serious. In the first place, he did not recognize that the two notebooks of the <u>Commentaries</u> were bound in a reverse order. So he published them in the order in which he found them, beginning his edition in the middle of the <u>Commentaries</u> with entry 400.

Secondly, many of Fraser's readings are wrong. Certainly he is to be pardoned for most of these, since he did not have the work of previous editors to help him. Nevertheless, these mistaken readings detract from the credibility of his transcription.

A more blameworthy fault is Fraser's whimsical or misguided omission of many of the recto entries. Some of these he omitted for a reason, though hardly a good one -- they are repetitious, he said. But he omitted many others for no apparent reason. He just ignored them.

Fraser's treatment of the verso entries is even more capricious. Some of them are omitted. Many are included in the text. Of these inclusions some bear no indication that they are from the verso; some are combined with recto entries without any indication of their distinction; some are printed in parentheses, but with no statement as to why; and others are printed in brackets, some with an explanation as to what they are, and some without. And many are relegated to the footnotes.

When we look more closely at the words of the <u>Commentaries</u> we see that Fraser also treated them with an unjustifiable freedom. He simply omitted many. Others -- often important words -- he changed (e.g., "Cartesian" to "philosopher"). And he added endings, etc., to some of Berkeley's words to make them grammatically correct.

The last in this series of serious weaknesses in Fraser's edition is his treatment of the marginal signs and symbols. He printed only Berkeley's capital letters, omitting completely the mathematical symbols. Of these letters he omitted many, omitting completely the stroked out letters.

Other shortcomings of Fraser's edition are of lesser importance. He gave no system of numbering, and did not indicate the folio numbers of the manuscript. These lacks are not in the category of errors in the transcription, but they are a serious handicap to the scholar who wishes to quote the entries or to use Fraser's edition in conjunction with the manuscript.

There are some inaccuracies in Fraser's edition which are of little or no importance. He often wrote out Berkeley's abbreviations, sometimes with brackets and sometimes without. He also frequently changed the spelling, capitalization, and punctuation.

All in all, the weaknesses of Fraser's first edition cry out for another edition. And he himself issued a second edition of the <u>Commentaries</u> in 1901, in the <u>Works of George Berkeley</u>, Vol. I. He merely changed some of the words, italicized others, added some, and omitted some. In fact, it is obvious from a comparison of Fraser's two editions that the many changes he made in the second edition were merely stylistic and whimsical. Of 100 consecutive entries which I examined in detail, I found that Fraser made forty changes from his first edition. In twenty instances the 1871 edition was correct but the 1901 edition was changed contrary to the manuscript. In six instances Fraser made changes consistent with the manuscript (one is punctuation and the others capitals). However, they are all merely accidental alterations for stylistic reasons (e.g., the capitalization of "Math." and "Space"). Other inconsistencies with the manuscript he left untouched. Therefore, it is evident that Fraser did not consult the manuscript in making his second edition and the second is not even as reliable as his first.[1] So even though Fraser did give us a first with his edition of the Commentaries -- and deserves much credit for doing so -- his editions are hardly a reliable source for scholarly work.

Johnston's Edition. The second in the series of editors of Berkeley's Philosophical Commentaries was G. A. Johnston. Johnston published his edition in 1930.[2] He justified his work by an appeal to the "defects" of Fraser's edition. His edition is an improvement over Fraser's, but it itself is far from being free of defects.

I would like to use a question by Aaron as a summary judgment on Johnston's edition of the Commentaries. Aaron asked, "We do not wish to be unkind, but has Dr. Johnston ever seen the MS. italics mine ?"[3] Johnston's own comments do not indicate that he had seen the manuscript. He said that the notebooks had been his "constant companion for over twenty years,"[4] but he did not say in what form. He said that his edition was "based on a careful examination of the manuscript . . . by Mr A. J. Watson,"[5] and elsewhere he spoke of "the careful collation of the manuscript made for the present edition by Mr A. J. Watson. . . ."[6] But Johns-

---

[1] Theodor Lorenz published a corrigenda to Fraser's second edition in Mind, XIII (1904), pp. 304ff. and in "Weitere Beiträge," pp. 554ff.
[2] Johnston, Berkeley's Commonplace Book.
[3] Aaron, "Locke and Berkeley's Commonplace Book," p. 454.
[4] Johnston, p. vii.
[5] Ibid.
[6] Ibid., p. xix.

ton nowhere claimed that he himself had worked with the manuscript.

Certainly an examination of his edition of the Commentaries reveals clear evidence that Johnston did not know the manuscript. He said that Fraser's 1871 edition ". . . was reprinted, with a few minor corrections, in vol. I of Campbell Fraser's 1901 edition of Berkeley's works, . . ."[1] We have already seen that Fraser's changes in his second edition were not corrections dictated by the manuscript. Johnston would have seen this too had he compared it with the manuscript.

In his actual "transcription" Johnston included a host of serious mistakes as we can see from Aaron's corrigenda which took up several pages in two issues of Mind.[2] It is interesting to note that of the second list of corrections to Johnston's edition Aaron said, "These additional errors were pointed out to me by Mr. A. J. Watson [Johnston's collaborator] of the British Museum."[3]

Let me comment on some of Johnston's errors that suggest his ignorance of the manuscript. He did print many of the verso entries in pointed brackets, as he promised in his introduction. Many others he printed either in square brackets, a convention that he supposedly reserved for marginal words and sentences, or else he did not note that they are from the verso pages. Also, some verso entries he printed as separate entries and some he combined with recto entries.

One of the least consistent of Johnston's conventions was

---

[1] Johnston, Berkeley's Commonplace Book, p. xviii.
[2] Aaron, "Locke and Berkeley's Commonplace Book," pp. 455-458; and R. I. Aaron, "Dr. Johnston's Edition of the Commonplace Book," Mind, XLI (April, 1932), p. 277.
[3] Aaron, "Dr. Johnston's Edition," p. 278. In my own correspondance with Mr. Watson, he wrote that in his eightieth year he could not recall the details of his and Dr. Johnston's work.

his use of square brackets. He said that this sign encloses words or sentences that Berkeley wrote in the margin of his manuscript. I could find only one instance in which Johnston used this convention correctly -- " Introd. " in 729. Otherwise he used it for: words which he added, but which are not in the manuscript; verso entries; Berkeley's own bracketing; words and phrases cancelled by Berkeley; and words that are in the text of the manuscript but not in the margin.

Johnston's treatment of particular words was equally inconsistent with the manuscript. He sometimes omitted words that Berkeley included, and sometimes included words of his own, not Berkeley's. In some cases he actually changed the words of the manuscript.

Of the spelling, capitalization, and punctuation Johnston said that he followed Berkeley's in all cases. But in fact he more often departed from the manuscript in these details that he followed it.

So Aaron's question requires a negative answer; Johnston had not seen the manuscript. The transcription was made by Watson. We can only wonder whether the major proportion of the mistakes were in Watson's transcription or in Johnston's obviously careless and inconsistent editing.

I should also add a few comments on weakness in Johnston's edition of the <u>Commentaries</u> that are matters of his judgment, not of respect for the manuscript. He did print the two notebooks in their correct order, following Theodor Lorenz. But he followed Lorenz in erroneously transposing entries 377-399 to the end.[1] Of the marginal signs and symbols, Johnston included only the unstroked letters, omitting

---

[1]However, even here Johnston showed ignorance of the manuscript. He printed entry 395 twice, once as his 933 and again as his 941 with one difference. Once he printed ". . . cannot. W^{ch} . . ." and then ". . . cannot, w^{ch} . . . ." Furthermore, he added his 946-953 which are not part of the <u>Commentaries</u>, as evidenced by their being inverted and having no marginal signs.

the mathematical symbols. He even printed Berkeley's key to the marginalia in his own introduction rather than in the text and did not indicate that it was Berkeley's rather than his own. He italicized words; Berkeley did not. And he numbered the verso entries consecutively with the recto entries, thus concealing their character as comments on the recto entries.

My concluding judgment can only be that Johnston's edition, though in some respects an improvement over Fraser's, is full of the most serious errors and cannot be relied on as a presentation of what Berkeley actually wrote.

<u>Luce's Editions</u>. A new day dawned for Berkeley's <u>Commentaries</u> with Luce's 1944 edition. It was a diplomatic edition. Luce reproduced the manuscript page for page, the only difference being that his version transcribed Berkeley's script into print. Moreover, he did a good job of it.

The principle defects in Luce's edition are errors in the transcription of the words and marginalia. Luce prepared this edition during World War II, when the manuscript was not available. He had to rely on a transcription that he had made ten years earlier. Therefore, it is not surprising to find transcription errors which could have been corrected by a comparison with the manuscript.

The virtues of Luce's edition far outweigh its weaknesses. In presenting the manuscript in detail Luce gave us "the text in the making." He included Berkeley's erasures, corrections, additions, spelling, punctuation, and capitalization. With this "text in the making" we can, in many cases, actually follow Berkeley's thoughts as he wrote, changed, and added to a passage. So we have a source for studying the development of his thought in a more detailed way than had been possible before Luce's edition.

Luce also included the erasures, changes, and additions in the marginalia. These are an indispensible aid in interpreting the <u>Commentaries</u>.

The other virtues of Luce's edition are his own contributions. He presented the notebooks in their proper order, even restoring entries 377-399 to their rightful place rather than at the end where Johnston had put them. He developed a good numbering system, giving the dependent verso entries the same number plus the letter "a" of the recto entry upon which it is a comment. He reproduced the folios page for page. He gave the folio number of each page, an invaluable aid in collating an edition with the manuscript. He revised an early article on the date, purpose, structure, and marginal signs of the Commentaries,[1] into an imaginative, informative, and scholarly introduction. And he wrote a very comprehensive set of notes on the individual entries and on general issues. Fraser had given a few comments in footnotes; Hecht and other translators prepared notes; Johnston included about forty pages of notes; but Luce gave us 150 pages of excellent notes -- a virtual encyclopedia of Berkeley studies.[2]

A regret, and yet part of the value, of Luce's edition is that it was a limited edition. The publisher printed only 400 numbered copies of it. These were quickly bought up by libraries, scholars, and collectors; and as a result copies of the diplomatic edition are extremely rare today.

In 1948 Luce included an edition of the Philosophical Commentaries in volume one of his and Jessop's The Works of George Berkeley. This edition is of the same kind as those of Fraser and Johnston. It is a clean text with all of Berkeley's erasures, blots, and stroked passages omitted and all signs of his corrections and additions removed. Furthermore, Luce's excellent notes from the diplomatic edition are, as he himself put it, "pruned severely." Of this type of edition, Luce's text is an improvement over those of Fraser and Johnston. It is a better transcription; it has a better numbering system; and it includes all the unstroked marginal signs. Yet even the best of this type of edition treats a fluid manuscript as a fixed text. Anyone

---

[1] Luce, "Berkeley's Commonplace Book."
[2] These are the notes that Luce has revised for the present edition of the Commentaries.

-xxxi-

who knows Luce's diplomatic edition would find his 1948 rather uninteresting.

The Text of the Present Edition

My principal goal in preparing a new edition of Berkeley's <u>Philosophical Commentaries</u> has been accuracy. I have sought to produce a text upon which scholars and students, for whom the manuscript is unavailable, can depend as a close second choice.

I would claim further that my transcription is as accurate, even in the smallest details, as is possible -- short of a photographic reproduction. It is not up to an editor to select among the details of a manuscript, including some and excluding others. He cannot anticipate which minor details future scholars may find significant. Therefore, I have followed the manuscript closely even in incomplete words ("n" for "in"), obviously wrong words ("nor" for "not," and "jnjure" for "injure"), and illegible letters and words (printed "xxx" or "x̶x̶x̶" [illegible and stroked out]). I have transcribed the ash (ae) where I could be sure of it. And I have included lines drawn across the pages on folios 3, 78, and 161, in my attempt at accuracy.

My procedure was to transcribe the <u>Commentaries</u> anew from the manuscript. In doing so I was, of course, helped by the editions of Fraser, Johnston, and especially Luce, as well as Aaron's corrigenda and Belfrage's suggestions and confirmations. I used a photocopy for most of the work, though I did check my edition carefully against the manuscript. At the beginning of my work I spent two days with the manuscript at the British Museum, mainly studying the marginal symbols and becoming acquainted with the manuscript. Then near the conclusion of my work I spent two weeks checking and rechecking my transcription against the manuscript. The conditions during my last study were ideal. Two weeks of almost nothing but sunny days in London enabled me to study the manuscript in the sunlight, which is a distinct advantage. In addition, I spent several hours using the Museum's ultraviolet reader, which was a great aid in reading the blotted and water-stained passages.[1]

All peculiarities of the manuscript have been reproduced. I have recorded the marginalia, completely and accurately. I have given Berkeley's abbreviations, spelling, and punctuation as they occur. I have observed his capitalization carefully. I should point out, however, some special problems here. One cannot always tell whether certain letters are capitals or small letters: "A," "M," "N," "S," "U," "V," and "W." In most cases I have been certain of my reading of these letters, but in a few ambiguous instances I had to make a personal decision. With the "S" I have made shape rather than size the determining factor. I have rendered a capital "S" if the letter was separated from the rest of the word and the loops closed, except in a few cases in which the small "s" shape was written very large on something as obvious as a proper name ("Spinoza").

There are several instances of words and blots that I think have been transcribed correctly for the first time in my edition. Some of the more significant words are: "e-verts" (272), "Mem:" (315), "Existere" (429), "near" (480), "meer" (763), "cant" (811), and the marginal "ob:" (36). Examples of significant blots printed for the first time are: "~~without him~~" (100), "~~good and bad~~" (158), "~~s under~~" (278), "~~its~~" (280), "~~clear1~~" (283), "~~minute~~" (284), "~~every~~" (349), "~~define~~" (516), and "~~Univer~~" (686). These examples are, of course, a major part of my claim to accuracy.

In addition to these comments on my transcription, a few words concerning the format of the present edition are

---

[1] The only water-stained passages that I found illegible even with the ultraviolet reader were: "a contradiction" (576a), "meaning" (581), "twixt per [ception]" (585), "from y^e" (614a), "i.e." and "[volition] s &" (643), "In" (651), "they themselves" (682), "Epistles" (709), "in ye 3^d." (717), "Gospels" (769), "as we do Hunger" and "Idea but sense or" (888). In these cases I have had to depend on the readings of previous editors.

in order. I have given a reproduction of the manuscript just short of a facsimile (Luce's format in his diplomatic edition was such a printed facsimile.). I have printed the marginalia complete and spaced approximately as it is in the manuscript, though without the varying sizes of Berkeley's script. I have used a much smaller type to indicate words and passages that Berkeley obviously added later in small squeezed-in script. I have separated the entries as in the manuscript. I have included the verso entries immediately following the recto entries to which they refer, each with the folio number on which it is to be found in the manuscript. As to the numbering of the entries, I have followed Luce's system. There are a few cases in which one could dispute Luce's division of an entry or his marking a verso as an independent entry. But there are sound reasons for following Luce's numbering. It is quite correct for the most part, and the introduction of a new system of numbering into the literature at this point in time would create more confusion than that which already exists with Fraser's pagination and Johnston's numbering in addition to Luce's. Therefore, there is no doubt in my mind but that we should accept Luce's numbering system.

With the accuracy of my transcription and the simplicity of my format, I trust that my edition will be a useful one. Though not always as smooth and readable as might be desired, it is accurate and dependable; it can be studied and quoted by scholars with confidence. In fact, I would be so bold as to predict that scholars of the future will hesitate to quote from Berkeley's <u>Philosophical Commentaries</u> without quoting from the present edition, or at least checking with it.

NOTEBOOK B

f.104

+	One eternity greater than another of ye same kind.	1
+	In w^t sense eternity may be limited.	2
G,T	Whether succession of ideas in ye divine intellect?	3
T	Time train of ideas succeeding each other.	4
+	Duration not distinguish'd from existence.	5
+	Succession explain'd by before, between, & after, & numbering.	6
+	Why time in pain, longer than time in pleasure?	7
+	Duration infinitely divisible, time not so.	8
T	The same το νυν not common to all intelligences.	9
+	Time thought infinitely divisible on account of it's measure.	10
12 X	Extension not infinitely divisible in one sense.	11
+	Revolutions immediately measure train of ideas, mediately duration.	12
T	Time a sensation, therefore onely in ye mind.	13
+	Eternity is onely a train of innumerable ideas. hence the immortality of ye Soul easily conceiv'd. or rather the immortality of the person, y^t of ye soul not being necessary for ought we can see.	14

f.105

+	Swiftness of ideas compar'd with y^t of motion shews the wisdom of God.	15
+	W^t if succession of ideas were swifter, w^t if slower?	16

M	ffall of Adam, rise of Idolatry, rise of Epicurism & Hobbism, dispute about divisibility of matter &c expounded by material substances	17
~~M~~ $	Extension a sensation, therefore not without the mind.	18
M$	In y^e immaterial hypothesis the wall is white, fire hot &c	19
1 ~~P~~	Primary ideas prov'd not to exist in matter, after the Same manner y^t secondary ones are prov'd not to exist therein.	20
X	Demonstrations of the infinite divisibility of extension suppose length without breadth ∧ wch is absurd.	21
	or invisible length	21a (f.104v.)
1 M	World wthout thought is nec quid nec quantum nec quale &c	22
M	'tis wondrous to contemplate ye world empty'd of intelligences.	23
+	Nothing properly but persons ~~do exist~~ i.e conscious things do exist, all other things are not so much existences as manners of ye existence of persons.	24
+	Qu: about the soul or ∧rather person whether it be not compleatly known.	25
X	Infinite divisibility of extension does suppose ye external existence of ~~exist~~ extension but the later is false, ergo ye former also.	26
13 X	Qu: Blind man made to see would he know motion at ist sight.	27

f.106

13X Motion, figure & extension perceivable by sight 28
are different from those ideas perceived by touch
wch goe by the same name.

+ Diagonal incommensurable wth ye side Quaere how 29
this can be in my doctrine?

N Qu: how to reconcile Newtons 2 sorts of motion wth 30
my doctrine

X Terminations of surfaces and lines not ~~compleat,~~ 31
~~positive ideas,~~ imaginable per se.

13X Molyneux's Blind man would not know the sphaere 32
or cube to ^be^ bodies or extended at first sight.

+~~&~~ Extension so far from being incompatible wth y^t 33
'tis impossible it should exist without thought.

M.S. Extension it self or any thing extended cannot think 34
these being meer ideas or sensations whose essence
we thoroughly know

13X No extension but ~~y^t of~~ surface perceivable by sight. 35

ob:
M.$. W^n we imagine 2 bowls v.g. moving in Vacuo, 'tis 36
onely conceiving a person affected wth those sensations.

^{1}M.$ Extension to exist in a thoughtless thing ^is^ a 37
contradiction.

M^1 or rather in a thing void of perception. Thought 37a
seeming to imply action. (f.105v.

f.107

+ Qu: if visible motion be proportional to tangible 38
motion

-4-

T	In some dreams succession of ideas swifter than at other times.	39
1 M	If a piece of matter have extension y.t must be determin'd to a particular bigness & figure, but &c.	40
+	Nothing corresponds to our primarys ideas w.thout but powers, hence a direct & brief demonstration of an active powerfull being distinct from us on whom we depend. &c.	41
+	The name of colours actually given to tangible qualitys by the relation of y.e story of y.e German Count.	42
13X✱	Qu: how came visible & tangible qualitys by the same name in all languages?	43
+	Qu: whether being might not be the substance of y.e soul. or (w.ch is much ex otherwise thus) whether being added to y.e faculties compleat the real essence and adaequate definition of the soul?	44

f.108

N ~~M.N.~~	Qu: whether on the supposition of ₍external₎ Bodies it be possible for us to know ~~wheth~~ that any Body is absolutely at rest, since that supposing ideas much slower than at present bodies now apparently moving would than be apparently at rest.	45
M~~S~~	Qu: w.t can be like a sensation but a sensation?	46
~~M↯~~	Qu: Did ever any man see any ₍other₎ things besides his own ideas, that he should compare them to these & make these like unto them?	47
T	~~The xxx~~ The age of a fly for ought that we know may be as long as y.t of a man.	48
31X	Visible distance heterogeneous from tangible distance demonstrated 3 several ways	49

31X 1ˢᵗ if a tangible inch be equal ~~in~~ or in any other reason to a visible inch, thence it will follow yᵗ unequals are equals wᶜʰ is absurd. for at wᵗ distance would the visible inch be placed to make it ~~like~~ equal to the tangible inch?

31X 2ᵈ One made to see yᵗ had not yet seen his own limbs or any thing he touch'd, upon sight of a foot length would know it to be a foot length if tangible foot & visible foot were the same idea, sed falsum id ergo & hoc.

31X 3ᵈˡʸ from Molyneux's problem wᶜʰ otherwise is falsely solv'd by Locke & h~~e~~im.

f.109

1$M Nothing but ideas perceivable.   50

~~M~~ $ A, man cannot compare 2 things together without perceiving them each, ergo he cannot say any thing wᶜʰ is not an idea is like or unlike an idea.   51

~~M~~+ Bodies &c do exist even wⁿ not perceiv'd they being powers in the active Being.   52

+ Succession a simple idea ∧ Locke cap. 7.   53

   Succession is an abstract ie. an unconceivable idea.   53a
                                                          (f.108v.)

31X Visible extension [is proportional to tangible extension, also] is encreas'd & diminish'd by parts, hence taken for the same.   54

X$ If extension be without the mind in bodies qu: 55
          abstratible or
    whether tangible or visible or ∧ both.

1X Mathematical propositions about extension & motion true in a double sense.   56

~~M.$~~ Extension thought peculiarly inert because not accompany'd wᵗʰ pleasure & pain; hence thought to exist in matter as also for yᵗ it was conceiv'd   57

-6-

common to 2 senses.

as also the constant perception of 'em   57a
                                                             (f.108v.)

11X   Blind at 1st sight could not tell how near w^t he saw   58
      was to him, nor even whether it be w^{th}out him or
      in his eye. Qu: would he not think ye later.

                                                              f.110

3X1   Blind at 1st sight could not know y^t w^t he saw was   59
      extended, untill he had seen & touch'd some one
      self same thing. Not knowing how minimum
      tangibile would look.

          Homogeneous particles
M.   Mem: y^t ~~Homoeomeries~~ be brought in to answer the   60
      objection of Gods creating sun, plants &c before
      Animals.

X   In every Bodie 2 infinite series of extension the one   61
    of tangible the other of visible.

+   All things to a Blind at 1st seen in a point   62

+   Ignorance of Glasses made men think extension to   63
    be in bodies.

    Homogeneous portions of matter
M.   ~~Homoeomeries~~: usefull to contemplate them   64

+   Extension if in matter changes its relation wth 65
    minimum visibile wch seems to be fixt.

+   Qu: whether M.V. be fix'd.   66

1M.   Each particule of matter if extended must be   67
      infinitely extended. or have an infinite series
      of extension.

1M   If the world be granted to consist of matter tis the   68
     mind gives it beauty & proportion

3X1 W^t I have said onely proves there is no proportion   69
      at all times & in all men between visible & tangible

inch v. g.

f.111

3X1   Tangible & visible extension heterogeneous because   70
they have no common measure, also because their
simplest, constituent parts or elements are specifically
distinct viz. punctum visibile & tangibile. **N.B. The
former seems** to be no good reason.

M.N.   By immateriality is solv'd the cohesion of bodies or   71
rather the dispute ceases.

X   Our idea ~~of~~ (we call) extension neither way capable of infinity.   72
i.e. either infinitely small or great.

+   Greatest possible extension seen under an angle wch 73
must be less than 180 degrees, the legs of wch angle
proceed from the ends of the extension.

$ M   Allowing there be extended solid &c substances   74
without the mind tis impossible the mind should
know or perceive them. the mind even according
to y^e materialists perceiving onely the impressions
made upon its brain or rather the ideas attending
those impressions.

X   Unite in abstracto not at all divisible it being as it   75
were a point or wth Barrow nothing at all. in concreto not divisible ad infinitum
there being no one idea diminishable ad infinitum.

M 1   Any subject can have of each sort of primary   76
qualities but one particular at once. Locke.
b. 4. c3. §15.

f.112

+   Qu: whether we have clear ideas of large numbers   77
themselves, or onely of their relations.

1M   Of solidity see L. b2. c4. §1. §5. §6. If any one ask   78
w^t solidity is let him put a flint between his hands
& he will know. Extension of Body is continuity

of solid &c, extension of Space is continuity of
unsolid &c.

3X1 Why may not I Say ˄visible extension is a continuity of 78a
visible points -- tangible extension is a continuity (f.111v.)
of tangible points.

M Mem. that I take notice that I do not fall in w:th 79
Sceptics Fardella &c, in y:^t I make bodies to
exist w:<s>th out us</s> ˄certainly, w:^{ch} they doubt of.

M I am more certain of y:^e existence & reality of 80
Bodies than <s>even</s> M:^r Locke, since he pretends
onely to w:^t he calls sensitive knowlege, whereas
I think I have demonstrative knowlege of their
Existence, by them meaning combinations of
powers in an unknown substratum.

1$ Our ideas we call figure & extension not images of 81
M   the figure & extension of Matter, these (if such
there be) being infinitely divisible, those not so.

+   Tis impossible a Material cube should exist, because 82
the edges of a Cube <s>can</s> ˄will appear broad to an acute
sense.
                                               f.113

+   Men die or are in state of annihilation ˄oft in <s>severall times</s> 83
a day.

S   Powers Quaere whether more or one onely? 84

+   Lengths abstract ˄from <s>of</s> breadths are the work of the 85
mind, such do ntersect in a point at all angles, after
the same way <s>extensi</s> colour is abstract ˄from <s>of</s> extension.
every position alters the line

X   Quaere, whether ideas of extension are made up of 86
other ideas v. g. idea of a foot made up of severall
ideas of an inch &c?

| | The idea of an inch length not one determin'd idea | 87 |
| + | Hence enquire the reason why we are out in judging of extension by the sight, for wch purpose 'tis meet also to consider the frequent & sudden changes of extension, by position. | |

2X$ ¹ No stated ideas of length without a minimum 88

MS. ~~Sub~~ Material substance banter'd by Locke b. 2c. 13. S.19 89

MS In my doctrine all absurditys from infinite space &c cease. 90

✗ 23X¹ Qu: whether ∧if (Speaking grosly) the things we see, were all of them at all times too small to be 91

felt ∧we ✗✗ should have confounded tangible & visible extension & figure?

f.114

T Qu: Whether if succession of ideas n the Eternal mind, a day does not seem to God a 1000 years rather than a 1000 years a day? 92

+ But one only Colour & it's degrees 93

+ Enquiry about a grand mistake in writers of Dioptricks in assigning the cause of Microscopes magnifying objects 94

+ X Qu. whether a blind made to see would at 1st, ~~call his~~ give the name of distance to any idea intromitted by sight since he would take distance y^t he had perceiv'd by touch to be something existing without his mind, but he would certainly 95

think that ~~every~~ ∧no thing seen was ~~not~~ without his mind.

S + Space wthout any bodies being in rerum natura, would not be extended as not having parts in that 96

parts are assigned to it wth respect to body ~~wch is~~
from whence also the notion of distance is taken,
now without either parts or distance ^or mind how can there
be space or any thing beside one uniform nothing?

  Two demonstrations that blind made to see would   97
+   not take
X   ~~think~~ all things he saw to be without his mind or not
  in a point, ye one from microscopic eyes, the other
  from not perceiving distance i.e radius of the visual
  sphere.

M.   The Trees are in the Park, that is, whether I will   98
  or no whether I imagine any thing about them or   (f.114v.)
  no, let me but go thither & open my Eyes by day
  & I shall not avoid seeing them.

                 f.115

+   Tho swiftness or slowness of motion depends on our   99
  ideas it does not therefore follow, that the same force
  can ~~be~~ impell a body over a greater or less Space in
  proportion to ~~swiftness or~~ slowness or swiftness of
  our ideas.

$3X^1$ By extension blind would mean either the perception 100
  caused in his touch by something he calls extended,
  or else the power of raising that perception, w^ch
  pow~~xx~~er is without in the thing term'd extended. Now
     not   visible
  he could ^know either of these to be in things ~~without him~~
  till he had try'd.

X   Geometry seems to have for it's object tangible   101
  extension, figures & motion, & not visible.

$3\overset{a}{X}^1$ The reason explain'd why we see things erect their   102
  images being inverted in the eye.

     Say
$32X^1$ A man will ^ a body will seem as big as before, tho   103
  the visible idea it yields be less that w^t it ~~is~~ was,
  therefore the bigness or tangible extension of the

body is different from the visible extension

X   Number not without the mind in any thing, because   104
    tis the mind by considering things as one that makes
    complex ideas of 'em, tis the mind combines into
    one, wch by otherwise considering it's ideas might
    make a score of w^t was but one just now.

                                                    f.116
          or Space
X   Extension$_\wedge$no simple idea, length, breadth &   105
    ~~De~~solidity being three severall ideas.

3X1 Depth or solidity nor perceiv'd by sight.   106

+   Strange impotence of men. Man ~~Less~~ without God.   107
    Wretcheder than a Stone or tree, he having onely
    the ~~will~~ power to be miserable by his unperformed
    wills, these having no power at all

X   Length, perceivable by hearing, length & ~~B~~breadth 108
    by sight, Length breadth & depth by touch.

    W^t affects us must be a thinking thing for w^t 109
G$ thinks
    ~~affects us~~ not cannot subsist.

+   Number not in bodies it being the creature of the   110
    mind depending entirely on it's consideration &
    being more or less as the mind pleases.

+S Mem: Quaere whether extension be equally a   111
    sensation with colour?

X   The Mob use not the word Extension. tis an abstract   111a
    term of the Schools.   (f.115v.)

P$ Round figure a perception or sensation in the mind   112
    but in the body is a power L. b2. c.8 S.8.

    Mem: mark well the later part of the last cited   113
    Section

f.117

	or any other tangible things	
$3X^1$	Solids ˄ are no otherwise seen than colours felt by the German ~~e~~Count	114
M$	Of & thing causes of mistake	115
$2X^1$	The visible point of he who has microscopical eyes will not be greater or less than mine.	116
X	Qu: whether the propositions & even axioms of Geometry do not divers of them suppose the existence of lines &c without the mind.	117
T	Whether motion be the measure of Duration see Locke. b.2 c.14 S.19	118
X	Lines & points conceiv'd as terminations different ideas from those conceiv'd absolutely.	119
X	Every position alters a line.	120
X S	Blind at 1st would not take colours to be without his mind, but colours would seem to be in the Same place with the colour'd extension, therefore extension would not seem to be without the mind.	121
$2X^1$	All visible concentric circles whereof the eye is the center are absolutely equall.	122

f.118

+	Infinite number why absurd. not rightly solv'd by Locke.	123
$3X^1$	Qu: how tis possible we should see flats or right lines.	124
$^2X^1$	Qu: why ~~we~~ the ~~m~~Moon appears greatest in the Horizon?	125
$3\overset{a}{X}1$	Qu: why we see things erect when painte'd inverted.	126

-13-

T	Question put ~~by~~ by Mʳ. Deering touching the thief & paradise.	127
M1 $	Matter tho' allow'd to exist may be no greater than a pin's head.	128
+	Motion is proportionable to Space describ'd in given time.	129
+	Velocity not proportionable to Space describ'd in given time.	130
M1	No active power but the will, therefore matter if it exists affects us not.	131

f.119

+	Magnitude when barely taken for the ratio partium extra partes or rather for ~~the~~ coexistence & succession without considering the parts coexisting & succeeding, is infinitely or rather indefinitely or not at all perhaps ∧divisible because it is it self infinite or indefinite, but definite, determin'd magnitudes ~~cons~~ i.e lines or surfaces consisting of points whereby ~~they~~ (together wᵗʰ distance & position) they are determin'd, are resoluble into these points.	132
+	Again, Magnitude taken for coexistence and succession is not∧at all divisible but is one simple idea.	133
+	Simple ideas include no parts n~~x~~or relations, hardly separated & consider'd in themselves. not yet rightly singl'd by any Authour. instance in power, red ~~colour~~, extension &c	134
$ M	Space not imaginable by any idea receiv'd from Sight, not imaginable, ~~by~~ without body moving not even then necessarily existing (I Speak of infinite Space) for wᵗ the body has past may be conceiv'd annihilated.	135

M $1   Qu: w.t can we see beside colours, w.t can we feel   136
       beside, hard, soft cold warm pleasure pain

                                                           f.120

3X1   Qu: why not taste & smell extension?   137

                                          thought
3x1   Qu: why not tangible & visible extensions ~~call'd~~   138
       heterogeneous extensions, so well as gustable &
       olfactible perceptions thought heterogeneous
       perceptions. or at least why not as heterogeneous
       as blue & red?

                        singling & abstracting
  +   Preliminary discourse about ~~sorting,~~ simple ideas.   139

2x1   Moon w.n Horizontal does not appear bigger as to   140
       visible extension than at other times, hence
                            things seen under
       difficulties & disputes about ʌ equal Angles &c cease.

  +   All Potentiae alike indifferent.   141

  +   A. B. w.t does he mean by his potentia, is it the will, 142
       desire, person or all or neither, or sometimes one
       some times t'other.

  +   No agent can be conceiv'd indifferent as to pain   143
       or pleasure,

                           in a Strict philosophical sense
  +   We do not properly speaking ʌ make objects more or   144
       less pleasant, but the laws of Nature do that.

                                                           f.121

  ✳   A finite intelligence might have foreseen 4 thousand   145
Mo. S years agoe, ~~every t~~ the place & circumstances,
       even the most minute & trivial of my present
       existence.

  ✳   This true on supposition that uneasiness determines   145a
S. Mo. the Will.   (f.120v.)

-15-

✗ S. Mo.	Doctrines of liberty, prescience &c explain'd by Billiard balls.	146
+	W^t should we think of an object plac'd as in the difficulty if we saw it clearly?	147
3✗1 ^{a}	W^t judgement would he make of uppermost & lowermost who had always seen thro' an inverting glass.	148
S. Mo.	According to Locke we have not liberty as to vertue & vice, the Liberty he allows consisting in an Indifferency of the operative Faculties, wch is consecutive to the will, but virtue & vice consist in the will ergo &c.	149

f.122

2✗1	All lines subtending the same optic angle congruunt (as is evident by an easy experiment) therefore they are equal.	150
+	We have not pure, simple ideas of blue, red or any other colour (except perhaps black) because all bodies reflect heterogeneal light.	151
+	Qu: whether this be true as to Sounds (& other sensations) there being, perhaps, Rays of air wch will onely exhibit one particular sound, as rays of light o~~x~~ne particular colour.	152
+	Colours not definable, not because they are pure, unmixt thoughts, but because we cannot ₐeasily distinguish & separate the thoughts they include, ~~✗✗~~ or because we want names for their component ideas.	153
+	~~My ✗~~ By Soul is meant onely a Complex idea made up of existence, willing & perception in a large sense. therefore its is known & it may be defin'd.	154
S	We cannot possibly conceive any active power but the Will.	155

f.123

+ ~~Vx~~In moral matters Men think (tis true) that they   156
are free, but this freedom is only the freedom of
doing as they please, wch freedom is Consecutive
to the Will, respecting onely the Operative faculties.

+ Men impute their actions to themselves because   157
they will'd them & that not out of ignorance but
whereas they knew the consequences of them whether
good or bad.

+ This does not prove men to be indifferent in respect 158
of desiring ~~good or bad~~.

+ If any thing is meant by the potentia of A. B. it must 159
be desire. but I appeal to any man if his desire be
indifferent, or (to Speak more to the purpose) whether
he himself be indifferent in respect of w^t he desires,
~~before~~ till after he has ~~chosen it~~ desir'd it. for as
for desire it self or the faculty of desiring that is
indifferent as all other faculties are.

f.124

+ Actions leading to heaven are in my power if I   160
will them, therefore I will will them.

+ Qu: concerning the progression of wills in infinitum. 161

+ Herein Mathematiques have the advantage over   162
Metaphysiques & Morality, Their Definitions being of
words not yet known to ye Learner are not Disputed,
but words in Metaphisiques & Morality being mostly
known to all the definitions of them may chance to
be controverted.

+   The short jejune way in Mathematiques will not do   163
M in Metaphysiques & Ethiques, for y^t about
Mathematical propositions men have no prejudices,
no anticipated opinions to be encounter'd, they not
having yet thought on such matters. tis not so in the
other 2 mention'd sciences, a Man must not onely

-17-

demonstrate the truth, he must also vindicate it against Scruples & establish'd opinions wch contradict it. In short the dry Strigose rigid way will not suffice.

f.125

he must be more ample & copious, else his demonstration tho never so exact will not go down wth most.

+$ Extension seems to consist in variety of homogeneal thoughts coexisting without mixture.   164

+$ or rather ˄visible Extension seems to be the coexistence of colours in y^e mind.   165

S. Mo.   Enquiring & judging are actions w^{ch} ~~require~~ depend on the operative faculties w^{ch} ~~require~~ depend on y^e will wch is determin'd by some uneasiness ergo&c.   166

Suppose an agent ˄wch is finite perfectly indifferent, & as to desiring not determin'd by any prospect o~~r~~ consideration of good I say, this Agent cannot do an action morally Good. Hence 'tis evident the suppositions of A:B: are insignificant.

+ Extension, motion, time ˄Number no simple ideas, but include Succession in them wch seems to be a simple idea.   167

X Mem: to enquire into the Angle of Contact. & into fluxions &c.   168

f.126

2X¹ The sphaere of vision is equal whether I look onely in my hand, or on the open firmament. for 1st in both cases the Retina is full. 2^d the Radius's of both spheres are equall or rather nothing at all to ye sight. 3^{d}ly equall number of points in one & t'other.   169

1X1	In the Barrovian Case purblind would judge aright	170
+X¹	Why the Horizontal Moon greater?	171
+X¹	Why objects seen erect?	172
N.	To w^t purpose certain figure & texture connected wth other perceptions?	173
2X¹	Men estimate magnitudes, both by angles & distance. Blind at 1st could not know distance, or by pure sight abstracting from experience of connexion of sight & tangible ideas we can't perceive distance. therefore by pure sight we cannot perceive or judge of extension.	174
2X¹	Qu: whether it be possible to enlarge our sight or make us see at once more ∧ than we do by ~~enlarging~~ diminishing the punctum Visibile below 30"? (or more points)	175

f.127

I.S.	Speech Metaphorial more than we imagine insensible things ~~be~~ & their modes circumstances &c being exprest for ye most part by words borrow'd from things sensible. the reason's plain. Hence Manyfold Mistakes.	176
S	The grand Mistake is that we think we ∧ ~~of~~ Ideas of (have) the Operations of our Minds. certainly this Metaphorical dress is an argument we have not.	176a (f.126v.)
G	Qu: How can our idea of God be ~~sim~~ complex ~~&~~ or compounded, w^n his essence his simple & uncompounded V. Locke b. 2. S. 35	177
G	omnes reales rerum proprietates continentur in Deo w^t means Le Clerc &c by this?	177a (f.126v.)
+	The impossibility of defining or discours~~xx~~ing clearly of most things proceeds from the fault & scantiness of language, as much, perhaps, as from	178

-19-

	obscurity & confusions of Thought. Hence I may clearly & fully understand my own soul, extension, &c & not be able to define them.	
M$✱	The substance wood a collection of simple ideas see Locke B. 2 C. 26. S. 1.	179

f. 128

+	Mem: concerning strait lines seen to look at them thro' an orbicular Lattice.	180
2X¹	Qu: whether possible that those visible ideas wch are now connected with greater extensions could have been connected wth lesser extensions. there seeming to be no necessary connexion ~~P~~between those thoughts.	181
+x	Speculums seem to diminish or enlarge objets not by altering the optique angle but by altering the ~~d~~Apparent distance.	182
+	Hence Qu: if blind would think things diminish'd by convexes, or enlarged by concaves?	183
P.N.	Motion not one idea, it cannot be perceiv'd at once.	184
M.P.	Mem: to allow existence to colours in the dark, persons not thinking &c but not an absolute actual existence. 'Tis prudent to correct mens mistakes without altering their language. This makes truth glide into their souls insensibly.	185
M.P	Colours in ye dark do exist really i.e. were there light or as soon as light comes we shall see them provided we open our eyes. & that whether we will or no.	185a (f.127v.)

f.129

+	How the Retina is fill'd by a Looking glass?	186
+	Convex speculums have the Same effect wth concave glasses.	187

-20-

+	Qu: whether concave speculums have the Same effect wth Convex glasses?	188
2X^1	The reason why convex speculums diminish & concave magnify not yet ~~righ~~ fully assign'd by any writer I know.	189
+	Qu: why not objects seen confus'd when y^t they seem inverted thro a ~~xx~~ convex lens?	190
+	Qu: How to make a glass or speculum which shall magnify or diminish by altering the distance without altering the angle?	191
+	No identity ^(other than perfect likeness) in any individuals besides persons.	192
	~~When there is no difference intrinsecal or extrinsecal of moment~~	192a (f.128v.)
N.	As well make ~~sweet~~ tastes, smells, fear, shame ~~&c move~~ wit, vertue, vice ^(& all thoughts) move wth Local motion as immaterial spirit.	193

f.130

+	On account of my doctrine the identity of ^finite substances must consist in some thing else than continued existence, or relation to determin'd ^time and place of beginning to exist. the existence of our ~~ideas~~ ^thoughts being combin'd (w^ch ^make all substances) being frequently interrupted, & they having divers beginnings, & endings.	194
S	Qu: Whether Identity of Person consists not in the Will	194a (f.129v.)
2X^1	No necessary connexion between great ~~&~~ or little optique angles & great or little extension.	195

2X¹ Distan~~x~~ce is not perceiv'd, optique angles are not 196
perceiv'd. how then is extension perceiv'd by sight?

2X¹ A~~xx~~pparent magnitude of a line is not ~~ds~~imply as 197
the Optique angle, but directly as the Optique angle,
& reciprocally as the confusion &c (i.e the other
sensations ~~x~~ or want of sensation that attend near
Vision) hence great mistakes in assigning the
magnifying power of glasses. Vid: Moly: p. 182.

      perhaps
Glasses or speculums may ^ magnify or lessen 198
2X¹   angle
without altering the Optique but to no purpose.

            f.131

2X¹ Qu: whether Purblind would think objects so much 199
✗ diminish'd by a convex speculum as another?

+ Qu: wherein consists identity of Person~~s~~? not in 200
actual consciousness, for then I'm not the Same
~~man~~ person I was this day twelvemonth, but wʰhile
I think of wᵗ I then did. Not in potential for then
all persons may be the Same for ought we know.

+ Mem: Story of Mʳ Deerings Aunt. 201

+ two sorts of Potential consciousnesses Natural & 202
praeternatural in the last § but one I mean the
latter.

     meant
If by magnitude be ^ the proportion any thing bears 203
2X¹ to a determin'd tangible extension as inch, foot &c
this 'tis plain cannot be properly & ~~in~~ per se
perceiv'd by sight. & as for determin'd visible
inches, feet &c there can be no Such thing obtain'd
by the meer act of seeing abstracted from
experience &c.

            f.132

2X¹ The greatness per se perceivable of the sight, is 204
onely the propo̸rtion any ~~thing bears vis~~ visible

appearance bears to the others seen at the Same time; or ~~the~~ (wch is the Same thing) the proportion of any particular part of the visual orb to the whole.

but mark that we perceive not ~~there~~ it is an orb, any more than a plain but by reasoning. This is all the greatness the pictures have perse.

2x¹ Hereby, meerly men cannot ~~absolut~~ at all judge of the 205
extension of any object, it not availing to know the object makes such a part of a sphaerical surface except we also know the greatness of the sphaerical surface. for a point ~~make~~ may subtend the Same angle w.th a mile & so create as great an image in the Retina, i.e take up as much of the Orb.

Men judge of magnitude by faintness & vigorousness, 206
2x¹ w.th Some other circumstances & little
by distinctness & confusion, by ~~little &~~ great angles. Hence 'tis plain the ideas of sight wch are now connected with greatness, ~~may~~ might have been connected w.th Smalness & vice versâ. there being no necessary reason why great angle, faintness & distinctness without Straining sould x stand for ~~greatness~~ great extension. ~~t~~ any more than than a ~~small a~~ great angle, vigorous ness & confusion.

f.133

My end is not to deliver ~~Genera~~ Metaphysics ~~in~~ ques 207
+ altogether ~~also~~ in Some measure
in a General Scholastique way but, to ~~to~~ accommodate them to the Sciences, & shew how they may be usefull in Optiques, Geometry &c.

2x¹ Qu: whether per se proportion of visible~~se~~ 208
magnitudes ~~per~~ be perceivable by Sight. this is put on account of distinctness & confusedness the act of perception seeming to be as great in viewing any point of the visual orb distinctly as in viewing

-23-

the whole confusedly.

+ Mem: to correct my Language & make it as   209
Philosophically nice as possible to avoid giving
handle.

$2X^1$ If men could without straining alter the   210
convexity of their Crystallines they might magnify
or diminish the apparent diameters of ~~bodies~~ objets
~~without~~ the Same optic angle remaining.

$2X^1$ The bigness of the pictures in one sense in the fund is not   211
determin'd, for the nearer a man views them,
the images of them
~~they~~ (as well as other objects) will ~~make x~~ take
up the greater room in the fund of his eye.

f.134

+ Mem: Introduction to contain the design, ~~of~~ of the whole the nature &   212
manner of demonstrating &c.

$2X^1$ Two sorts of bigness accurately to be distinguish'd   213
they being perfectly & Toto Coelo different. the one
the proportion that any one appearance has to the sum
of appearances perceiv'd at the same time wth it, w^{ch}
is proportional to angles or ~~rather~~ if a surface to segments of
Sphaerical surfaces, the other is tangible bigness.

$2X^1$ Qu: w^t would happen if the sphaerae of the Retina   214
were enlarg'd or diminish'd?

X^+ We think by ~~meer sight~~ the meer act of vision we   215
perceive ~~surface~~ distance from us, yet we do not.
~~We think~~ also that we perceive Solids yet we do
not, also ~~that~~ the inequality of things seen under
the Same angle, yet we do not. Why may I not add?
we think we see extension by meer vision, yet we
do not.

X^+ Extension seems to be perceiv'd by the eye as   216
thoughts by the ear.

f.135

X We seem to have clear & distinct ideas of large 217
numbers v.g. 1000 no otherwise than by considering
'em
ₐas form'd by the multiplying of small numbers.

$2x^1$ As long as the Same angle determines the minimum 218
visibile to two persons, no different conformation
of the Eye can make a different appearance of
magnitude in the Same thing. But it being possible
to try the Angle, we may certainly know whether
the Same thing appears differently big to 2 persons
on account of their Eyes.

$2x^1$ If a man could see " objects would appear larger to 219
him than to another; hence there is another Sort
purely
ofₐVisible magnitude beside the proportion any
appearance bears to the Visual sphere, viz. its
proportion to the M.V.

1⊕B Were there but one & the Same Language in the 220
world, & did children Speak it naturally as soon
X as born, & were it not in the Power of men to
conceal their thoughts or deceive others but that
there were an inseparable connexion between words
and thoughts, soy^t posito uno ponitur alterum by
the Laws of nature. Qu: would not men think they
heard thoughts as much as that they see [extension].

Distance   220a
                                          (f.134v.)

f.136

+ All our ideas are adaequate, our knowlege of the 221
Laws of nature is not perfect & adaequate.

M.P. Men are in the right in judging their simple ideas 222
$ to be in the things them selves, certainly Heat &
colour is as much without the mind as figure,
motion, time &c

-25-

We know many things wch we want words to 223
express. Great things discoverable upon this
Principle, for want of considering wch divers
men have run into sundry mistakes endeavouring
to set forth their knowlege by sounds, w^ch
  foundring them
~~seeming difficult~~ they thought the defect was in
their knowlege w^n in truth it was in their Language.

$3\overset{a}{X}1$ Query whether the sensations of sight arising from 224
a man's head be liker the sensations of touch
proceeding from thence or from his legs?

     it constant & long
$3\overset{a}{X}1$ Or is ⋏onely the⋏ association of ideas entirely 225
different that makes me judge them the same?

              f.137

$1\overset{a}{X}3$ W^t I see is onely variety of colours & light. w^t 226
I feel is hard or soft, hot or cold, rough or smooth
&c. w^t resemblance have these thoughts wth those?

A picture painted wth great variety of colours 227
$13\overset{x}{X}$ affects the touch in ~~the s~~one uniform manner. I
cannot therefore conclude that because I see 2 I
shall feel 2, because I see angles or inequalitys
I shall feel angles or inequalitys. How therefore
can I before experience teaches me know that the
visible leggs are (because 2) connected wth the
tangible ones, or the visible head (because one)
connected wth the tangible head?

1M   All things by us conceivable are 1st thoughts, 2dly 228
powers to receive ~~those~~ thoughts, 3dly powers to
$ cause
~~occasion~~ thoughts neither of all wch can possibly
exist ~~w^thout the~~ in an inert, senseless thing.

         seen
An object w^thout a glass may be⋏under as great an 229
1X2   angle as wth a glass. a glass therefore does not
magnify the appearance by the angle.

-26-

S	Absurd that men should know the soul by idea, ideas being inert, thoughtless. Hence Malbranch confuted.	230

f.138

1×1 23	I saw gladness in his looks, I Saw Shame in his face so I see figure or Distance	231
1 X2	Qu: why things seen confusedly thro a convex glass are not magnify'd?	232
1 X2	Tho we should judge the Horizontal Moon to be more distant, why whould we therefore judge her to be greater what *Connexion betwixt, the Same Angle, ~~wider dist~~ farther distant & greaterness?	233
N.	My Doctrine affects the Essences of the Corpuscularians.	234
X	Perfect Circles &c exist not without (for none can so exist whether perfect or no) but in the mind	235
X	Lines thought ~~th~~Divisible ad infinitum because they are suppos'd to exist without. Also because they are thought the same when view'd by the naked eye & w^n view'd thro magnifying glasses.	236
X	They who knew not Glasses had not so fair a pretense for the Divisibility ad infinitum.	237
X	No idea of Circle &c in abstract.	238
+	Metaphisiques as capable of Certainty as Ethiques but not So capable to be demonstrated in a ~~M~~Geometrical way because men see clearer & have not So many prejudices in Ethiques.	239

f.139

$	Visible ideas come into the mind very distinct, so do tangible ideas, Hence Extension seen & felt.	240

3X1 Sounds tastes &c are more blended.

3X1 Qu: why not extension intromitted by the taste in   241
conjunction wth the smell seeing tastes & smells
are very distinct ideas.

X Blew & yellow particles mixt while they exhibit an   242
uniform green, their extension is not perceiv'd,
but as soon as they exhibit distinct sensations of
Blew & yellow than their Extension is perceiv'd.

3$X $\frac{1}{}$ Distinct perception of Visible ideas not so perfect   243
as of tangible, tangible ideas being many at once
equally Vivid. Hence heterogeneous ~~distinction.~~
Extension.

2X^1 Object: Why a mist encreases not the Apparent   244
Magnitude of an object in proportion to the
faintness?

+ Mem: to Enquire touching the Squaring of the   245
Circle &c.

3$\overset{a}{X}$1 That wch seems smooth & round to the touch may   246
to sight seem quite otherwise. Hence no necessary
connexion betwixt visible ideas & tangible ones.

<u>f.140</u>

X In Geometry it is not prov'd that an inch is   247
divisible ad infinitum.

X Geometry not conversant about our compleat   248
determin'd ideas of figures, for these are not
divisible ad infinitum.

$ Particular Circles may be Squar'd, for the   249
circumference being given a Diameter may be
X found betwixt w^{ch} & y^e true there is not any
perceivable difference. therefore there is no
difference. Extension being a perception & a
perception not perceiv'd is contradiction, nonsense,
nothing. In vain to alledge the difference may be

seen by Magnifying Glasses. for in y.ᵗ case there is ('tis true) a difference perceiv'd but not between the Same ideas but others much greater entirely different therefrom.

X | Any visible circle possibly percevable of any man may be Squar'd, by the Common way most accurately, or even perceivable by any other being see he never so acute i. e never so small an arch of a Circle this being w.ᵗ makes the distinction between acute & dull sight, & not y.ᵉ m̶M:V: as men are, perhaps apt to think. | 250

X | The Same is True of any Tangible Circle, therefore farther Enquiry of Accuracy in Squaring or other Curves is perfectly needless & time thrown away. | 251

f.141

X | Mem: to press w.ᵗ last precedes more homely & to think on't again. | 252

X | A meer line or distance is not made up of points, does not exist, cannot be imagin'd or have an idea fram'd thereof no more than meer colour without extension. | 253

X$ | Mem: a great difference between considering a̶ ̶length w.ᵗʰout breadth, and having an idea of or imagining length without breadth. | 254

+ | Malbranch out touching the Xtallines m̶a̶g̶ diminishing. O̶ v 1. 1. c6. | 255

¹X2 | Tis possible, (& perhaps not very improbable that is is Sometimes so) we may have the greatest pictures w̶.ᵗʰ from the least objects. therefore no ₐ connexion betwixt visible & tangible ideas, these ideas viz. great relation to the sphaera Visualis or to the M:V: (w.ᶜʰ is all that ̶s̶ₐ meant by | 256

necessary

I would have

-29-

our having a greater picture) and faintness, might possibly have stood for or signify'd small tangible extensions. Certainly the greater relation to S.V: & M:V. does frequently in y̴ Men view little objects near the Eye.

12X   Malbranch out in asserting we cannot possibly know   257
whether there are 2 men in the world that see a
thing of the Same bigness. V. L. 1c. 6

X   Diagonal of particular square commensurable wth 258
its side they both containing a certain number of
M:V:

f.142

X   I do not think that surfaces consist of lines i.e   259
meer distances. Hence perhaps *may be solv'd
that sophism wch would prove the oblique line
equal to the perpendicular between 2 parallels.

X ⊕   Suppose an inch represent a mile. 1/1000 of an   260
inch is nothing, but 1/1000 of ye mile represented
is something therefore 1/1000 of an inch tho' nothing
is not to be neglected, because it represents
Something i.e 1/1000 of a Mile

X   Particular Determin'd lines are not divisible ad   261
infinitum, but lines as us'd by Geometers are so
they not being determin'd to any particular finite
number of points. Yet a Geometer (He knows not
why) will very readily Say he can demonstrable an
inch line is divisible ad infinitum.

1_{X3} A Body moving in the Optique axis not perceiv'd to   262
move by sight meerly & wthout experience. there
is (tis true) a successive change of ideas it seems
less & less, but besides this there is no visible
change of place.

f.143

X   Mem: To Enquire most diligently Concerning the   263
Incommensurability of Diagonale & side. whether
it Does not go on the Supposition of ~~Unit~~ unit being
divisible ad infinitum, i.e of ~~an~~ the Extended thing
spoken of being divisible ad infinitum (unite being
nothing also V. Barrow Lect. Geom:). & so the
infinite indivisibility deduc'd therefrom is a
petitio principii.

X   The Diagonal is commensurable with the side.   264

M   ffrom Malbranch, Locke & my first arguings it   265
P   cant be prov'd that extension is not in matter ffrom
Lockes arguings it can't be prov'd that Colours,
~~smells &c~~ are not in Bodies.

Mem: that I was ~~Sceptical~~ distrustful at 8 years old and   266
Consequently by nature disposed for these new
Doctrines.

X   Qu: How can a line consisting of an~~x~~ unequal   267
number of Points be divisible [ad infinitum] in
two equals

f.144

1X/2   Mem: To discuss copiously how & why we do not   268
see The Pictures.

M.   Allowing extensions to exist in matter, we cannot   269
P.   know even their proportions Contrary to Malbranch.

1M   I wonder how men cannot see a truth so obvious,   270
$ as that extension cannot exist without ~~n~~ a
thinking substance.

M   Species of all sensible things made by the mind,   271
This prov'd either by turning Mens Eyes into
magnifyers or diminishers.

-31-

2 1X	Y.ʳ M. V. is suppose less than mine. Let a 3.ᵈ person have perfect ideas of both our M. Vs. His idea of my M. V. contains his idea of y.ʳˢ & sombewhat more, therefore tis made up of parts, therefore his Idea of my V. M: is not perfect or just w.ᶜʰ everts the Hypothesis.	272
2X¹	Qu: whether a M. V, or T. be extended?	273

f.145

1X2   Mem. The Strange errours men run into ~~on account~~ 274
       ~~of~~ about the pictures.

  ˣ2   We think them small, because shou'd a man be   275
1   suppos'd to see them their Pictures would take up
       but little room in the fund of his Eye.

  X   It seems all lines can't be bisected in 2 equall   276
       parts, Mem: to examine how the Geometers prove
       the contrary.

   2   Tis impossible there should be a M. V. less than   277
X1   mine. if there be mine may become equal to it
       (because they are homogeneous) by detraction of
       some part or parts, but it consists not of parts
       Ergo. &c

   ᵃ   Suppose ~~an~~ inverting perspectives bound to ᵞ.ᵉ eyes   278
X13   of a child, & continu'd to the years of Manhood,
       When he looks up or turns up his head he shall
       behold w.ᵗˢ ~~under~~ we call under. Qu: w.ᵗ would
       he think of up & down?

1M   I wonder not at my sagacity in discovering the   279
$ obvious tho' Amazing truth, I rather wonder at
       my stupid inadvertency in not finding it out before.
       'tis no Witchcraft to see ~~we know nothing but our~~
       ~~thoughts or w.ᵗ these think.~~

f.146

       Our simple ideas are so many simple thoughts or   280

¹M perceptions, & that a perception ~~exists no longer than its' perception~~ cannot exist without a thing to perceive it or any longer than it is perceiv'd, that a thought cannot be in an unthinking thing, that one uniform simple thought can be ~~onely~~ like ~~an~~ to nothing but another uniform simple thought. Complex thoughts or ideas are onely an assemblage of simple ideas and can be the image of nothing or like unto nothing but another assemblage of simple ideas. &

The ~~Belief of~~ Cartesian opinion of light & Colours 281
&c is orthodox enough ~~tho'~~ even in their eyes who
M   the   expression
think∧ Scripture∧ may favour the common opinion.
why may not mine also? But there is nothing in
Scripture that can possibly be wrested to make
against me, but, perhaps, many things for me.

+ Bodies &c do ~~really~~ exist whether we think of 'em 282
   or no, they being taken in a twofold sense.
$ Collections of thoughts & collections of ~~ideas~~
   powers to cause those thoughts. these later exist,
   tho perhaps a parte rei it may be one simple
   perfect power.

f.147

Qu. whether the extension of a plain look'd at 283
11X2 ~~straight~~ straight & slantingly, survey'd minutely
& ~~clearl~~ distinctly or in the Bulk and confusedly
at once, be the Same. N.B. the plain is suppos'd
to keep the same distance.

the ideas we have by a successive, curious, ~~minute~~ 284
⑪X2 ye minute parts of
inspection of∧ a plain do not seem to make up the
extension of that plain view'd & consider'd all
together.

+ Ignorance in ~~a measure~~ some sort requisite in ye 285
   Person that should Discover the Principle.

+ Thoughts do ~~xx~~ most properly signify ~~the~~ or are 286
mostly taken for the interiour operations of the
mind, wherein the mind is active, those y^t ~~follow~~
obey not the acts of Volition, & in wch the mind is
passive are more properly call'd sensations or
perceptions. But y^t is all a case.

X
$ Extension being the Collection or distinct 287
coexistence ~~of perception~~ of Minimums i.e of
perceptions intromitted by sight or touch, ~~to~~ it
cannot be conceiv'd without a perceiving substance.

f.148

P Malbranch does not prove that the ~~species are not~~ 288
figures & extensions exist nt w^n the are not
perceiv'd. Consequently he does not prove nor can
it be prov'd on his principles that ye sorts are the
work of the mind & onely in the mind.

M.P.1 The great argument to prove that Extension cannot 288a
be in an unthinking substance is that it cannot be (f.147v.)
conceived distinct from or without all tangible or
Visible quality

Tho matter be extended wth an indefinite Extension, 289
yet the mind makes the Sorts, they were not before
M1   even
the mind perceiving them. &ₐnow they are not
without the mind. Houses trees, &c tho indefinitely
extended matter do exist. are not without the mind.

M The great danger of making extension exist without 290
$ the mind. in y^t if it does it must be acknowleg'd
infinite immutable eternal &c. wch will be to make
either God extended (wch I think dangerous) or an
eternal, immutable, infinite, increate being beside
God.

f.149

M1 The Principle easily prov'd by plenty of arguments 291
$ ad absurdum.

-34-

IX	finiteness of our mind no excuse for the Geometers.	292 (f.148v.)
+	The twofold signification of Bodies viz. combinations of thoughts ~~a~~ & combinations of powers to raise thoughts. These, I say, in conjunction wth homogeneous particles, may solve much better the objections from the Creation. than ye supposition that matter does exist ^upon^ wch supposition, I think, ~~it~~they cannot be solv'd.	293
+	Bodies taken for Powers do exist w^n not perceived but this existence is not actual. w^n I say a power exists no more is meant than that if in ye light I open my eyes & look that way ^I^ shall see it ^i.e ye body^. &c	293a (f.148v.)
+	Quer: whether Blind before sight may not have an idea of light & colours & visible extension. After the same manner as we perceive them wth Eyes shut or in ye dark. not imagining but seeing after a sort.	294
X^{13}	Visible extension cannot be conceiv'd added to tangible extension. visible & tangible points can't make one sum. therefore these extensions are heterogeneous.	295
^{1}X^1	A Probable method propos'd whereby one may judge whether in near vision there is a greater distance between the Xtalline & fund than usual. or whether ye Xtalline be onely render'd more convex	296

f.150

if the former, then the V.S is enlarg'd & ye M.V. corresponds to less than 30" or w^{t}ever it us'd to correspond to.

12X	little extension, by distinction made great	296a (f.149v.)

-35-

1 X³   Stated measures, inches, feet &c are tangible   297
not visible extensions.

M   Locke, Moor, Raphson &c seem to make God   298
extended. 'tis nevertheless of great use to religion
to take ~~away~~ extension out of our idea of God & put
a power in its place. it seems dangerous to suppose
extension wch is manifestly inert in God.

M   But, say you, the thought or perception I call   299
             it self
$ extension is not ‸ in an unthinking thing or matter
But it is like something wch is in matter. Well,
says I, do you apprehend & conceive w^t you say
extension is like unto or do you not. If the later,
how know you they are alike, ~~if the former~~ how
can you compare any things besides y^r own ideas.
if the former it must be an idea i. e. perception
thought, or sensation wch to be in an unperceiving
thing is a Contradiction.

                         & figures
I.   I abstain from all florish & pomp of words ‸ using   300
                      Stile
a great plainness & simplicity of ~~speech~~ hav~~e~~ing oft

f.151

found it difficult to understand those that use the
Lofty & Platonic or subtil & Scholastique strain.

M1   Whatsoever has any of our ideas in it must   301
perceive, it being that very having, that passive
$ reception of ideas that denominates the mind
perceiving. th~~is~~at being the very essence of
perception, or that wherein perception consist~~e~~s.

1X2   The faintness wch alters the Appearance of the   302
Horizontal Moon, rather proceeds from the quantity
or Grossness of the intermediate Atmosphere, than
from any change of Distance wch is ~~Almost inconsiderable.~~ perhaps not considerable enough
to be a total ~~t~~Cause but may be a partial cause of
the Phaenomenon. N. B. the Visual angle is less

in the Horizon.

1   We Judge of the distance of bodies as by other   302a
1X things so also by the situation of their pictures   (f.150v.)
in the eye. (wch is the Same thing) according as they appear higher or lower those wch seem higher are farther of &c.

12X Qu: why we see objects greater in ye dusk whether   303
this can be solv'd by any but my principles.

M The Reverse of ye Principle introduc'd Scepticism.   304

M N.B. On my Principles there is a reality, there   305
are things, there is a rerum Natura.

                                                    f.152

X Mem. The surds. Doubling the Cube &c   306

X13^a ~~We think that if just made to~~ We think that if just   307
made to see we shou'd Judge of the Distance &   (f.151v.)
Magnitude of things as we do now. but this is false.
So also w^t we think positively of the situation of objects.

X Hays's Keil's &c method of proving the infinitesimals 308
of y^e 2^d order absurd, & perfectly contradictious.

X Angles of Contact, & vr̄ly all angles comprehended   309
by a right line & a curve, cannot be measur'd, the
arches intercepted not being similar.

$+   The danger of Expounding the H: Trinity by extension. 310

M.P. 1 Qu: why should the magnitude seen at a near   311
distance be deem'd the true one rather than that
seen at a farther distance? Why should the sun be
thought many 1000 miles rather than one foot in
diameter. both being ~~onely~~ equally apparent diameters?
Certainly Men judg'd of the Sun not in himself but
wth relation to themselves.

M 4 Principles whereby to answer objections viz. 312
1. Bodies do really exist tho not perceiv'd by us.
2. There is a law or course of Nature.
~~4~~3. Language & knowlege are all about ideas, & words stand for nothing else.

f.153

4. Nothing can be a proof against one side of a contradiction that bears equally hard upon the Other.

$X What shall I say? dare I pronounce the admir'd 313
ἀκριβεια Mathematica: that Darling of ~~this~~ the Age a trifle?

X Most certainly no finite Extension divisible ad Infinitum. 314

X Mem:Difficulties about Concentric Circles. 315

N. Mem. to Examine & accurately discuss the Scholium of the 8th. Definition of M^r. Newton's Principia. 316

X$ Ridiculous in the Mathematicians to despise sense 317

+ Qu. is it not impossible there shou'd be General ideas? All ideas come from without, ~~the mind~~ they are all particular. The mind, tis true, can consider one ~~xd~~ thing wthout another, but then consider'd asunder they make not 2 ideas. both together can make but one as for instance Colour & Visible extension. 318

f.154

X The end of a Mathematical line is nothing. Locke's argument that the end of his pen is black or white concludes nothing here. 319

X Mem: take care how you pretend to define extension, for fear of the Geometers. 320

X Qu: why difficult to imagine a minimum. Ans. because we are not us'd to take notice of 'em singly, they not being able singly to pleasure or hurt us thereby to deserve our regard.   321

X Mem. to prove against Keil y^t the ^infinite^ divisibility of matter makes ~~a less bx~~ the half ~~of~~ have an equal number of equal parts with the whole.   322

X Mem. to examine how far the not comprehending infinity may be admitted as a plea.   323

X Qu. why may not the Mathematicians reject all the ~~xx~~ extensions below the M. as well as the dds &c wch are allow'd to be Somthing & consequently may be magnify'd by glasses into inches, feet &c as well ~~tas~~ as the quantitys next below the M?   324

f.155

$+ Bigg, little & number are the works of the mind. How therefore can y^e extension you suppose in matter be big or little how can it consist of any number of points?   325

P. Mem: Strictly to remark L.b2.c.8S.8   326

+ Schoolmen compar'd with the Mathematicians   327

X Extension is blended wth tangible or visible ideas, & by the mind praescinded therefrom.   328

X Mathematiques made easy the Scale does almost all. the Scale can tell us the Subtangent in ye Parabola is 2ble the abscisse.   329

X W^t need of the Utmost accuracy w^n the Mathematicians own in rerum natura they cannot find any thing correspond~~ed~~ing wth their nice ideas.   330

X Newton in Sad plight about his Cave intellexeris finitas.   331

X   One should indeavour to find a progression by trying w.th the Scale.   332

X   Newtons fluxions needless. any thing below a M. might serve for Leibnitz's Differential Calculus.   333

f.156

X   How can they hang together so well since ~~therein~~ there are in them (I mean the mathematiques) so many Contradictoriae argutiae v. Barrow Lect: 334

X   A man may read a book of Conics with ease knowing how to try if they are right. he may take 'em on the credit of the Authour.   335

X   Where's the ~~good~~ need of certainty in Such trifles? the ~~onely~~ thing that makes it so much esteem'd in them is x that we are thought not capable of getting it elsewhere. But we may in Ethiques & Metaphysiques.   336

X   The not Leading men into mistakes no argument for the truth of the infinitesimals. they being nothings may, perhaps, ~~be~~ do neither good nor harm. except w.ⁿ they are taken for som thing. & then the~~y~~ contradiction begets a Contradiction.   337

X $a + 500$ nothings $= a + 50$ nothings an innocent silly truth   338

M   My Doctrine excellently corresponds w.th the Creation I suppose no matter, ~~nor any~~ no Stars, sun &c to have existed before.   339

X   It seems all Circles are not similar figures there not being the same proportion betwixt all circumferences & their diameters.   340

f.157

X   When a small line upon Paper represents a mile the Mathematicians do not calculate the 1/10000   341

of the Paper line they Calculate the 1/10000 of the
mile tis ~~x~~to this the have regard, tis of this the
think if they think or have any idea at all. the inch
perhaps might ~~be~~ represent to their imaginations
the mile but ye 1/10000 of the inch can be ~~mad~~ not
made to represent any thing it not being imaginable.

X   But the 1/10000 of a mile being somwhat they think   341a
the 1/10000 of the inch is somwhat, w.^n they   (f.156v.)
think of y.^t they imagine they think on this.

     3 ~~prob~~ faults occur in the arguments of the   342
Mathematicians, for divisibility ad infinitum.
X   1. they suppose extension to exist without the mind
or not perceiv'd. 2. they suppose that we have an
idea of length without breadth. *or that length without
breadth does exist. 3. that ~~Number~~ unite is divisible ad
infinitum.

X*   or rather that invisible length does exist.   342a
                                                                              (f.156v.)
     To suppose a M.S. divisible is to Say α there are   343
X   distinguishable ideas where there are no distinguishable
ideas.

X   The M.S. is not near so inconceivable as this   344
signum in magnitudine individuum.

X   Mem: To examine the Math: about their point w.^t   345
it is Something or nothing, & how it differs from
the M.S.

                                                                            f.158

X   All might be demonstrated by a new method of   346
indivisibles, easier perhaps & juster than that
of Cavallerius.

M.P.1   Unperceivable perception a contradiction.   347

     Proprietates reales rerum omnium in Deo tam   348

G   corporum quam Spirituum continentur. Clerici
Log: cap. 8.^{m}

+   Let my adversaries answer ~~every~~ ^{any} one of mine i'll   349
yield -- If I don't answer every one of theirs I'll
yield.

+   The Loss of the excuse may hurt Transubstantiation,   350
but not the Trinity

    By ye excuse is meant the finiteness of our mind   350a
making it possible for contradictions to appear   (f.157v.)
true to us.

X   We need not Strain our Imaginations ~~x~~to conceive   351
such little things. Bigger may do as well for
intesimals since the integer must be an infinite.

X   Evident y^t wch has an infinite number of parts must   352
be infinite.

X   Qu: whether extension be resoluble into points id   353
does not consist of.

    Axiom. No reasoning about things whereof we   354
X have no idea. Therefore no reasoning about
Infinitesimals.

X   Nor can it be objected that we reason about   354a
Numbers wch are only words & not ideas, for   (f.157v.)
these Infinitesimals are words of no use
if not supposed to stand for Ideas.

                                                                       f.159

X   Much less infinitesimals of infinitesimals &c   355

X   Axiom. No word to be used without an idea.   356

S   If uneasiness be necessary to set the will at work.   357
Qu: How shall we will in Heaven.

+   Malbranche's & Bayle's arguments do not seem to   358

-42-

   prove against Space, but onely Bodies.

M. P. 1 Our Eyes & senses inform us not of the existence of 359
   Matter or ideas existing existing without the mind.
   They are not to be Blam'd for the mistake.

 X I defy any man to assign a Right line equal to a   360
   Paraboloeid, but that w^n look't at thro a Microscope
   they may appear unequall.

 M Newtons Harangue amounts to no more than that   361
   gravity is proportional to gravity.

 X One can't imagine an extended thing without colour. 362
   v. Barrow. L. G.

        not
   Qu: whether I had ˄ better allow Colours to exist   362a
M without the Mind taking the Mind for the Active   (f.158v.)
P thing wch I call I, my self. y^t seems to be distinct
   from ye Understanding.

          not
   Men allow colours, sounds &c ˄ to exist without the 363
     had
P. mind tho they ~~have~~ no Demonstration they do not.
   Why may the not allow my Principle with a
   Demonstration.

 P. The taking extension to be distinct from all other   363a
   tangible & visible qualities & to make an idea by   (f.158v.)
   it self, has made men take it to be without the Mind.

                f.160

 X Keils filling the world with a mite this follows from 364
 M the Divisibility of extension ad infinitum.

 * Extension or length without breadth seems to be   365
 X+ nothing ~~the~~ save the number of points that lie betwixt
   any 2 points. it seems to consist in meer proportion
   meer reference of the mind.

 X Extension without breadth i.e. invisible, intangible 365a
 X ~~b~~length is not conceivable tis a mistake we are   (f.159v.)

-43-

	led into by the Doctrine of Abstraction.	
X⁺	To what purpose is it to Determine the Focus's of Glasses Geometrically.	366
M	Innumerable vessels if Matter v. Cheyne.	367
X⁺	I'll not admire the Mathematicians. tis w:t any one of common sense might attain to by repeated acts. I know it by experience, I am but one of common sense, and I &c	368
+	By thing I ~~onely mean~~ either mean Ideas or that w.ᶜʰ has ideas.	369
+	Nullum Praeclarum ingenium unquam fuit magnus Mathematicus. Scaliger.	370
+	Genius A Great ~~wit~~ cannot Stoop to such trifles & ~~they~~ minutenesses ~~&~~as they consider.	371
+	in I see no wit any of them but Newton, The rest are meer triflers, meer ~~Nothin~~ Nihilarians.	372 (f.159v.)
X	The folly of the Mathematicians in not judging of sensations by their senses. Reason was given us for nobler uses.	373 (f.159v.)
X	Sir Isaac owns his book could have been demonstrated on the Supposition of indivisibles.	374 (f.159v.)
+	Mathematicians have some of them good parts, the more is the pity. Had they not been Mathematicians they had been good for nothing. they were Such fools they knew not how to employ their parts.	375 (f.159v.)
X⁺	The mathematicians could not somuch as tell wherein truth & certainty consisted till Locke told 'em. I see the best of them talk of light & colours as if w.ᵗʰout the mind.	376 (f.159v.)
M. 1	an idea cannot exist unperceiv'd.	377 (f.160v.)

f.161

+1 All significant words Stand for Ideas   378

2 All knowlege about our ideas

+3 All ideas come from without or from within.

4 If from without it must be by the Senses & they are call'd sensations.

+5 If from within they are the operations of the mind & are called thoughts.

6 No sensation can be in a senseless thing.

7 No thought can be in a thoughtless thing.

+8 All our ideas are either sensations or thoughts, by 3, 4, 5.

9 None of ^our ideas can be in a thing wch is both thoughtless & senseless. 6, 7, 8.

10 the bare passive reception or having of ideas is call'd perception

11 whatever ~~therefore~~ has ^in it an idea, tho it be never so passive, tho it exert no manner of act about it, yet it must perceive. 10.

12 all ideas either are ~~ar~~Simple, ~~uniform~~ ideas, or made up of Simple ~~uniform~~ ideas.

+13 that thing wch is like unto another thing must agree wth it in one or more Simple ideas.

f.162

+14 whatever is like a Simple idea must either be another Simple idea of the Same Sort or contain a Simple idea of the Same Sort. 13.

-45-

15 nothing like ~~a Simple~~ an idea can be in an unperceiving thing. 11. 1~~3~~4.

    another demonstration of the same thing

16 Two things cannot be Said to be alike or unlike till they have been compar'd

17 Comparing is the view_ing two ideas together, & marking w^t ~~Simple ideas~~ they agree in & w^t they disagree in.

18 The mind can compare nothing but it's own ideas. 17.

19 Nothing like an idea can be in an ūperceiving thing. 11. 16. 18.

    Th~~is~~ese arguments must be propos'd shorter & more separate in the Treatise.   378a (f.160v.)

N.B. Other arguments innumerable, both a priori & a posteriori drawn from all the Sciences, from the clearest plainest most obvious truths ~~for~~ whereby to Demonstrate the Principle ~~viz.~~ i.e. that neither our Ideas nor any thing like our ideas can possibly be in an unperceiving thing.   379

N.B. not one argument ~~of any Sort~~ of any kind w^t soever, certain or pro~~xxx~~bable, a priori or a posteriori from any art or Science, from either sense or reason against it.   380

f.163

X Mathematicians have no right idea of angles. hence angles of Contact wrongly apply'd to prove extension divisible ad infinitum.   381

X We have got the Algebra of pure intelligences   382

X We can prove Newtons ~~prin~~ propositions* more accurately more easily & upon truer principles than himself.   383

*	to the utmost accuracy wanting nothing of	383a
X	of Problems	(f.162v.)
	perfection. their solutions_∧ themselves must own to fall infinitely short of perfection	

	Barrow owns the Downfall of Geometry However	384
	it	
X	Ill Endeavour to Rescue it so far as_∧ is usefull or real or imaginable or intelligible, but for the nothings I'll leave them to their admirers.	

X	Ill teach any one the whole course of Mathematiques in 1/100 part the time that another will.	385

X	~~P~~Much Banter got from the prefaces of the Mathematicians.	386

+	Innumerable vessels if Matter v. Cheyne.	387

P.	Newton~~s~~ says colour is in the subtil matter hence Malbranch proves nothing or is mistaken in asserting there is onely figure & motion therein.	388

	use	
X	The Billys ~~take~~ a finite visible line for an 1/m	389 (f.163v.)
T	Marsilius ficinus his appearing the moment he died solv'd by my idea of time.	390 (f.163v.)

	The Philosophers lose their Matter, The	391
M	Mathematicians loose their insensible	(f.163v.)
	the Profane their extended Deity	
	sensations_∧. Pray w^t do the Rest of Mankind lose, as for bodies &c we have them still. N.B the future P~~hl~~hilosoph: & Mathem: get vastly by ye bargain.	

	There are men who Say there are insensible	392
P.	extensions, there are others who Say the Wall	(f.163v.)
	is not white, the fire is not hot &c We Irish men cannot attain to these truths.	

	The Mathematicians think there are insensible	393
X	lines, about these they harangue, these cut in a	(f.163v.)
	all angles	
	point, at these are divisible ad infinitum. We Irish	

X men can conceive ~~no such thing~~ no such lines.

X The Mathematicians talk of ~~Something~~ w^t they call a 394
point, this they ~~they~~ Say is not altogether nothing (f.163v.)
nor is it downright somthing, now we Irish men
are apt to think something & nothing are next
neighbours.

f.164

X I can Square the Circle, &c they cannot, wch goes on the 395
best principles

+ Engagements to P. on account of ye treatise that 396
grew up under his Eye, on account also of his
approving my harangue. Glorious for P. To ~~pxr~~
be the Protectour of usefull tho Newly discover'd
Truths.

+ How could I venture thoughts into the World before 397
I knew the would be of use to the world? and how
could I know that till I had try'd how the suited
other men's ideas.

+ I publish not this so much for any thing else as to 398
know whether Other Men have the Same Ideas as
we Irishmen. this is my end and not to be Inform'd
as to my own Particular.

+ The Materialists & Nihilarians need not be of a 399
party.

NOTEBOOK A

f.3

    I -- Introduction

    M -- Matter

    P -- Primary & Secondary Qualities

    E -- Existence

    T -- Time

    S -- Soul -- Spirit

    G -- God

    Mo -- Moral Philosophy

    N -- Natural Philosophy

f.4

1X3	Qu: if there be not two kinds of visible extension. one perceiv'd by a confus'd view, the other by a distinct successive direction of the optique axis to each point.	400
I	No general Ideas, the contrary a cause of mistake or confusion in Mathematiques &c. this to be intimated in ye Introduction.	401
+	The Principle may be apply'd to the difficulties of Conservation cooperation &c.	402
N	Trifling for the Philosophers to enquire the cause of Magnetical attractions &c, They onely search after coexisting ideas.	403
M.P.	Quaecunqx in Scriptura militant adversus Copernicum, militant pro me.	404

-50-

M. P   All things in the Scripture wch side with the Vulgar   405
against the Learned side with me also. I side in all
things with the Mob.

I know there is a mighty Sect of Men will oppose   406
me. but yet I may expect to be Supported by those
whose minds are not so far overgrown wth madness,
these are far the greatest part of mankind.
Especially Moralists, Divines, Politicians, in a
word all but Mathematicians

f.5

& Natural Philosophers (I mean only the
Hypothetical Gentlemen). Experimental
Philosophers have nothing whereat to be offended
in me.

+ Newton begs his Principle, I Demonstrate mine.   407

M. E.   I must be very particular in explaining w^t is meant   408
by things existing in Houses, chambers, fields,
      not
caves &c w^n ∧ perceiv'd as well as w^n perceiv'd.
& shew how the Vulgar notion agrees with mine
when we narrowly inspect into the meaning &
definition of the word Existence wch is no simple
idea distinct from ~~perception~~ perceiving & being
perceiv'd.

+ The Schoolmen have ~~a~~ noble subjects but handle   409
them ill. The Mathematicians have trifling subjects
but reason admirably about them. certainly their
Method & arguing are excellent.

+ God knows how far our knowlege of Intellectual   410
beings may be enlarg'd from th~~is~~e Principle.

f.6

The Reverse of the Principle I take to have been   411
M   chief
the ∧ Source of all that Scepticism & folly all those

-51-

contradictions & inextricable puzling absurdities, ~~all~~that have in all ages been a reproach to Human Reason. as well as of that Idolatry ~~of~~ whether of Images or of Gold &c that blinds the Greatest part of the World. as well as of that shamefull immorality that turns us into Beasts.

E   היה   vixit & fuit.   412

E+   ουσια   the name for substance used by Aristotle   413
the ffathers &c.

X   If at the same time we shall make the Mathematiques   414
much more easie & much more accurate. w^t can
be objected to us?

X   We need not force our Imagination to conceive such   415
very small lines for infinitessimals. they may
every whit as well be imagin'd big as little since
that the integer must be infinite.

                                                                              f.7

X   Evident that wch has an Ifinite number of parts   416
must be infinite.

X   We cannot imagine a line or space infinitely great   417
therefore absurd to talk or make propositions
about it.

X   We cannot imagine a line, space &c quovis dato   418
majus. since y^t what we imagine must be datum
aliquod. & a thing can't be greater than it self.

X   If you call infinite that wch is greater than any   419
assignable by another. then I say in that sence
there may be an infinite square, sphere or any
other figure wch is absurd.

X   Qu: if extension be resoluble into points it does   420
not consist of.

X	No reasoning about things whereof we have no ideas therefore no Reasoning about Infinitesimals.	421
+	No word to be used without an idea.	422
S	If uneasiness be necessary to set the will at work. Qu: How shall we will in Heaven.	423

f.8

+	Bayle's Malbranchs &c arguments do not seem to prove against space, but onely against Bodies.	424
M / P	I agree in Nothing wth the Cartesians as to ye existence of Bodies & qualities	424a (f.7v.)
+	Aristotle as good a Man as Euclid but He was allow'd to have been mistaken.	425
X	Lines not proper for Demonstration	426
⊕M	We see the Horse it self, the Church it self ~~xxxxxxx~~ it being an Idea & nothing more.	427
M	The Horse it self the Church it self is an Idea i.e. immediate object object ∧ of thought	427a (f.7v.)
X	Instead of injuring our Doctrine much Benefits Geometry.	428
E	Existere is percipi or percipere∧. the horse is in the Stable, the Books are in the Study as before.	429
	∧ or velle i.e agere have	429a (f.7v.)
N	In Physiques I ~~see~~ have a vast view of things soluble hereby but have not Leisure.	430
N	Hyps & such like unaccountable things confirm my Doctrine.	431

-53-

f.9

X   Angle not well Defin'd see Pardie's Geometry by   432
Harris &c. this one ground of Trifling

+   One idea not the cause of another, one power not   433
the cause of another. the cause of all natural things
is onely God. Hence trifling ∧ after second Causes. (to enquire)
This Doctrine gives a most suitable idea of Divinity.

N   Absurd to study Astronomy & other the like   434
Doctrines as Speculative Sciences.

N   The absurd account of Memory by the Brain &c   435
makes for me.

+   How was light created before man? even so were   436
Bodies created before man.

E^1 Impossible any thing Besides that wch thinks & is   437
thought on should exist.

Making thought to be active   437a
(f.8v.)

f.10

X   That wch is visible cannot be made up of invisible   438
things.

X   M.S. is that wch wherein there are not contain'd   439
distinguishable sensible parts. now how can that
wch hath not sensible parts be divided into sensible
parts? if you Say it may be be divided into insensible
parts. I Say these are nothings.

X   Extension abstract from sensible qualities is no   440
Sensation, I ~~axx~~, grant, but then there is no such
idea as any one may try. there is onely a
Considering the number of points without the sort
of them, & this makes more for me since it must
be in a Considering thing.

-54-

1x12	Mem: before I have shewn the Distinction between visible & tangible extension I must not mention them as distinct, I must not mention M.T. & M.V. but in general M.S. &c.	441
X	this belongs to Geometry	441a (f.9v.)
1X3	Qu: whether a M.V. be of any colour? a M.T. of any tangible quality?	442
1x3	If visible extension be the object of Geometry 'tis that which is survey'd by the Optique axis.	443
P	I may say the pain is in my finger &c according to my Doctrine.	444

f.11

X	Mem: nicely to discuss w^t is meant when we say a line consist~~s~~ of a certain number of inches or points &c A Circle of a certain number of Square inches, points &c. Certainly we may think of a Circle, or have it's idea in our mind without thinking of points or Square inches &c. whence it should seem the idea of a Circle is not make up of ∧the ideas of points square inches &c.	445
X	Qu: is any more than this meant by the foregoing Expressions viz. that Squares or points may be perceived in or made∧of a ~~Line~~ Circle &c. or that squares points &c are actually in it i.e. are perceivable in it.	446
X$^+$	A line in abstract or distance is the number of points between two points. there is also distance between a slave & an Emperour, between a Peasant & Philosopher, between a drachm & a pound, a farthing & a Crown &c in all wch distance signifies the number of intermediate ideas.	447

f.12

X   Halley's Doctrine about the Proportion between   448
Infinitely great quantities vanishes. When men
speak of Infinite quantities, either they mean finite
*   quantities or else talk of [that whereof they have]
no idea. both wch are absurd.

*   that need not have been blotted out, 'tis good Sense   448a
if we do but determine w^t we mean by thing and   (f.11v.)
Idea.

If the Disputations of the Schoolmen ~~xx~~are blam'd   449
            triflingness
for intricacy ∧ & confusion, yet it must be acknowleg'd
X   that in the main they treated of great & important
subjects. If we admire the Method & acuteness of
the Math: the length, the subtilty, the exactness of
their Demonstrations, we must nevertheless ~~th~~ be
forced to grant that they are for the most part about
trifling subjects & perhaps nothing at all.

+   Motion on 2^d thoughts seems to be a simple idea   450

p1   Motion distinct from ye thing moved is not   450a
Conceivable.   (f.11v.)

N   Mem: to take notice of Newton for Defining it also   451
of Locke's wisdom in leaving it undefin'd.

ut ordo partium Temporis est immutabilis, sic   452
etiam ordo partium Spatii. Moveantur hae de locis
+   suis et movebuntur, (ut ita dicam) de seipsis. truly
Number is immoveable that we will allow wth
Newton.

f.13

Ask a Cartesian whether he is wont to imagine his   453
globules without colour. pellucidness is a colour.
P   The Colour of ordinary light of the Sun is white.
Newton in the right in assigning colours to the rays
of light.

1X1   A man born Blind would not imagine Space as we   454
do. we give it always some dilute or duskish or
dark colour. in short we imagine it as visible or
intromitted by the Eye wch. he would not do.

N   Proinde vim inferunt Sacris literis qui voces hasce   455
(v. tempus, spatium, motus) de quantitatibus
mensuratis ibi interpretantur. Newton p. 10.

N   I differ from Newton in that I think the recession   456
ab axe motus is not the effect or index or measure of motion,
but of the vis impressa. it sheweth not w^t is truly
moved but w^t has the force impress'd on it. or
rather that wch. hath an impressed force.

X   D & P are not proportional in all Circles. dd is to 1/4   457
dp as d to p/4 but d & p/4 are not in the same
proportion in all Circles. Hence tis nonsense to
seek the terms of one general proportion whereby
to rectify all peripheries or of another whereby
to Square all Circles.

                                                     f.14

X   N.B. if the Circle be Squar'd Arithmetically, 'tis   458
Squar'd Geometrically. Arithmetic or numbers
being nothing but lines & proportions of lines
when applyd to Geometry.

X$^+$ Mem. to remark Cheyne & his Doctrine of infinites   459

X   Extension, motion, Time do each of them include   460
the idea of Succession. & so far forth they seem to
be of Mathematical Consideration. Number
consisting in Succession & distinct perception w^{ch}.
also consists in Succession for things at once
perceiv'd are jumbled & mixt together in the mind.
Time and motion cannot be conceiv'd without
Succession, & extension qua Mathemat: cannot be
conceiv'd but as consisting of parts w^{ch}.
may be distinctly & Successively perceiv'd.

Extension perceiv'd ~~much~~ at ~~xx~~ once & in confuso does not belong to Math.

+ The~~ ^Simple idea ~~of~~ call'd Power seems obscure or rather none at all. but onely the relation 'twixt cause & Effect. W^n I ask whether A can móve B. if A be an intelligent thing. I mean no more than whether the volition of A that B move be attended wth the motion of B. if ~~a~~A be senseless whether the   461

f.15

impulse of ~~a~~A against B be follow'd by ye motion of B.

X Barrows arguing against indivisibles, lect. x 1. p. 16 is a petitio principii, for the Demonstration of Archimedes supposeth the circumference to consist of more than 24 points. moreover it may perhaps be necessary to suppose the divisibility ad infinitum, in order to Demonstrate that the radius is equal to the side of the Hexagon.   462

X Shew me an argument against indivisibles that does not go on some false supposition.   463

X A great number of insensibles. or thus. two invisibles say you put together become visible therefore that M.V. contains or is made up of Invisibles. I answer. the M.V. does not comprise, is not compos'd of Invisibles. all the matter amounts to this viz. whereof I had no idea a while agoe I have an idea now. It remains for you to prove that I came by the present ^idea because there were 2 invisibles added together. I say the invisibles are nothings, cannot exist, include a contradition.   464

+ I am young, I am an upstart, I am a pretender, I am vain, very well. I shall Endeavour patiently to bear up under the most lessening, vilifying ap-   465

f.16

    pride
pellations the ~~wit~~ & rage of man can devise. But
one thing, I know, I am not guilty of. I do not pin
my faith on the sleeve of any great man. I act not
out of prejudice & prepossession. I do not adhere
to any opinion because it is an old one, a receiv'd
       or
one, a fashionable one, ~~&~~ one that I have spent much
time in the study and cultivation of.

X Sense rather than Reason & demonstration ought 466
to be employ'd about lines & figures, these being
things sensible, for as for those you call insensible
we have proved them to be nonsense, nothing.

I If in some things I differ from a Philosopher I 467
profess to admire, 'tis for that very ~~account on w^{ch}~~
thing on account whereof I admire him namely
 the
~~a free & unprejudic'd search after~~ love of truth.
this &c

I Wherever my Reader finds me talk very positively 468
I desire he'd not take it ill. I see no reason why
certainty should be confin'd to the Mathematicians.

f.17

X I Say there are no incommensurables, no surds, 469
~~Say you~~ I Say the side of any Square may be
assign'd in numbers. Say you assign unto me the
side of the Square 10. I ask w^t 10, 10 feet, inches
&c or 10 points. if the later; I deny there is any
Such Square, 'tis impossible 10 points should
compose a Square. if the former, resolve y^r ~~Square~~
10 Square inches, feet &c into points & the number
of points must necessarily be a Square number
whose side is easily assignable.

X A mean proportional cannot be found betwixt any 470
two given lines. it can onely be found betwixt those
the numbers of whose points multiply'd together

-59-

produce a Square number. thus betwixt a line of 2
geometrical
inches & a line of 5 inches, a mean ˄ cannot be found
except the number of points contain'd in 2 inches
multiply'd by ye number of points contain'd in 5
inches make a Square number.

X   If the wit & industry of the Nihilarians were   471
employ'd about the usefull & practical Mathematiques,
w^t advantage had it brought to Mankind?

                                                                            f.18

M. E   You ask me whether the books are in the study ˄ now w^n 472
no one is there to see them. I answer yes. you ask
me are we not in the wrong for imagining things to
exist w^n they are not actually perceiv'd by the
senses. I answer no. the existence of our ideas
consists in being perceiv'd, imagin'd thought on.
whenever they are imagin'd or thought on they do exist.
Whenever they are mention'd or discours'd of they
are imagin'd & thought on therefore you can at no
time ask me whether they exist or no, but by reason
of y^t very question they must necessarily exist.

E   But say you then a Chimaera does exist. I answer   473
it doth in one sense. i.e it is imagin'd. but it must
be well noted that existence is vulgarly restrain'd
to actuall perception. & that I use the word Existence
in a larger sense than ordinary.

+   N. B. according to my Doctrine all things are entia   474
rationis i.e. solum habent esse in Intellectu.

E   according to my Doctrine all are not entia rationis   474a
the distinction between Ens rōnis & ens reale is   (f.17v.)
kept up by it as well as any other Doctrine.

X   You ask me whether there can be an infinite Idea?   475
I answer in one sense there may. thus the visual
sphaere tho ever so small is infinite. i.e. has no
end. But if by infinite you mean extension

-60-

f.19

consisting of innumerable points. then I ask y.̅ͬ
pardon. points tho never so many may be number'd
⁎ the multitude of points or feet, inches &c hinders
not their numberableness in the least. Many or most
are numerable as well as few or least. also if by
infinite idea you mean an idea too great to be
comprehended or perceiv'd all at once. you must
excuse me. I think such an infinite ~~xx~~ is no less
than a contradiction.

* i.e hinders not their being Nameable. 475a
(f.18v.)

M^1 The sillyness of the Currant Doctrine makes much 476
for me. they commonly suppose a Material world,
figures, motions, bulks of va~~x~~rious sizes &c
according to their own confession to no purpose, all
our sensations may be & sometimes actually are
without them. nor can men so much as conceive it
possible they should concur in any wise to ~~*~~the
production of them.

I mean a Cartesian
M^1 Ask a man˄why he supposes this vast Structure, 477
this compages of Bodies. & he shall be at a Stand,
he'll not have one word to say. w.̅ͨʰ suf-

f.20

ficiently shews the folly of the hypothesis.

M. or rather why he supposes all y.ˢ Matter, for bodies 477a
& their qualitys I do allow to exist indepently of (f.18v.)
Our Mind.

Qu: how is the Soul distinguish'd from it's ideas? 478
S certainly if there were no sensible ideas there
could be no Soul, no perception, remembrance,
love, fear &c no faculty could be exerted.

S The soul is the will properly speaking & as it is 478a
distinct from Ideas. (f.19v.)

-61-

S   The grand, puzling question whether I sleep or   479
wake? easily Solv'd.

X   Qu: whether minima or near minima may not be   480
compar'd by ~~their~~ their Sooner & later evanescency
as well as by more or less points. So that one
sensibile may be greater than another tho it
exceeds it not by one point.

X   Circles ~~are not~~ o~~r~~n several radius's are not   481
similar figures they having neither all nor any an
infinite number of sides. Hence in Vain to enquire
after 2 terms of ∧ one & ye same ~~a~~ proportion that should constantly
express the reason of the d to the p in all Circles.

X   Mem: to remark Wallis's harangue that the   482
aforesaid ~~h~~Proportion can neither be express'd
by rational numbers nor surds.

<u>f.21</u>

X   We can no more have an idea of length without   483
breadth or Visibility than of a General figure.

X   One idea may be like another idea tho' they Contain   484
+   no common simple idea. thus the Simple idea red
is in some sense like the Simple idea blue. tis liker
it than sweet or shrill. But then those ideas wch are so
said to be alike agree ~~either~~ both in their connexion
with another simple idea viz. extension & in their
being receiv'd by one & ye same sense. But after
all nothing can be like an idea but an idea.

This I do not altogether approve of   484a
(f.20v.)

+   No sharing betwixt God & Nature or second Causes   485
in my Doctrine.

M   Materialists must allow the Earth to be actually   486
mov'd by the Attractive power of every Stone that
falls from the air. with many other the like
absurditys.

X   Enquire concerning the Pendulum Clock &c.   487
whether those inventions of Huygens &c may be
attained to by my Doctrine.

                                                                     f.22

\+   The $''''$ & $'''''$ & $''''''$ &c of time are to be cast   488
away & neglected as So many noughts or nothings.

\+   Mem. to make experiments concerning Minimums   489
& their colours. whether they have any or no. &
whether they can be of that green wch seems to be
compounded of yellow & blue.

S   Qu: whether it were not better not to call the   490
operations of the $_\wedge^{mind}$ ideas, confining this term to
things sensible?

E   Mem: Diligently to set forth how $_\wedge^{that}$ many of the   491
Ancient Philosophers run into so great absurditys
as even to deny the existence of motion and those
other things they perceiv'd actually by their senses.
this sprung from their not knowing w^t existence
was and wherein it consisted this the source of all
their Folly, 'tis on the Discovering of the nature &
meaning & import of Existence that I chiefly insist.
This puts a wide difference betwixt the Sceptics &c
& me. This I think wholly new. I am sure 'tis
new to me.

                                                                     f.23

X   We have learn'd from Mr Locke that $_\wedge^{there}$ may be and   492
that there are several glib, coherent, methodical
Discourses wch nevertheless amount to just nothing.
this by him intimated with relation to the Scholemen.
We may apply it to the Mathematicians.

\+   Power no simple Idea. it means nothing but the   493
Relation between Cause & Effect.

\+   Qu: How can all words be Said to Stand for ideas?   494

The word Blue stands for a Colour without any
extension or abstract from extension. But we have
not an idea of Colour without extension. we cannot
imagine Colour without extension.

+ Locke seems wrongly to Assign a Double use of   495
words one for communicating & the other for
recording our thoughts. Tis absurd to use words
for the recording our thoughts to our selves. or
in our private meditations.

f.24

                 two
No one abstract simple idea like another ~~one~~ simple 496
ideas may be connected with one & the same 3^d.
+ simple idea, or be intromitted by one & the same
sense. But consider'd in themselves they can have
no thing common & consequently no likeness.

Qu: How can there be any abstract ideas of   497
+ Colours? it seems not so easily as of tastes or
sounds. But then all abstract ideas whatsoever
are particular. I can by no means conceive a
general idea. 'Tis one thing to abstract one idea
from another of a different kind. & another thing
to abstract an idea from all particulars of the
Same kind.

N Mem. much to Recommend & approve of   498
Experimental Philosophy

What means Cause as distinguish'd from Occasion? 499
S nothing but a Being wch wills w^n the Effect follows
the volition. Those things that happen from without
we are not the Cause of therefore there is some
other Cause of them

f.25

i.e. there is a being that wills those perceptions
in us.

S.	it should be Said Nothing ^but a Will a being wch wills being unintelligible.	499a (f.23v.)
X	One Square cannot be double of another. Hence the Pythagoric Theorem is false.	500
1X1	Some writers of Catoptrics absurd enough to place ^the apparent place of ye object ~~image~~ in the Barrovian Case behind the eye.	501
+	Blew & yellow chequers still diminishing terminate in green. This may help to prove the composition of green.	502
+	There is in green 2 foundations of 2 relations of likeness to blew & yellow. therefore Green is compunded.	503
+	A mixt cause will produce a mixt Effect therefore Colours are all compounded that we see.	504
+	Mem: to Consider Newton's two Sorts of Green.	505
+	N.B. My Abstract & general Doctrines ought not to be condemn'd by the Royall Society Tis w^t Their Meeting did Ultimately intend. v. Sprat's History S.R.	506

f.26

I	Mem: to Premise a Definition of Idea.	507
Mo.	The 2 great Principles of Morality. the Being of a God & the Freedom of Man: these to be handled in the beginning of the Second Book.	508
X	Subvertitur Geometria ut non practica sed Speculativa.	509
X	Archimedes's proposition about Squaring the Circle has nothing to do with circumferences containing less than 96 points. & if the circumference contain ^96 points it may be apply'd but nothing will follow	510

against indivisibles. v. Barrow.

      Curve
X Those˄ lines that you can Rectify Geometrically.   511
Compare them with their equal right lines & by a
Microscope you shall discern an inequality. Hence
my Squaring of the Circle as good & exact as the
best.

                                                         f.27

   Qu: whether the substance of Body or any thing else, 512
M be any more than the Collection of Ideas included
                                         any particular
in that thing. Thus the substance of˄ Body is
extension Solidity figure. & of General Body no
idea.

   Mem: ~~Care~~ most carefully to inculcate & set forth 513
I how that the Endeavouring to Express abstract
philosophic Thoughts by words unavoidably runs a
man into Difficulties. This to be done in the ~~Pre~~---
Introduction.

   Mem: to Endeavour most accurately to understand 514
X w$\overset{t}{\cdot}$ is meant by this axiom: Quae sibi mutuo
congruunt aequalia sunt.

   Qu: w$\overset{t}{\cdot}$ the Geometers mean by equality of lines & 515
X whether according to their definition of equality a
curve line can possibly be equal to a right line.

              call
   If w$^{th}_{\cdot}$ me you ~~define~~ those lines equal w$^{ch}_{\cdot}$ contain 516
X an equal number of points. then there will be no
difficulty. that curve is equal to a right line w$^{ch}_{\cdot}$
contains as many

                                                         f.28

points as the right, one doth.

   I take not away substances. I ought not to be 517
M accus'd of Discarding Substance out of the reasonable
World. I onely reject the Philosophic sense (w$^{ch}_{\cdot}$ in

effect is no sense) of the word substance. Ask a
man non tainted with their jargon wt he means by
corporeal substance, or the substance of Body.
He shall answer Bulk, Solidity & such like sensible
qualitys. These I retain. the Philosophic nec quid
nec quantum nec quale whereof I have no idea I
discard. if a man may be Said to discard that wch never had
any being was never so much as imagin'd or
conceived.

M N.B. I am more for reality than any other   517a
Philosophers, they make a thousand doubts &   (f.27v.)
know not certainly but we may be deceiv'd. I
assert the direct Contrary.

M In short be not angry you lose nothing. whether   518
real or chimerical w{t}ever you can in any wise
conceive or imagine be it ever so wild so
extravagant & absurd much good may it do you
with it. I'll let you may enjoy it for me. I'll nere
deprive you of it.

   A line in the sense of Mathematicians is not meer   519
X distance. this evident in that there are curve lines.

X Curves perfectly incomprehensible, inexplicable,   520
absurd except we allow points.

                                                  f.29

   If men look for a thing wehere it's not to be found.   521
I be they never so Sagacious it is lost labour. if
a simple clumsey man know where the Game lies.
He tho afoot shall catch it sooner than the most
fleet & dexterous that seek it elsewhere. Men
choose to hunt for truth & knowlege any where
rather than in their own Understanding where 'tis
to be found.

1M All knowlege onely about ideas. V. Locke. B.4c.1. 522

S   It seems improper & liable to difficulties to make   523
    the Word Person stand for ~~Ideas~~ an Idea. or to
    make our selves Ideas or thinking things ideas.

I   General Ideas Cause of much Trifling & Mistake.   524

X   Mathematicians seem not to speak clearly &   525
    coherently of Equality. They no where define w^t
    they mean by that word when apply'd to Lines.

+   Locke says the modes of simple Ideas besides   526
    extension & number are ~~simple~~ counted by degrees.
    I deny there are any modes or degrees of simple
    Ideas. W^t He terms such are complex Ideas as I
    have prov'd in Green.

f.30

X   W^t do the Mathematicians mean by Considering   527
    Curves as Polygons? either they are Polygons or
    they are not. if they are why do they give them the
    Name of Curves? why do not they constantly call
    them Polygons & treat them as such. If they are
    not polygons I think it absurd to use polygons in
    their Stead. w^t is this but to pervert language to
    adapt an idea to a name that belongs not to it but
    to adifferent idea?

X   The Mathematicians should look to their axiom   528
    Quae congruunt sunt aequalia. I know not what
    they mean by bidding me put one Triangle on
    another. the under Triangle is no Triangle, nothing
    at all, it not being perceiv'd. I ask must sight be
    judge of this Congruentia or not. if it must then all
    Lines seen under the Same Angle are equal w^{ch}
    ~~is absurd~~ they will not acknowlege. Must The
    Touch be Judge? But ~~the~~ we cannot touch or feel
    Lines & surfaces, Such as Triangles &c according
    to the Mathematicians themselves. Much less can
    we feel a line or Triangle that's cover'd by another
    Line or Triangle.

    D~~x x~~o you mean by Saying one triangle is equall to   529

X another that they both take up equal Spaces. But
then the Question recurrs w.^{t} mean you by equal
Spaces. if you mean Spatia congruentia answer the
above difficulty truly.

              f.31

X I can mean (for my part) nothing else by equal   530
Triangles than Triangles containing equal numbers
of Points.

X I can mean nothing by equal lines but lines wch tis   530a
indifferent whether of them I take, lines in wch I (f.30v.)
observe by my senses no difference, & wch therefore
have the Same Name.

Must the Imagination be Judge in the aforemention'd 531
X Case. but then Imagination cannot go beyond the
Touch & sight. Say you Pure Intellect must be Judge.
I reply that Lines & Triangles are not operations
of the Mind.

If I Speak positively & with the air of a   532
✝ Mathematician in things of which I am certain.
tis to avoid Disputes to make Men careful to think
before they censure. To Discuss my Arguments
before they go to refute them. I would by no means
jnjure truth & Certainty by an affected modesty &
submission to Better Judgements. W.^{t} I lay before
you are undoubted Theorems not plausible
conjectures of my own nor learnd opinions of
other Men. I pretend not to prove them by figures,
analogy or Authority. Let them stand or fall by
their own Evidence.

N When you speak of the Corpuscularian Essences of   533
Bodys Mem: to reflect on Sect: 11 & 12 b. 4. c. 3.
            meer
Locke. Motion supposes not solidity a ^ Colour'd
Extension may give us the Idea of ~~solidity~~ Motion.

-69-

f.32

P | Any subject can have of each Sort of primary Qualities but one particular at once. Lib. 4. c. 3 S. 15 Locke. | 534

M | Well say you according to this new Doctrine all is but meer Idea, there is nothing wch is not an ens rationis. I answer things are as real, & exist in rerum natura as much as ever. the distinction betwixt entia Realia & entia rationis may be made as properly ^now^ as ever. Do but think before you Speak. Endeavour rightly to comprehend my meaning & you'll agree with me in this. | 535

N | ffruitless the Distinction twixt real & nominal Essences. | 536

We are not acquainted with the meaning of our words. Real, Extension, Existence, power, matter, Lines, Infinite, point. & ~~innumer~~ many more are frequently in our mouths when little clear & determin'd answers them in our Understandings. This must be well inculcated. | 537

M | Vain is the Distinction twixt Intellectual & Material World V. Locke Lib. 4. c. 3. S. 27 where he says that is far more beautifull than this. | 538

S. Mo. | ffoolish in men to despise the senses. if it were not for them ye Mind could have no knowlege no thought at all. All xxxxxxxxxxx of Introversion, meditation, contemplation & spiritual acts as if these | 539

f.33

could be exerted before we had ideas from without by the Senses are manifestly absurd. This may be of great Use in that it makes the Happyness of the Life to come more conceivable & agreeable to our present nature. The Schoolemen & Refiners in Philosophy Gave the Greatest part of Mankind no more tempting Idea of Heaven or the Joys of the Blest.

X | The Vast, Wide-spread, Universal Cause of our Mistakes. Is that we do not consider our own notions, I mean consider them in them selves, fix, settle & determine them. We regarding them with relation to each other on~~e~~ly. In short we are much out in study the relations of things before we Study them absolutely & in themselves. Thus we study to find out the Relations of figures to one another, the Relations also of Number. without Endeavouring rightly to understand the Nature of Extension & Number in themselves This we think is of no concern of no difficulty but If I mistake not tis of the last Importance. | 540

Mo | I allow not of the Distinction there is made twixt Profit & Pleasure. | 541

Mo | I'd never blame a Man for acting upon Interest. he's a fool that acts on any other Principle. the not considering these things has been of ill consequence in Morality. | 542

f.34

+ | My positive Assertions are no less modest than those that are introduc'd wth it seems to me, I suppose &c since I Declare once for all, that all I write or think is entirely about things as they appear to me. It concerns no man else any farther than his thoughts agree with mine. This in the Preface. | 543

I | Two things are apt to confound men in their Reasonings one with another. 1st words signifying the operations of the mind are taken from sensible Ideas. 2dly words as Used by the Vulgar are taken in some Latitude, their signification is confused. ~~So y^{t} if~~ Hence if aman use y^{m} in a Determin'd settled signification he is at a hazard either of not being understood or of Speaking improperly. | 544

	All this remedyed by studying the Understanding.	
X	Unite no simple Idea. I have no Idea ₐ answering [meerly] the word one. all Number ~~is onely~~ consists in Relations.	545
+	Entia realia & Entia rationis a foolish Distinction of the Schoolemen.	546
	Words there not so foolish neither	546a (f.33v.) f.35
M. P.	We have an intuitive Knowlege of the Existence of other Things besides our selves & even praecedaneous to the Knowlege of our own Existence. in that we must have Ideas or else we cannot think.	547
S	We move our Legs our selves. 'tis we that will their movement. Herein I Differ from Malbranch.	548
Mo†X	Mem: nicely to discuss Lib. 4. c. 4. Locke.	549
	it is of ye Reality of Knowlege	549a (f.34v.)
M	Mem:again & again to mention & illustrate the Doctrine of the Reality of Things Rerum Natura &c.	550
† Ml	W^t I Say is Demonstration, perfect Demonstration. Whenever men have fix'd & determin'd Ideas annex'd to their words they can hardly be mistaken. Stick but to my Definition of Likeness & tis a Demonstration y^t Colours are not simple Ideas. All Reds being like &c. So also in other things. This to be heartily insisted on.	551
E	The abstract Idea of Being or Existence is never thought of by the Vulgar. they never use those words standing for abstract Ideas.	552
		f.36
	I must not Say the words thing, substance &c have	553

M	been the Cause of mistakes. But the not reflecting one their meaning. I will be still for retaining the words. I only desire that men would ~~speak before~~ think before they speak & settle the Meaning of their words.	
Mo +X	I approve not of that which Locke Says viz truth consists in the joyning & separating of signs.	554
I	Locke cannot Explain general Truth or Knowlege without treating of words & propositions. This makes for me against general Ideas -- V. Locke Lib. 4:ch:6.	555
I	Men have been very industrious in travelling forward they have gone a great way. But ~~N~~few or none have gone backward beyond the Principles. On that side there lys much terra incognita to be travell'd over & discover'd by me. A vast field for invention:	556
X	Twelve inches not the Same Idea with a foot. Because a Man may perfectly conceive a foot who never thought of an inch.	557
		f.37
X	A foot is equal to or the Same with twelve inches in this respect viz. the contain both the Same number of points.	558
+	[Forasmuch as] to be used	559
	Mem: to mention somewhat wch may Encourage the study of Politiques & testify of me ∧^{yt} I am well dispos'd toward them.	560
I	If men did not use words for Ideas they would never have thought of abstract ideas. certainly Genera & Species ~~Stan~~ are not abstract general ideas. these include a contradiction in their nature v. Locke Lib. 4 S. 9. c. 7.	561

          or mixt
+ A various ^ cause must necessarily produce a   562
various or mixt effect. This demonstrable from
the Definition of a Cause. wch way of Demonstrating
must be frequently made use of in my Treatise &
to that end Definitions often praemis'd. Hence
'tis evident that according to Newton's Doctrines
Colours can not be simple ideas

f.38

M   I am the farthest from Scepticism of any. man.   563
I know with an intuitive knowlege the existence of
other things as well as my own Soul. this is w^t
Locke nor Scarce any other Thinking Philosopher
will pretend to.

I   Doctrine of Abstraction of very evil consequence in   564
all the Sciences. Mem: Bacon's remark. Entirely
owing to Language.

+ Locke greatly out in ~~making words be one of the~~   565
~~proper uses of~~ reckoning the recording our Ideas
                                                        & not
~~one use of xx~~ by words amongst the uses ~~rather than~~
the abuses of Language.

Of great use & ye last Importance to Contemplate   566
                    alone
I   a man put into the World ^ wth admirable abilitys.
& see how after long experience he would know
wthout words. Such a one would never think of
Genera & species or abstract general Ideas.

                w^n advanc'd in years at all
I   Wonderful in Locke that he could ^ see ^ thro a mist   567
y^t had been so long a gathering & was consequently
thick. This more to be admir'd than y^t he did not
see farther.

f.39

+ Identity of Ideas may be taken in a Double sense   568
either as including or excluding Identity or
Circumstances. Such as time, place &c.

-74-

Mo — I am glad the People I converse with are not all richer, wiser &c than I. This is agreeable to Reason, is no sin. Tis certain that if the Happyness of my Acquaintance encreases & mine not proportionably, mine much decrease. The not understanding this & the Doctrine about relative Good discuss'd with French, Madden &c to be noted as 2 Causes of Mistake in Judging of Moral Matters. 569

+ Mem: to observe (w^n you talk of the Division of Ideas into Simple & complex) that there may be another cause of the Undefinableness of certain Ideas besides that which Locke gives viz. the want of Names. 570

M — Mem: To begin the 1st Book not with mention of Sensation & Reflection but instead of those to use perception or thought in general. 571

f.40

S — I Defy any man to Imagine or conceive Perception without an Idea or an Idea without perception. 572

E — Locke's very supposition that matter & motion should exist before thought is absurd, includes a manifest Contradiction. 573

X — Locke's harangue about coherent, methodical Discourses amounting to nothing, apply'd to the Mathematicians. 574

X — They talk of determining all the points of a Curve by an Aequation w^t mean they by this. w^t would they signify by the word points. ~~Do~~ Do they stick to the Definition of Euclid? 575

S — We think we know not the Soul because we have no imaginable or sensible Idea annex'd to that sound. This the Effect of prejudice. 576

S   Certainly we do not know it. this will be plain if   576a
we examine w^t we mean by the Word knowlege.   (f.39v.)
Neither doth this argue any defect in Our knowlege
no more than our not knowing a contradiction

f.41

+   The very existence of Ideas constitutes the soul.   577

S   Consciousness, perception, existence of Ideas   578
seem to be all one.

Consult, ramsack y^r Understanding w^t find you   579
+ there besides several perceptions or thoughts. W^t
mean you by the word mind you must mean something
that you perceive or y^t you do not perceiv'de. a
thing not perceived is a contradiction. to mean also
a thing you do not perceive is a contradiction. We
are in all this mattr Strangely abused by words.

+   Mind is a congeries of Perceptions. Take away   580
Perceptions & you take away the Mind ~~take~~ put the
Perceptions & you put the mind.

+   Say you the Mind is not the Perceptions. but that   581
thing wch perceives. I answer you are abused by
the words that & thing these are vague empty words
without a meaning.

f.42

The having Ideas is not the Same thing with   582
S   Perception. a Man may have Ideas when he only
Imagines. But then this Imagination presupposeth
Perception.

That wch extreamly strengthen's us in prejudice is   583
M   y^t we think we see an empty Space. wch I shall
Demonstrate to be false in the 3^d Book.

There may be Demonstrations used even in   584
+   Divinity. I mean in reveal'd Theology, as

contradistinguish'd from natural. for tho the Principles may be founded in Faith yet this hinders not but that legitimate Demonstrations might be ~~drawn~~ built thereon. Provided still that we define the words we use & never go beyond our Ideas. Hence 'twere no very hard matter for those who hold Episcopacy or Monarchy to be establish'd jure Divino. to demonstrate their Doctrines if they are true. But to pretend to demonstrate or reason any thing about the Trinity is absurd here an implicit Faith becomes us.

S Qu: if there be any real Difference betwixt certain Ideas of Reflection & others of sensation. e.g. 'twixt perception & white, black, sweet &c. wherein I pray you does the perception of white differ from white. Meanxxxxxx   585

f.43

† I shall Demonstrate all my Doctrines. the Nature of Demonstration to be set forth & insisted on in the Introduction. In that I must needs differ from Locke forasmuch as he makes all Demonstration to be about abstract Ideas wch I say we have not nor can have.   586

S The Understanding seemeth not to differ from its perceptions or Ideas. Qu: w^t must one think of the Will & passions.   587

E A good Proof that Existence is nothing without or distinct from Perception may be Drawn from Considering a Man put into the World without company.   588

E There was a Smell i.e. there was a Smell perceiv'd. Thus we see that common Speech confirms my Doctrine.   589

No broken Intervals of Death or Annihilation Those   590

T Intervals are nothing. Each Person's time being measured to him by his own Ideas.

f.44

I We are frequently puzzl'd & at a loss in obtaining clear & determin'd meanings of words commonly in use. & that because we imagine words stand for general Ideas which are altogether inconceivable. 591

I A Stone is a Stone. This a nonsensical Proposition. & such as the Solitary Man would never think on. nor do I believe he would ever think on this viz. The whole is equal to it's Parts. &c. 592

E Let it not be Said that I take away Existence. I onely declare the meaning of the Word so far as I can comprehend it. 593

I If you take away abstraction, how do men differ from Beasts. I answer by Shape. By Language rather by Degrees of more & less ~~chiefly~~. 594

+ W^t means Locke by inferences in words, consequences, of Words as Somthing different from consequences of Ideas. I conceive no Such thing. 595

I N.B. Much Complaint about the Imperfection of Language. 596

f.45

M But perhaps Some man may ~~say~~ say an inert thoughtless substance may exist tho' not extended, moved &c ~~*~~but wth other properties whereof we have no Idea. But even this I shall demonstrate to be Impossible w^n I come to treat more particularly of Existence. 597

+ Will not rightly distinguish'd from Desire by Locke. it seeming to superadd nothing to the Idea of an 598

Action but the Uneasiness for it's absence or non Existence.

S | Mem: to enquire diligently into that Strange Mistery viz. How it is that I can cast about, think of this or that Man, place, action w^n nothing appears to Introduce them into my thoughts w^n they have no perceivable connexion wth the Ideas suggested by my senses at the present. | 599

I | Tis not to be imagin'd w^t a marvellous emptiness & Scarcity of Ideas that man shall descry who will lay aside all use of Words in his Meditations. | 600

M | Incongruous in Locke to fancy we want a sense proper to see substances withal. | 601

<u>f. 46</u>

I | Locke owns that Abstract Ideas were made in order to naming. | 602

1xM | The common Errour of the Opticians, that we judge of Distance by Angles strengthen's men in their prejudice that they see things without and distant from their mind. | 603

E | I am persuaded would Men but examine w^t they mean by the Word Existence they wou'd agree with me. | 604

X | C. 20 S. 8 B. 4 of Locke makes for me against the Mathematicians. | 605

M | The supposition that things are distinct from Ideas takes away all real Truth, & consequently brings in a Universal Scepticism, since all our knowlege & contemplation is confin'd barely to our own Ideas. | 606

I | Qu: whether the Solitary Man would not find it necessary to make use of words to record his Ideas if not in memory or meditation yet, at least, in Writing without which he could Scarce retain his Knowlege. | 607

f.47

+   We read in History there was a time when fears,   608
      & Jealousies, Privileges of Parliament, Malignant
      Party & such like expressions of too unlimited &
      doubtfull a meaning were Words of much Sway.
      Also the Words Church, Whig, Tory &c contribute
      very Much to faction & Dispute.

S   The Distinguishing betwixt an Idea and perception of   609
      the Idea has been one great cause of Imagining
      material substances.

S   That God & Blessed Spirits have Will is a manifest   610
      Argument against Lockes proofs that the will cannot
      be conceiv'd put into action without a Praevious
      Uneasiness.

S   The act of the Will or volition is not uneasiness for   611
      that uneasiness may be without volition.

S   It is not so very evident that an Idea or at least   611a
      Uneasiness may be without all Volition or act.   (f.46v.)

S   Volition is distinct from the object or Idea for the   612
      Same reason.

S   Also from uneasiness & Idea together.   613

✱   The Understanding not distinct from particular   614
      perceptions or Ideas.

*   The Understanding taken for a faculty is not really   614a
      distinct from ye Will.   (f.46v.)

✱   The Will not distinct from ~~idea~~ Particular volitions.   615

*   This alter'd hereafter   615a
      (f.46v.)

f.48

S   To ask whether a man can will either side is an   616
      absurd question. for they word can praesupposes

-80-

volition.

N | Anima Mundi. Substantial fforms, Omniscient radical Heat. Plastic vertue. Hylarchic principle. All these Vanish. | 617

M | Newton proves that gravity is proportional to gravity. I think that's all. | 618

\+ | Qu: whether it be the vis inertiae that makes it difficult to move a stone or the vis attractrix or both or neither. | 619

Mem: to express the Doctrines as fully & copiously & clearly as may be. also to be full and particular in answering objections. | 620

S | To say ^y^e Will is a power. Volition is an act. This is idem per idem. | 621

\+ | W^t makes men despise ~~the~~ extension motion &c & separate them from the ~~Idea o~~ essence of the soul is that they imagine them to be distinct from thought & to exist in Unthinking substance. | 622

f.49

\+ | An extended may have passive modes of thinking, not action. | 623

\+ | There might be Idea, there might be uneasiness. there might be the greatest uneasiness. wthout ~~xxxxi~~ any volition. therefore the | 624

M.+ | Matter once allow'd. I defy any man to prove that God is not matter. | 625

S | Man is free. Th~~is~~ere is no difficulty in this proposition if we but settle the signification of the word free, if we had an Idea annext to the word free & would but contemplate that Idea. | 626

S   We are imposed on by the words, Will, determine,   627
agent, free, can &c.

S   Uneasiness precedes not every Volition. This   628
evident by experience.

S   Trace ~~a xx~~ an Infant in the Womb. mark the train   629
& successions of its Ideas. observe how volition
comes into the Mind. This may perhaps acquaint
you with it's nature.

S   Complacency seems rather to determine or   630
precede or coincide wth & constitute the Essence
of Volition than uneasiness.

f.50

S   You tell me according to my Doctrine a Man is not   631
free. I answer. tell me w^{t} you mean by the word
free & I shall resolve you.

N   Qu: w^{t} do men mean when they talk of one Body's   632
touching another. I say you never saw one Body
touch. or (rather) I say I never saw one Body that
I could say touch'd this or that other. for that if
my optiques were improv'd I should see intervalls
& other bodies ~~wch xxx~~ betwixt those wch now
seem to touch.

X   Mem: upon all occasions to use the Utmost Modesty.   633
to Confute the Mathematicians wth the utmost
civility & respect. not to stile them Nihilarians &c:

N. B. to rein in y^{r} Satyrical Nature.   634

S   Tis folly to define Volition an act of the mind   635
          neither   nor
ordering. for ~~both~~ act ~~and~~ ordering can them selves
be understood without Volition.

f.51

Blame me not if I use my words sometimes in some   636

latitude. 'tis w:t cannot be helpt. Tis the fault of
Language that you cannot always apprehend the
clear & determinate meaning of my Words.

+ Say you there must be a thinking substance. 637
Somthing unknown wch perceives & supports &
ties together the Ideas. Say I, make it appear
there is any need of it & you shall have it for me.
I care not to take away any thing I can see the
least reason to think should exist.

+ I affirm 'tis manifestly absurd. no excuse in ye 638
world can be given why a man should use a word
without an idea. Certainly we shall find that w:tever
word we make use of in matter of pure reasoning
has or ought to have a compleat Idea annext to it.
i.e. it's meaning or the sense we take it in must
be compleatly known.

+ Tis demonstrable a Man can never be brought to 639
Imagine any thing shoud exist whereof he has no
Idea. Whoever says he does, banters himself with
Words.

G We Imagine a great difference & distance in respect 640
of Knowlege, power &c betwixt a Man & a Worm.
the like distance

f.52

betwixt Man & God may be Imagin'd. or Infinitely
greater.

                                  different
We find in our own minds a great Number of˄Ideas. 641
G We may Imagine in God a Greater Number i.e. that
Our's in Number or the Number of ours is
inconsiderable in respect thereof. the Words
difference & Number old & known we apply to that
wch is Unknown. but I am embrangled in Words.
tis Scarce possible it should be otherwise.

  the Chief thing
~~All~~ I do or pretend to do is onely to remove the 642
Mist or veil of Words. This has occasion'd

Ignorance & confusion. This has ruin'd the
Scholemen & Mathematicians, Lawyers & Divines

 The grand Cause of perplexity & darkness In   643
treating of the Will, is that we Imagine it to be
  an
S ~~the~~ object of thought (to speak wth the vulgar), we
think we may perceive, contemplate & view it like
any of our Ideas whereas in truth 'tis ~~xx~~ no idea.
Nor is there an Idea of it. tis toto coelo different
from the Understanding i.e. from all our Ideas.
If you say the Will or rather a Volition is something
I answer there is an Homonymy in the word ~~will~~
thing w^{n} apply'd to Ideas & volitions & Understanding
& will. All ideas are passive, volitions active.

              f.53

 Thing & Idea are much w^{t} words of the Same   644
S extent & meaning. Why therefore do I not use the
word thing? Answ: because thing is of greater
latitude than Idea. Thing comprehends also
Volitions or actions. now these are no ideas.

S There can be perception wthout Volition. Qu: 645
whether there can be Volition without perception.

E Existence not conceivable without perception or   646
Volition not distinguish'd therefrom.

 N.B. Severall distinct Ideas can be perceiv'd by   647
T Sight & Touch at once. not So by the other senses.
'Tis this diversity of sensations in other senses
chiefly but sometimes in touch & sight x (as also
diversity of Volitions whereof there cannot be more
than one at once, or rather it seems there cannot
for of that I doubt) gives us the Idea of Time. or is
Time it self.

X W^{t} would the Solitary Man think of number?   648

S There are innate Ideas i.e. Ideas created with us.   649

S   Lockes seems to be mistaken w.ⁿ he says thought   650
is not essential to the Mind.

Certainly the Mind always & constantly thinks &   651
we know this too In

f.54

Sleep & trances the mind exists not there is no time
no Succession of Ideas.

S   To say the mind exist's without thinking is a   652
Contradiction, nonsense, nothing.

Folly to enquire w.! determines the Will.   653
S   Uneasiness &c are Ideas, therefore unactive,
therefore can do nothing therefore cannot determine
the Will.

S   Again. w.! mean you by determine?   654

for want of rightly Understanding, time, motion,   655
N. T.   existence &c Men are forc'd into such absurd
contradictions as this v. g. light moves 16 diameters
of Earth in a Second of Time.

Twas the opinion that Ideas could exist unperceiv'd   656
S   or before perception that made Men think perception
was somewhat different from the Idea perceived, y.!
it was an Idea of Reflexion whereas the thing
perceiv'd was an idea ₍of₎ Sensation. I say twas this
made 'em think the understanding took it in
receiv'd it from without w.ᶜʰ could never be did not
they think it existed without.

f.55

S   To ask have we an idea of ₍yᵉ₎ Will ₍or volition₎ is nonsense. an   657
idea can resemble nothing but an idea.

Properly speaking Idea is the picture of the   657a
(f.54v.)

M Imaginations making this is ye likeness of & refer'd to the real Idea or (if you will) thing.

S If you ask w^t thing it is that wills. I answer if you mean Idea by the Word thing or any thing like any Idea, then I Say tis no thing at all that ~~thinks~~ will's. This how extravagant soever it may Seem yet is a certain truth. we are cheated by those general terms, thing, is &c.   658

+ S Again if by is you mean is perceived or do's perceive. I say nothing wch is perceived or does perceive Wills.   659

S The referring Ideas to things wch are not Ideas, the using the Terms, Idea of, is one great cause of mistake as in other matters so also in this.   660

S Some words there are wch do not stand for Ideas v.g particles, Will &c   661

S particles stand for volitions & their concomitant Ideas   661a (f.54v.)

+ There seem to be but two Colours wch are simple Ideas. viz. those exhibited by the most & least refrangible Rays. being the Intermediate ones may be framed by composition.   662

S I have no Idea of a Volition or act of the Mind. neither has any other Intelligence for that were a contradiction.   663

f.56

+ N.B. Simple Ideas viz. Colours are not devoid of all sort of Composition. tho it must be granted they are not made up of distinguishable Ideas. yet there is another sort of composition. Men are wont to call those things compounded in which we do not actually discover the component ingredients. Bodies are said to be compounded of Chymical Principles wch nevertheless come not into view till after the   664 dissolution of the Bodies. & wch were not could not be discerned in the Bodies whilst remaining entire.

S | If by Idea you mean object of the Understanding. Then certainly the Will is no Idea, or we have no idea annext to the word Will. | 665

I | All our knowlege is about particular ideas according to Locke. All our sensations are particular Ideas as is evident. w^t use then do we make of general Ideas, since we neither know, nor perceive them. | 666

S | Tis allow'd that Particles stand not for Ideas &
        they are not Said to be
yet ~~there not~~ empty useless sounds. The truth on't is they stand for the Operations of the Mind i.e. Volitions. | 667

f.57

+
Mo. | Locke Says all our knowlege is about Particulars. if So, pray w^t is the following ratiocination but a jumble of words Omnis Homo est animal, omne animal vivit, ergo omnis Homo vivit. it Amounts (if you annex particular Ideas to the Words Animal & vivit) to no more than this. Omnis Homo est Homo, Omnis Homo est Homo, ergo Omnis Homo est Homo. A ~~perfect~~ meer Sport & trifling with sounds. | 668

Mo | We have no Ideas of Vertues & Vices, no Ideas of Moral Actions wherefore it may be Question'd whether we are capable of arriving at Demonstration about them, the morality consisting in the Volition chiefly. | 669

E | Strange it is that Men should be at a loss to find their Idea of Existence since that (if such ^there be distinct from Perception) it is brought into the mind by all the Ways of Sensation & Reflection; methinks it should be most familiar to us & we | 670 best Acquainted with it.

E | This I am sure I have no *such* idea of Existence or annext to the Word Existence. & if others have that's nothing to me they can Never Make me sensible of it, simple Ideas being uncommunicable by Language. | 671

f.58

S | Say you the unknown substratum of Volitions & Ideas, is somthing whereof I have no Idea. I ask is there any other Being wch has or can have an Idea of it. if there be then it must be it self an Idea wch you will think absurd. | 672

S | There is somwhat active in most perceptions i.e such as ensue upon our Volitions, such as we can prevent & stop v.g I turn my eyes towards the Sun I open them all this is active. | 672a (f.57v.)

S | Things are two fold active or inactive, The Existence of Active things *is* to act, of inactive to be perceiv'd. | 673

S.E. | Distinct from or without perception there is no Volition; therefore neither is their existence without perception. | 674

G | God may comprehend all Ideas even the Ideas wch are painfull & unpleasant without being in any degree pained thereby. Thus we our selves can imagine the pain of a burn &c without any misery or uneasiness at all. | 675

†:N.Mo.X | Truth. three Sorts thereof Natural, Mathematical & Moral | 676

†Mo X | Agreement of relation onely where Numbers do obtain. of Coexistence in Nature, of signification or Including or thinking by Including in Morality. | 677

f.59

I — Gyant who shakes the Mountain that's on him must   678
be Acknowleg'd I or rather Thus. I am no more to
be reckon'd Stronger than Locke than a pigmy
should be reckon'd Stronger than a Gyant because
he could throw of the Molehill wch lay upon him,
& the Gyant could onely shake or shove the Mountain
that oppressed him. This in the Preface.

I — Promise to extend our knowlege & clear it of those   679
shamefull Contradictions wch Embarrass it.
something like this to begin the Introduction in
a Modest Way.

I — ~~H~~Wow ever shall pretend to censure any part -- I   680
desire He would read out the Whole, else he may
perhaps not Understand me. in the Preface or Introd:

S — Doctrine of Identity best explain'd by Taking the   681
Will for Volitions, the Understanding for Ideas.
~~Hence~~ The difficulty of Consciousness of w^{t} are
never acted &c solv'd Hereby.

I — I must acknowlege my self beholding to the   682
Philosophers have gone before me. They have
given good rules tho perhaps they do not always
observe them. Similitude of Adventurers who tho
they themselves

f.60

attained not the desir'd Port, they by their wrecks
have Made known the Rocks & Sands, whereby the
Passage of after Comers is made more Secure &
easy. Pref: or Introd:

Mo — The opinion that Men had Ideas of Moral actions   683
has render'd the Demonstrating ~~xh~~ Ethiques very
~~perplex'd~~ difficult to them.

S — An Idea being it self unactive cannot be the   684
re~~m~~semblance or image of An Active thing.

I | Excuse to be made in the Introduction ~~to be made~~ for the using the Word Idea viz. because it has obtain'd. But a Caution must be added. | 685

† | Scripture & possibility are the onely proofs with Mabranch add to these ~~Univer~~ w^t he calls a great propenson to think so. this perhaps may be question'd. ~~I cant conceive how a man should be inclin'd to think any thing does exist whereof he has no Idea.~~ perhaps men if they think before they Speak will not be found so thoroughly perswaded of the Existence of Matter. | 686

M | On second thoughts I am on t'other extream I am certain of that wch Malbranch seems to doubt of. viz the existence of Bodies. | 686a (f.59v.)

I. &c. | Mem: to bring the killing blow at the last v. g. in the Matter of Abstraction to bring Lockes general triangle at the last. | 687

I | They give good rules tho perhaps they themselves do not always observe them. they ~~sxxx~~ Speak much of clear & distinct Ideas. tho at the Same they talk of General, abstract ideas &c I'll instance | 688

f.61

in Lockes opinion of abstraction he being as clear a writer as I have met with. Such was the Candour of this great Man that I perswade my Self were he alive. he would not be offended that I differ from him seeing that even in so doing. I follow his advice viz. to use my own Judgement, see with my own eyes & not with anothers. Introd:

S | The Word thing as comprising or standing for ~~an~~ Idea & Volition usefull. as Standing for Idea and Archetype without the Mind Mischievous & useless. | 689

Mo | To demonstrate Morality it seems one need only Make a Dictionary of Words & see Which included which. at least. This is the greatest part & bulk | 690 of the Work.

+Mo. Lockes instances of Demonstration in Morality are according to his own Rule trifling Propositions. 691

P.S. Qu: How comes it that Some Ideas are confessedly allow'd by all to be onely in the mind, & others ~~generally~~ as generally taken to be without the mind. if according to you All are equally only in the Mind. Ans: because ~~these that are pleasant~~ that in proportion to the Pleasure & pain Ideas are attended with desire aversion & other actions wch include Volition now volition is by all grant'd to be in Spirit. 692

<u>f.62</u>

I If Men would lay aside words in thinking 'tis impossible they should ever mistake Save only in Matters of Fact. ~~or Conject~~ I mean it seems impossible they should Be positive & secure ~~of any~~ that any thing was true wch in truth is not so. certainly I cannot err in matter of simple perception. ~~except th~~ So far as we can in reasoning go without the help of signs there we have certain knowlege. indeed in long deductions made by signs there may be slips of Memory. 693

Mo. From my Doctrine there follows a cure for Pride. we are only to $_\wedge$be praised for those things wch are our own, or of our own Doing, Natural Abilitys are not consequences of Our Volitions. 694

M Mem: $_\wedge$candidly to take Notice that Locke holds some dangerous opinions. such as the Infinity $_\wedge$& eternity of Space. The Possibility of Matter's Thinking. 695

I Once more I desire my Reader may be upon his guard against the Fallacy of Words, Let him beware that I do not impose on him by plausible empty talk that common dangerous way of cheating men into absurditys. Let him not regard my Words any 696

-91-

otherwise than as occasions of bringing into his mind
      significations
determin'd ~~ideas~~ so far as they fail of this they are
Gibberish, Jargon & deserve not the name of
Language. I ~~entreat him to make my Book the occ~~
desire & warn him not to expect to find truth in my
Book or any where but in

f.63

his own Mind. w^tever I see my Self tis impossible
I can paint it out in Words.

Mo.　N. B.　To Consider well w^t is meant by that w^{ch}　697
Locke Saith Concerning Algebra that it supplys
intermediate Ideas.　Also to think of a Method
affording the same use in Morals &c that this doth
in Mathematiques.

✝　Homo is not proved to be Vivens by means of any　698
Mo　intermediate Idea.　I dont fully agree wth Locke in
X　w^t he says concerning Sagacity in finding out
Intermediate Ideas in Matter capable of
Demonstration & the use thereof; as if that were the
Onely Means of Improving & enlarging Demonstrative
Knowlege.

S　There is a difference betwixt Power & Volition.　699
There may be Volition without Power.　But there
can be no Power without Volition.　Power implyeth
Volition & at the Same time a Connotation of the
Effect's following the Volition.

M.S.　We have assuredly an Idea of Substance. twas　700
absurd of Locke to think we had A Name ~~fo~~ without
a Meaning. this Might prove Acceptable to the
Stillingfleetians.

M.S　The Substance of Body we know, the Substance of　701
Spirit we do not know it not being knowable. it being
purus Actus.

f.64

I | Words have ruin'd & over run all the Sciences, Law Physique &c Chymistry, Astrology. &c | 702

I | Abstract Ideas only to be had amongst the Learned. The Vulgar never think they have any such, nor truly do they find any want of them. Genera & Species & abstract Ideas are terms unknown to them. | 703

S | Locke's out. The case is different. we can have an Idea of Body without motion, but not of Soul without Thought. | 704

Mo. | God Ought to be worship'd. This Easily demonstrated when once we ascertain the signification of the word God, worship, ought. | 705

S | No Perception according to Locke is active. Therefore no perception (i.e. no Idea) can be the image of or like unto that wch is altogether active & not at all passive i.e. the Will. | 706

S | I can will the calling to mind somthing that is past, tho at the Same time that wch I call to mind was not in my thoughts before that Volition of mine, & consequently I could have had no uneasiness for the want of it. | 707

S | The will & the Understanding may very well be thought two distinct beings. | 708

S | Sed quia Voluntas raro agit nisi ducente desiderio. V. Locke's Epistles p. 479 ad Limburgum. | 709

f.65

$_1X^3$ | You cannot say the M. ⩒T. is like or one with the M. V. because they be both Minima, just perceiv'd & next door to nothing. you may as well say the M. T. is the Same with or like unto a sound so small that it is scarce perceiv'd. | 710

-93-

+   Extension seems to be a Mode of some tangible or   711
sensible quality according as it is seen or f~~x~~elt.

The Spirit the Active thing that wch is Soul & God   712
S   is the Will alone The Ideas are effects impotent
things.

The Concrete of of the Will & understanding I must   713
Call ~~the~~ Mind not person, lest offense be given,
S   there being but one volition acknowleged to be God.
Mem: Carefully to omit defining of Person, or
making much mention of it.

You ask do these volitions make one Will. w^t you   714
S   ask is meerly about a Word. Unite being no more.

N.B. To use utmost Caution not to give the least   715
Handle of offence to the Church or Church-men.

Even to speak somwhat favourable of the Schoolmen   716
I   & shew that they who blame them for Jargon are not
free from it themselves. Introd:

Introd: Locke's great oversight seems to be that he did   717
✝   not Begin wth his Third Book at least that he had
not some thought of it at first. Certainly the 2 1st
books don't agree wth w^t he says in ye 3^d.

                                                                  f.66

                                      of beards
If Matter is once allow'd to exist Clippings ^ &   718
M.   parings of nails may Think for ought that Locke
can tell Tho he seems positive of the Contrary.

                            in
Since I say men cannot mistake ✗^ short reasoning   719
about things demonstrable if they lay aside Words.
✝   treatise
it will be expected This ^ will Contain nothing but w^t
is certain & evident Demonstration. & in truth I
~~Think it contains~~ Hope you will find nothing in it
but w^t is such. certainly I take it all for such. Introd:

When I say I will reject all Propositions wherein   720

I   I know not ~~the full ordinary~~ fully & adequately &
so far as knowable
clearly_∧ the Thing meant thereby This is not to be
extended to propositions in the Scripture. I speak
of Matters of Reason & Philosophy not Revelation,
In this I think an Humble Implicit faith becomes us
just (where we cannot ~~fully~~ comprehend & Understand the
proposition) such as a popish peasant gives to
propositions he hears at Mass in Latin. This proud
~~m~~men call blind, popish, implicit, irrational. for
my part I think it more irrational to pretend to
dispute at cavil & ridicule ~~things~~ holy mysteries i.e that are altogether
above our knowlege out of our reach. propositions about things out of our reach W.ⁿ I shall come
to plenary knowlege of the Meaning of any Text then
I shall yield an explicit belief. Introd:

f.67

✱   Complexation of Ideas twofold. y.^s refers to colours   721
being complex Ideas.

X   C̄osidering length without breadth is considering   722
any length be the Breadth w.^t it will.

M   I may say earth, plants &c were created before   723
Man there being other intelligences to perceive
them before Man was created.

   There is a Philosopher who says we can get an idea   724
of substance by no way of Sensation or Reflection.
M   &_∧ imagin~~es~~ seems to that we want a sense proper for it.
Truly if we had a new sense it could only give us a
new Idea. now I suppose he will not say substance
according to him is a_n Idea. for my part I own I
have no Idea can stand for substance in his or y.^e
Schoolmens sense of that Word. But take it in the
common Vulgar sense & then we see & feel substance.

-95-

E	N.B. That not common usage but the Schools coined the Word Existence supposed to stand for an abstract general Idea.	725

f.68

1x	Writers of Optics mistaken in their principles both in judging of Magnitudes & distances.	726
I	Tis evident y^t wⁿ the Solitary Man should be taught to Speak the Words would give him no other new Ideas (Save only the Sounds)∧ beside w^t he had before. If he had not could not have an abstract Idea before, he cannot have it after he is taught to speak.	727
I	& complex Ideas wch tho' unknown before may be signify'd by Language.	727a (f.67v.)
Mo †	Homo est Homo &c comes at last to Petrus est Petrus &c Now if these identical Propositions are sought after in the Mind they will not be found. there are no identical Mental Propositions tis all about sounds & terms.	728
Mo †	Hence we see the Doctrine of Certainty by Ideas & proving by intermediate Ideas comes to Nothing.	729
Mo † X	We may have certainty & knowlege without Ideas∧.	730
Mo †	∧ i.e without other Ideas than the Words & their Standing for one idea i.e. their being to be used indifferently.	730a (f.67v.)
* † Mo X	It seems to me that we have no certainty about Ideas but onely about Words. tis improper to say I am certain I see, I feel &c. there are no Mental propositions form'd answering to these Words & in simple perception tis allowed by all there is no affirmation or negation & consequently no certainty.	731
*	real certainty this seems wrong certainty∧ is of s✗✗ensible Ideas pro hic & nunc. I may be certain without	731a (f.67v.)

-96-

affirmation or negation.

+Mo/X 732 The reason why we can demonstrate ~~only~~ ^(So well) about signs is that they are perfectly arbitrary & in our power, made at pleasure.

f.69

Mo/X+ 733 The Obscure ambiguous term Relation wch is said to be the largest field of Knowlege confounds us, deceives us.

Mo/X+ 734 Let any Man shew me a Demonstration ^(not verbal) that does not depend either on some false principle or at best on some principle of Nature which is ^(y^e) effect of God's will and we know not how soon it may be changed.

I 735 Qu: w^t becomes of the aeternae veritates? Ans^r they vanish.

I 736 But Say you I find it very difficult to look beneath the words & Uncover my Ideas. Say I use will make it easy. In the sequel of My Book the Cause of this difficulty shall be more clearly made out.

I 737 To view the deformity of Errour we need onely undress it.

E 738 Cogito ergo sum, Tautology, no mental Proposition. answering thereto.

+N. Mo X 739 Knowlege or certainty or perception of agreement of Ideas as to Identity & diversity & real existence Vanisheth of relation becometh meerly Nominal of Coexistence remaineth. Locke thought in this later our knowlege was little or nothing whereas in this onely real knowlege seemeth to be found.

f.70

P+M 740 We must wth the Mob place certainty in the senses.

-97-

+ Tis a mans duty, tis the fruit of friendship, to 741
speak well of his friend, wonder not therefore that
I do w! I do.

I A Man of slow Parts may overtake Truth &c 742
Introd: Even my shortsightedness might perhaps
be aiding to me in this Matter, twill make me bring
the object nearer to my thoughts A Purblind Person
&c Introd:

S Locke to Limborch &c Talk of Judicium I͞tellectus 743
preceding the Volition I think Judicium includes
Volition I can by no means distinguish ~~betwixt~~
these Judicium, Intellectus, indifferentia,
    so many things
Uneasiness∧ ∀Accompanying or praeceding every
Volition as e.g. the Motion of my hand.

        you
Qu: w! Mean∧ by My perceptions, my Volitions? 744
            or conceive &c
S Res, all the perceptions I perceive∧ ~~xxx~~ are mine,
all the Volitions I am Conscious to are mine.

S Homo est agens liberum. w! mean they by Homo 745
& agens in this place?

f.71

              yᵉ
E Will any Man Say that Brutes have∧ ideas, Unity & 746
Existence? I believe not. yet if they are suggested
by all the ways of sensation, tis strange they should
want them.
It is
I ~~Tis xx~~ a Strange thing & deserves our attention, 747
that the more time & pains men have consum'd in
the Study of Philosophy by so much the more they
look upon themselves to be ignorant & weak
Creatures, they discover flaws & imperfections in
their Faculties wᶜʰ Other Men never spy out. they
find themselves under a Necessity of admitting
                                  opinions
                                  ~~opinions~~
many inconsistant, irreconcilable ~~things~~ for true.

> with their hand or behold

There is nothing they touch ~~or Handle~~ but has it's

> with their eyes

dark sides much larger & more numerous tha~~t~~n w^t.

^& at length turn Scepticks at least in most things is perceiv'd.^ &c I ⁂ imagine all this proceeds from &c Exord: Introd:

I These Men with a supercilious Pride disdain the 748
common single informations of sense. they grasp
at Knowlege by s~~☓~~heaves & bundles ('tis well if
catching at two Much at once they hold nothing but
emptyness & air). they in ~~profound meditations contem~~ y^e depth of their understanding Contemplate
Abstract Ideas. &c Introduction

1_X2 It seems not improbable that the most 749
comprehensive, & sublime Intellects see more M.
V.s at once i.e. that their Visual spheres are the
largest.

f.72

✝.X Words (by them meaning all Sort of signs) are so 750
necessary that instead of being (w^n duly us'd or in
their own Nature) prejudicial to the Advancement
of knowlege, or an hindrance to knowlege that w^{th}out
them there could in Mathematiques themselves be
no demonstration.

Mem: To be eternally banishing Metaphisics &c 751
& recalling Men to Common Sense.

S We cannot Conceive other Minds besides our own 752
but as so many selves. We suppose ourselves
affected wth such & Such thoughts & Such & Such
sensations.

S.I. Qu: whether Composition of Ideas be not that 753
faculty which chiefly serves to discriminate us
from Brutes. I question whether a Brute ~~can or~~
does or can imagine a Blue Horse or Chimera.

N. Naturalists do not distinguish betwixt Cause & occasion. Useful to enquire after coexisting Ideas or occasions.   754

Mo. Morality may be Demonstrated as mixt Mathematics. 755

<u>f.73</u>

S Perception is passive but this not distinct from Idea therefore there can be no Idea of Volition.   756

M.✢. Why I use not the Word thing instead of Idea? Introd. 757

X Algebraic Species or letters are denominations of Denominations. therefore Arithmetic to be treated of before Algebra.   758

X 2 Crowns are called ten shillings hence may appear the nature of Numbers.   759

X Complex Ideas are the Creatures of the Mind. hence may appear the Nature of Numbers. this to be deeply discuss'd.   760

X I am better inform'd & shall know more by telling me there are 10000 men than by shewing me them all drawn up. I shall better be able to Judge of the Bargain﹀ w$^{\underline{n}}$ you'd have me make you tell me how much (i.e the name of y$^{\underline{e}}$) mony lies on y$^{\underline{e}}$ Table than by offering & shewing it without Naming. In short I regard not the Idea the looks but the Names. hence may appear the Nature of Numbers.   761

<u>f.74</u>

X Children are unacquainted with Numbers till they have made some ⁎Progress in language. This could not be if ⁎they were Ideas suggested by all the senses.   762

X Numbers are nothing but Names, meer Words.   763

X   Mem: Imaginary roots to ~~un~~ravel that M~~i~~ystery.   764

X   Ideas of Utility are annexed to Numbers.   765

X   In Arithmetical Problemes Men seek not any Idea of Number. they onely seek a Denomination. this is all can be of ~~no~~ use to them.   766

X   Take away the signs from Arithmetic & Algebra, & pray w.^t remains?   767

X   Those are sciences purely Verbal, & entirely useless but for Practise in Societys of Men. No Speculative knowlege, no comparing of Ideas in them.   768

Mo.   Sensual Pleasure is the Summum Bonum. This the Great Principle of Morality. This once rightly understood all the Doctrines even the severest of the Gospels may cleerly be Demonstrated.   769

f.75

X   Qu: whether Geometry may not properly be reckon'd, among the Mixt Mathematics. Arithmetic and Algebra being the Only abstracted pure i. e. entirely Nominal. Geometry being an application of these to Points.   770

I. X. Mo.   Locke of Trifling Propositions. Mem: well to observe & con over that chapter.   771

E. X   Existence, Extension &c are abstract i. e. no ideas. they are words unknown & useless to the Vulgar.   772

Mo.   Sensual Pleasure qua Pleasure is Good & desirable by a Wise Man. but if it be Contemptible tis not quâ pleasure but qua pain or Cause of pain. or (wch is the same thing) of loss of greater pleasure.   773

I   W.ⁿ I consider the More objects we see at once the more distant they are, & that Eye wch beholds a great many things can see none of them near.   774

I. M.   By Idea I mean any sensible or imaginable ~~thing. or intelligible thing~~ thing.   775

f.76

S   Agreeable to my Doctrine of Certainty. He that acts not in order to the obtaining of eternal Happyness must be an infidel at least he is not certain of a future Judgement.   776

S   To be sure or certain of w^t we do not actually perceive (I Say perceive not imagine) We must not be altogether Passive, there must be a disposition to act, there must be assent, wch is active. nay w^t do I talk There must be Actual Volition.   777

X   W^t do we demonstrate in Geometry but that lines are equal or unequal i.e. may or may not be called by the Same Name?   778

I. M.   I approve of this axiom of the Schoolemen nihil est in intellectu quod non prius fuit in sensu. I wish they had stuck to it. it had never taught them the Doctrine of Abstract Ideas.   779

S.G.   Nihil dat quod non habet or the effect is contained in ye Cause. is an axiom I do not Understand or believe to be true.   780

f.77

E   Whoever shall Cast his eyes on the Writings of Old or New Philosophers & see the Noise is made about formal & objective Being Will &c.   781

G   Absurd to Argue the Existence of God from his Idea. we have no Idea of God. tis impossible!   782

M. E.   Cause of Much errour & Confusion that Men Knew not w^t was meant by Reality.   783

Descartes in Med:2. says the Notion of this particular wax is less clear than that of Wax in   784

I General. & in the Same Med: a little before he
forbears to Consider Bodies in general because
(says he) those General Conceptions are usually
confused.

   Descartes in Med: 3. Calls himself a thinking   785
   substance & a Stone an extended substance. & adds
M.S. that they both agree in this that they are substances.
   & in the next paragra~~x~~ph he Calls extension a
   Mode of substance.

  Tis commonly said by the Philosophers that if the   786
   soul of Man were self existent it would have given
S it self all possible perfection. this I do not
  Understand.

                      f.78

  Mem. to excite men to the pleasures of the Eye &   787
Mo the Ear wch surfeit not, nor bring those evils after
  them as others.

  We see no variety or difference betwixt the   788
S Volitions, only between their effects. Tis One
  Will one Act distinguish'd by the effects. This
  will, this Act is the spirit, operative, Principle,
  soul &c.
        lou
No Mention of fears & jea$_\wedge$sies, nothing like a party. 789

  Locke in his 4th book & Descartes in Med. 6. use   790
M. the same argument for the Existence of objects.
  viz. th~~e~~at sometimes we see feel &c against our
  will.

  While I exist or have any Idea ~~xx~~ I am eternally,   791
S constantly willing, my acquiescing in the present
  State is willing.

  The Existence of any thing imaginable is nothing   792
E different from Imagination or perception.

or Will
Volition, wch is not imaginable regard must not be had to it's existence at least in the first Book.

f.79

Mo. There are four sorts of Propositions. Gold is a Metall, Gold is yellow; Gold is ~~fusible~~ fixt, Gold is not a Stone. of wch ye 1st 2^d & 3^d are only Nominal & have no Mental propositions answering them.   793

Also of non-coexistence as Gold is not blue.   793a (f.78v.)

M   Mem. in Vindication of the senses effectually to confute w^t Descartes Saith in the last par. of ye last Med: Viz. that the senses oftener inform him falsly than truely. That sense of pain tells me not my foot is bruised or broken but ✱ I having
viz
frequently observed those two Ideas of that peculiar pain & bruised foot go together do erroneously take them to be inseparable by a necessity of Nature as if Nature were any thing but the Ordinance of the free Will of God.   794

M.S. Descartes owns we know not a substance immediately by it self but by this alone that it is the subject of several acts. Answer to 2^d objection of Hobbs.   795

f.80

S   Hobbs in some degree falls in wth Locke saying thought is to the Mind or him self as dancing to the Dancer. object: 796

S   Hobbs in his object. 3. ridicules those expressions of the Scholastiques the Will wills &c so does Locke. I am of another Mind.   797

S   Descartes in answer to Object: 3. of Hobbs owns he is distinct from thought as a thing from it's modus or manner.   798

E.S. Opinion that existence was distinct from perception 799
of Horrible Consequence it is the foundation of
Hobbs's doctrine. &c

M.P.E. Malbranch in his Illustration differs widely from 800
me He doubts of the existence of Bodies I doubt
not in the least of this.

P. I differ from ~~xxxxxxxx~~ the Cartesians in that I make 801
extension, Colour &c to exist really in Bodies &
independent of Our Mind. All y^S carefully &
lucidly to be set forth.

f.81

M.P. Not to mention the Combinations of Powers but to 802
say the things the effects themselves to really exist
even w^n not actually ~~seen~~ perceiv'd but still with
relation to perception.

X The great use of the Indian figures above the Roman 803
shews Arithmetic to be about Signs not Ideas, or
not Ideas different from the Characters themselves.

Mo.X Reasoning there may be about things or Ideas Actions but 804
N. Demonstration can be only Verbal. I question, no
matter &

G Quoth Descartes the Idea of God is not made by me 805
for I can neither add to nor subtract from it. No
more can he add to or take from any other Idea
even of his own making.

S The not distinguishing twixt Will & Ideas is a 806
Grand Mistake wth Hobbs. He takes these things
for nothing wch are not Ideas.

f.82

M. Say you, at this rate all's nothing but Idea meer 807
phantasm. I answer every thing as real as ever.
I hope to call a thing Idea makes it not the less real.

truly I should have (perhaps) stuck to y̅e̅ word thing and not
mention'd the Word Idea were it not for a Reason
& I think a good one too w̅c̅h̅ I shall give in y̅e̅
Second Book.

I.S.   Idea is y̅e̅ object or subject of thought; y̅t̅ I think on w̅t̅ever   808
it be, I call Idea. thought it self, or Thinking is no
Idea tis an act i.e. Volition i.e. as contradistinguish'd
to effect, the Will.

I. Mo.   Locke in B. 4. c. 5. assigns not y̅e̅ right cause why   809
Mental Propositions are so difficult. it is not
because of Complex but because of abstract Ideas.
y̅e̅ Idea of a Horse is as complex as that of
Fortitude. yet in saying y̅e̅ Horse is White I form
a Mental Proposition with ease but w̅n̅ I say
Fortitude is a Vertue I shall find a Mental
proposition hardly or not at all to be come at.

                                                                    f.83

S.   Pure Intellect I understand not.   810

Locke is in y̅e̅ right in those things wherein He   811
differs from y̅e̅ Cartesians & they cannot but allow
of his Opinions if they stick to their own principles
or cant of Existence & other abstract Ideas.

G. S.   The propertys of all things are in God i.e. there   812
is in the Deity Understanding as well as Will. He
is no Blind agent & in truth a blind Agent is a
Contradiction.

G   I am certain there is a God, tho I do not perceive   813
him have no intuition of him. this not difficult if
we rightly understand w̅t̅ is meant by certainty.

S   It seems that the Soul taken for the Will is   814
immortal, Incorruptible.

S   Qu: whether perception must of necessity precede volition?   815

S. Mo.   Errour is not in the Understanding but in ye Will. w^t I understand or perceive, that I understand there can be no Errour in this.   816

f.84

Mo. N.   Mem: to take notice of Lockes Woman afraid of a wetting in ye Introd: to shew there may be reasoning about Ideas or things.   817

M.   Say Descartes & Malbranch God hath given us strong inclinations to think our Ideas proceed from Bodies. ~~pray w^t mean they~~ or that Bodies do exist. Pray w^t mean they by this. Would they have it that the Ideas of imagination are images of & proceed from the Ideas of sense. this is true but cannot be their meaning for they speak of Ideas of sense themselves as proceeding from being like unto I know not w^t.   818

M. S.   Cartesius per Ideam Vult omne id quod habet esse objectivum in Intellectu. V. Tract: de Methodo.   819

S   Qu: may not there be an Understanding without a Will.   820

S   Understanding is in some sort an Action.   821

S   Silly of Hobbs &c to speak of ye Will as if it were Motion wth wch it has no likeness.   822

f.85

M.   Ideas of Sense are the Real things or Archetypes. Ideas of Imagination, Dreams &c are copies, images of those.   823

M.   My ~~rig~~ Doctrines rightly Understood all that Philosophy of Epicurus, Hobbs, Spinoza &c wch has been a Declared Enemy of Religion ~~xx~~ Comes   824 to y̆e Ground.

G.   Hobbs & Spinosa make God Extended. Locke also seems to do the Same.   825

I. E.   Ens, res, aliquid dicuntur termini transcendentales. Spinosa p. 76. prop. 40. Eth. part: 2. gives an odd account of their original. also of the original of all Universals Homo, Canis &c.   826

G.   Spinosa (vid: Pref: oper: Posthum:) will Have God to be Omnium Rerum Causa immanens & to countenance this produces that of S^t. Paul, in him we live &c. ✷ Now this of S^t. Paul may be explain'd by my Doctrine as well as Spinosa's or Locke's or Hobbs's or Raphson's &c.   827

f.86

S   The Will is purus actus or rather pure Spirit not imaginable, not sensible, not intelligible. in no wise the object of y̆e Understanding, no wise perceivable.   828

S.   Substance of a Spirit is that it acts, causes, wills, operates, or if you please (to avoid the quibble y^t may be made on y̆e word it) to act, cause, will, operate & it's substance is not knowable not being an Idea.   829

G.   Why may we not conceive it possible for God to create things out of Nothing. certainly we our selves create in some wise whenever we imagine.   830

G. N.   Ex nihilo nihil fit. this (saith Spinoza op: posth: p. 464) & y̆e like are called veritates aeternae because nullam fidem habent extra Mentem. to make this axiom have a positive signification, one should express it thus. Every Idea has a Cause i. e. is produced. by a Will.   831

P. | The Philosophers ~~Speak~~ Talk much of a distinction twixt absolute & relative things, or twixt things consider'd in their | 832

f.87

own nature & the Same things considered with respect to us. I know not w.^t they mean by things consider'd in themselves. This is nonsense, Jargon.

S. | It seems there can be no perception, no Idea without Will, being there are no Ideas so indifferent but one had rather ~~be without them~~ Have them than annihilation, or annihilation than them. or if there be such an equall Ballance there must be an equal mixture of pleasure & pain to Cause it. there being No Ideas perfectly Void of all pain & uneasiness But w.^t are preferable to annihilation. | 833

X | Recipe in animum tuum per cogitationem Vehementum rerum ipsarum non literarum aut sonorum imagines. Hobbs against Wallis. | 834

X | Tis a perfection we may imagine in Superior Spirits that they can see a great deal at once with the Utmost Clearness & distinction whereas we can only see a point. | 835

M. | Treating of Matter I had better Say the proportion & Beauty of Things than their Species (wch Locke hath proved already) are the Workmanship of the Mind. | 836

f.88

X | Mem: w.ⁿ I treat of Mathematiques to enquire into ye Controversy twixt Hobbes & Wallis. | 837

G. | Every sensation of mine wch happens in Consequence of the general, known Laws of nature | 838

&. is from without i.e. independent of my Will
demonstrates the Being of a God. i.e: of an ~~xxx~~
unextended incorporeal Spirit wch is omniscent,
om_ni_potent. &c.

Mo. One great Cause of Miscarriage in Men's affairs   839
is that they too much regard the Present.

M I say not with J.S. that we see Solids I reject his   840
Solid Philosophy. Solidity being only perceived
by touch.

S It seems to me that Will & understanding Volitions   841
& ideas cannot be severed, that either cannot be
possibly without the Other.

E.S. Some Ideas or other I must have so long as I exist   842
or Will. But no one Idea or Sort of Ideas is essential.

f.89

M. The distinction between Idea & Ideatum I cannot   843
one or consequence
otherwise conceive than by making the effect of
Dream, reverie, Imagination the Other of sense
& the Constant laws of Nature.

P. Dico quod Extensio non concipitur in se & per se   844
contra quam dicit Spinoza in ep: 1^a ad Oldenburgium.

G My Definition of ye Word God I think Much clearer   845
than that of Descartes & Spinoza viz. ens Summè
perfectum, & absolute Infinitum or ens constans
infinitis attributis quorum unumquodque est
infinitum.

X. Tis chiefly the Connexion betwixt Tangible &   846
Visible Ideas that deceives & not the visible Ideas
them selves.

S. But the Grand Mistake is that we know not w^t we   847
mean by ~~x~~ we our selves, our mind &c. tis most

sure & certain that our Ideas are distinct from the Mind i.e. the Will, the Spirit.

f.90

S. I must not Mention the Understanding as a faculty or part of the Mind, I must include Understanding & Will &c in the word Spirit by wch I mean all that is active. I must not Say that the Understanding differs not from the particular Ideas, or the Will from particular Volitions. T 848

S. The Spirit, the Mind, is neither a Volition nor an Idea. 849

N.S. I Say there are no Causes (properly Speaking) but Spiritual, nothing active but Spirit. Say you, this is only Verbal, tis only annexing a new sort of signification to the word Cause, & why may not others all as well retain the old one & call one Idea the Cause of another wch always follows it. I answer, if you do so, I shall drive you into many absuridtys, I say you cannot avoid running into opinions yo'll be glad to disown if you stick firmly to that signification of the Word Cause. 850

Mo. In Valuing Good we reckon too much on ye present & our own. 851

Mo. There be two Sorts of Pleasure the one is ordain'd as a spur or incitement to Somewhat else & has a Visible relation & Subordination thereto, the other is not. Thus the pleasure of eating is of the former Sort, of Musick is ye later Sort. These may be used for recreation, those not but in order to their End. 852

f.91

Mo. N. X Three Sorts of usefull knowlege, that of coexistence to be treated of in our dioxx Principles of Natural Philosophy, that of Relation in Mathematiques, that of definition, or inclusion, or Words (wch perhaps 853

-111-

differs not from that of Relation) in Morality.

S — Will, Understanding, desire, Hatred &c so far forth as they are acts or active differ not, all their difference consists in their objects, circumstances &c. 854

N. — We must carefully distinguish betwixt two Sorts of Causes Physical & Spirituall: 855

N. — Those may more properly be Called occasions yet but then we must mean Causes yt do nothing. (to comply) we may term them Causes. ʌ 856

S — According to Locke we must be in an Eternal uneasyness so long as we live, bating the time of sleep or Trance &c. for He will have even the Continuance of An action to be in his Sense an action & so requires a Volition & this an uneasiness. 857

I. — I must not pretend ~~at least near the beginning~~ to promise much of Demonstration, I must Cancell all passages that look like that Sort of Pride, that raising of Expectation in my Readers. 858

f.92

I. — If this be the Case, Surely a Man had better not Philosophize at all, No more than a Deform'd Person Ought to ʌ behold himself by the Reflex light of a Mirrour.   *covet to*   859

I. — Or thus, like Deformed Persons who having beheld themselves by the reflex light of a Mirrour are displeas'd with their ~~xxx~~ Discoery. 860

M.1 — What can an Idea be like, but another Idea, we can compare it with Nothing else, a Sound like a Sound, a Colour like a Colour. 861

-112-

M. 1	Is it not nonsense to say a Smell is like a thing wch cannot be smelt, a Colour is like a thing which cannot be seen.	862
M. S.	Bodies exist without the Mind i. e. are not the Mind, but distinct from it. This I allow, the Mind being altogether different therefrom.	863
P.	Certainly we should not see Motion if there was no diversity of Colours.	864
P.	Motion is an abstract Idea i. e. there is no such Idea that ~~th~~ Can be conceived by it Self.	865
I	Contradictions cannot be both true. Men are oblig'd to answer Objections drawn from Consequences. Introd:	866
S.	The Will & Volition are Words not used by the Vulgar, the Learned are banter'd by their meaning abstract Ideas.	867

f.93

X	Speculative Math: as if a Man was all day making hard knots on purpose to unty them again.	868
X132	Tho it might have been otherwise yet it is convenient the same thing wch is M. V. should be also M. T. or very near it.	869
S	I must not give the Soul or Mind the Scholastique Name pure act, but rather pure Spirit or active Being.	870
S	I must not Say the Will & Understanding are all one but that they are both Abstract Ideas i. e. none at all. they not being even ratione different from the Spirit, Qua faculties, or Active.	871
S	Dangerous to make Idea & thing terms Convertible, tha~~xt~~ were the Way to prove Spirits are Nothing.	872

Mo. X	Qu: whether Veritas Stands not for an Abstract Idea.	873
M	Tis plain the Moderns must by their own Principles own there are no Bodies i.e. no Sort of Bodies without the Mind i.e. unperceived.	874
S.G.	Qu: whether the Will can be the object of Praescience or any knowlege.	875
P	If there were only one Ball in the World it Could not be Moved. there could be no Variety of Appearance.	876

f.94

X	According to the Doctrine of Infinite Divisibility there must be some smell of a Rose v. g. at an infinite distance ~~of~~ from it.	877
M.	Extension tho it exist only in the Mind, yet is no Property of the Mind, The Mind can exist without it tho it cannot without the Mind. But in Book 2 I shall at large shew the difference there is betwixt the Soul & Body or Extended being.	878
S	Tis an absurd Question wch Locke puts whether Man be free to Will?	879
X	Mem. to enquire into the reason of the Rule for Determining Questions in Algebra.	880
X	It has already been observ'd by others that names are no where of more necessary use than in Numbering.	881
M.P.*	I will grant you that extension, Colour &c may be Said to be without the Mind in a double respect i.e. as independent of our Will & as distinct from the Mind.	882
Mo.N.X	Certainly it is not impossible but a Man may arrive at the knowlege of all real truth as well without as with signs had he a Memory & imagination most	883

strong & capacious. therefore reasoning & Science doth not Altogether depend upon Words or Names.

N. I think not that things fall out of necessity, the connexion of no two Ideas is necessary, 'tis all the result of freedom i.e. tis all Voluntary.   884

M.1 One simple Idea can be the pattern or resemblance only of Another. So far as they differ one cannot resemble the Other.   885

M.S. If a Man with his Eyes shut Imagines to Himself the Sun & firmament you will not say he or his Mind is the Sun or Extended. tho Neither sun or firmament be without his Mind.   886

S Tis Strange to find Philosophers doubting & disputing whether they have Ideas of y̅e̅ ~~Mind~~ spiritual things or no. Surely tis easy to know. Vid. De Vries de id: In: p. 64   887

S. De Vrie will have it that we know the Mind as we do Hunger not by Idea but sense or Conscientia So will Malbranch. This is a Vain distinction   888

NOTES ON THE ENTRIES*
by
A. A. LUCE

---

*Notes as revised by Professor A. A. Luce from his <u>Philosophical Commentaries generally called the Commonplace Book -- George Berkeley</u> (London: Thomas Nelson and Sons, Ltd., 1944)

NOTES ON THE ENTRIES BY A. A. LUCE

A General Note

The <u>Philosophical Commentaries</u> abounds in entries which are quite clear when explained, but which need explanation, e.g., "Of & thing causes of mistake" (115). My first aim has been to state simply what, in my opinion, each entry means, or to enable the reader to find out for himself by looking up the references given. I have had also in mind the requirements of scholars who are seeking light on disputed points in the Berkeleian philosophy, or who are studying the genesis and development of Berkeley's early thought. For their sakes I have included references to (a) other entries in the <u>Commentaries</u> which deal with the same topic, (b) corresponding passages in Berkeley's publications, especially the <u>Theory of Vision</u> and the <u>Principles</u>, which were on the stocks along with the <u>Commentaries</u>, and (c) corresponding passages in the books he is known to have used at the time, especially Locke's <u>Essay</u>.

For the most part I have given each entry a separate note, but where consecutive or adjacent entries are obviously connected, I have combined the notes. I have consulted the notes of Johnston and of Hecht, but have written mine <u>de novo</u>. The numbers are those assigned to <u>my</u> edition of the text.

To avoid repetition where topics recur frequently (e.g., abstract ideas, or infinite divisibility), I have as a rule given one comprehensive note on the first occurrence, referring back to it in the subsequent entries. The multitude of references and cross-references could not be avoided; for I have aimed at making my annotations at once adequate and brief.

The subjects of my key doctrinal notes with numbers of the entries on which they comment are given in the following table:

Table of Key Doctrinal Notes

Abstract general ideas, 318

Archetypes, 689

Body, reality of, 41, 52

Books projected, 508, 676

Causation, 403

Certainty, 163, 693

Connection of ideas, 181

Deity, 107

Demonstration, 163; in ethics, 669

Existence, 408

Hedonism, Berkeley's, 541-542

Heterogeneity of sight and touch, 28

Idea, "of", 115; and thing, 369; and spirit, 490

Identity, 192, 200

Imagination and pure intellect, 531

Indifference, 143, 158-159

Infinite divisibility, 8, 11

Laws of nature, 144

Liberty, 149, 156-157

Minimal points, 59

Mind, see Soul

Molyneux problem, 27

Optical angle, 73

Perceivable, the, see Body

Powers, 41

Principle, the, 285

Quadrature of the circle, 245

Relations, 540

Resemblances, ideas as, 46-47

Retinal image, 102, 211

Scepticism, 79

Senses, reliability of the, 317

Simple ideas, 53

Solidity, 78

Soul, 14, 154, 576

Substance, 80

"Thoughts" as objects, 153

Time, 4

Truth, 554

Understanding, 362a

Uneasiness, 145

Will, 131; see Liberty

Words and thought, 178

Numbered Notes on the Entries

1.2. "Neither again can it be conceived how eternity has flowed down to the present day; for that distinction which is commonly received of infinity in time past and in time to come can by no means hold; for it would thence follow that one infinity is greater than another. . ." (Bacon, Nov. Org. I xlviii). Locke (II xvii 10) refers to eternity a parte post and ante without comparing them, and in section 20 he argues that man has no positive idea of eternity, because (if he had) "he could add two infinities together; nay, make one infinity bigger than another: absurdities too gross to be confuted!"

The purport of Berkeley's two observations is not clear; he would certainly, with Locke, regard as absurd an infinite greater than an infinite (he attacked infinite divisibility on that very ground); but taking eternity as "onely a train of innumerable ideas" (14), he seems prepared to admit that there may be limited eternities, such as the duration (i.e., experience) of finite spirits, which has a beginning, if not an end. The clue of the precise meaning of these entries was contained, no doubt, in Berkeley's essay on time, on which see 4n.

3. For the same question see 92, and Locke II xvii 16; the answer, for Berkeley, is in the negative. In his letter to Johnson of March 24, 1730 (Works II 293) he says that the supposition of a succession in Deity is one of the causes of confusion about time.

4. In the same letter he writes, "One of my earliest inquiries was about time which led into several paradoxes that I did not think fit or necessary to publish; particularly the notion that the resurrection follows the next moment to death." That early inquiry is, no doubt, represented here in these entries on time and eternity. Probably Berkeley wrote an essay on time as part of his first study of immaterialism, subsequently noting here those problems and features of the subject which required further examination. Time is discussed briefly in Princ. 97-98, and is there stated to be "nothing abstracted from the succession of ideas in our minds"; the same teaching is contained in the PC. Time is the succession of ideas in our minds here, 167, 460, 647, 651; it cannot exist outside the mind, i.e., there is no abstract, absolute time, infinitely divisible, 5, 8, 10, 13, 48, 655; time being relative to mind has no gaps, and there are no intervals of mere existence without thought, 127, 390, 590, 651; questions are raised about variations in the rate of succession of ideas, 7, 16, 39, 92.

5. In Princ. 98 Berkeley closely connects the existence, the duration, and the cogitation of a finite spirit. Locke (II xiv 3) distinguishes duration as the distance between any parts of the succession of our ideas.

6. "before, between, ≰ after," i.e., the train of our ideas, which for Berkeley, as for Locke, measures succession. Berkeley adds "numbering," because number, he holds (see 460), requires "distinct perception," i.e., successive perceptions.

7. Malebranche (I viii) adduces this fact as evidence that we have no exact knowledge of duration or motion; pain, he says, makes us consider the parts of duration with closer attention; but mirth and joy carry the soul out of itself.

8.10. In his next paragraph Malebranche argues for the infinite divisibility of duration. Similarly Locke (II xv 9) says, "Every part of duration is duration too; and every part of extension is extension; both of them capable of addition or division in infinitum." With regard to the concrete succession of ideas which, for him, is time, Berkeley differs from both of them; for he denies, directly or by implication, the infinite divisibility of time here, and in 132-133, 488, Princ. 98. The "measure" of time, he holds, leads men to suppose space infinitely divisible; just as the inch representing the mile leads them to suppose space infinitely divisible (see Princ. 126-127).

What, then, are we to understand by "Duration infinitely divisible"? I find no such concession in his published works. The phrase must refer to some intermediate position which he held for a time, or was thinking of holding; he may have been prepared to grant infinite divisibility to the abstract "perseverare in existendo," just as we find him in 11 and <u>TV</u> 54 prepared to allow infinite divisibility to abstract space; cf. <u>Princ.</u> 97, 111.

9. This may be a comment on "this present moment is common to all things that are not in being" (Locke II xv 11)).

Two questions arise: (a) Does " το νυν " refer to time or to eternity? (b) Does "not common" involve a solipsist view of time?

(a) The entry is marked T, and therefore must have at least an application to the problem of time; but if Berkeley had been originally thinking of the present moment of time, I do not think he would have troubled to write the Greek term, which had long been technical for the <u>punctum stans</u>. Writing to Johnson on March 24, 1730 (<u>Works</u> II 293), Berkeley says, "By the το νυν I suppose to be implied that all things, past and to come, are actually present to the mind of God, and that there is in Him no change, variation, or succession." Moreover the term "intelligences" was often used technically of celestial beings, as in 723, but it may be used more broadly, as in 663. Perhaps there is an implied <u>a fortiori</u> argument; as in heaven intelligences do not all experience the instant of eternity in the same way, so on earth human minds do not all experience the instant of time in the same way.

(b) Berkeley says that το νυν is not common to "all intelligences"; to assume that he meant <u>any</u> when he says <u>all</u> is rash. The words, therefore, do not necessarily imply that Berkeley held, even for a time, a solipsist view. Entries 48 (perhaps) and 590 stress the privacy of the <u>measure</u> of time; so, too, do the letter to Johnson and <u>Princ.</u> 98 ("estimated");

but there can be a private measure of a public continuum. On the other hand, it is important to note that in Princ. 98 the words "is participated by all beings" are used with a clear reference to the Newtonian conception of time, which Berkeley is attacking; but, again, it would be rash to force into those words an implicit denial of all public time, especially as he has just before mentioned "such a time" which is common at least to master and servant.

Berkeley denies abstract and absolute time, and I think we might say that he denies impersonal time; but he did not publish any full theory of time; he certainly held that time is the succession of ideas in the mind; but there is no need to give a subjectivist, much less a solipsist, turn to that phrase; the ideas have their private and personal aspect; in so far as they are in my mind, they are mine and not yours, as is the air I breathe. But they have their public aspect too; they are God's ideas, given by Him to all, forming the course of nature, shared by many, accessible to all, as is the air we breathe.

11. "in one sense," Berkeley consistently denies that finite, sensible extension is infinitely divisible, and the limitation here is to be interpreted by his words, "Whatever may be said of extension in abstract, it is certain sensible extension is not infinitely divisible" (TV 54); he was prepared to admit that abstract extension, or the "extension of matter" (PC 81) could be in thought infinitely divided.

Infinite divisibility was accepted almost universally in Berkeley's day (Bayle was a notable exception), and he devotes much attention to the problem in the early part of the PC viz., 17, 21, 26, 67, 72, 75, 81, 132-133, 236-237, 247-248,

261, 263, 314, 322-323, 342, 364, 393, 462 (cf. 877). He touches on the infinite divisibility of time (see 8n.) and of magnitude in general (see 132-133), but he is chiefly concerned with that of extension.

From these entries and from the discussion of the problem in Princ. 123ff. we see that Berkeley objected to infinite divisibility on the following grounds: (1) it gives rise to many geometrical paradoxes, and fosters that extreme subtlety of mathematical reasoning exemplified in the doctrine of fluxions; (2) it entails a depreciation of our faculties, especially of our senses; (3) it encourages false abstraction; (4) it runs directly counter to his New Principle, for when the mathematician takes his doctrine objectively, that is, when he goes beyond the assertion, "I can go on dividing," and asserts, "This is infinitely divisible and consists of an infinite number of parts," he has to assume the existence of what is not perceived, the "something we know not what." In opposition to the infinite divisibility Berkeley advanced his own theory of indivisible, sensible points, or minima, on which see 59n.; on extension, see 18n.

12. Cf. 118, which gives the reference to Locke II xiv 19, "The revolutions of the sun and moon the properest measures of time." Being immediately perceived they immediately measure our train of ideas (see 4n.), and since our train of ideas, in its turn, measures our duration, the "revolutions" measure our duration "mediately," i.e., indirectly.

13. "onely" is not depreciatory, but is an implicit denial of the Newtonian view (see Berkeley in Princ. 110) that there is an absolute time outside the mind, as well as a relative time

within the mind; on time, see 4n.

14. Locke (II xvii 16) rejects the classical conception of eternity as simultaneity, and resolves it into infinite succession. Berkeley here adopts this suggestion, and tries to explain immortality as an indefinite continuance of the train of ideas.

In *Princ*. 141 (1st ed.) he declares the immortality of the soul "a necessary consequence" of his doctrine, and the hesitation expressed in this entry does not represent any serious doubt about immortality, but merely reflects the fluidity, at this stage, of his psychologial terms. In 814 the immortality of the soul "taken for the Will" is admitted; but it must be rememered that the identification of "mind, spirit, soul, or my self" with one another and with the will or active being was worked out very gradually in the *PC*.

A study of the phases through which the terms "soul" and "mind" pass in the *PC* is needed for a full understanding of Berkeley's doctrine of existence in the mind.

In this entry the soul is unimportant compared with the person, which is the bearer of immortality; in 25 the two are almost equated, and the question is asked whether they are completely known; in 44 and 154 attempts are made to define the soul; but perhaps the souls may be known, and yet not defined, 178; in any case it is not to be known by idea, 230; in 286 we reach the important transitional position of mind active and mind passive. A big step forward is taken in 478 by the raising of the question, How is the soul distinguished from its ideas? Hitherto soul and ideas have not been distinguished; hence the doubt in our present entry about the soul's immortality. After an interval we reach the striking series of entries, 576-581, where the identity of soul and mind with their contents is roundly asserted; in 622 extension and motion are virtually united to the soul's essence; in 637 the possibility of an unknown thinking substance of ideas is granted. Another pause for reflection, and the early phase is over; in 712 the soul is the active thing, the will, and therefore distinct from ideas, which are passive; 478a, a verso addition, is to the same effect; 788 fixes the terminology, as in the <u>Principles</u>, of will, spirit, and soul; and in 863, 878, and 882 mind is distinguished from body and extension.

15. 16. Reflections on the rate of succession of ideas, probably founded on <u>Locke</u> II xiv 6-12, cf. <u>Princ</u>. 14; on time, see 4n.

17. Cf. 824. Epicurism, Hobbism, Atheism, and idolatry are traced to materialism in <u>Princ</u>. 35, 92-94. The mention of the fall of Adam is curious; presumably Berkeley means that materialism is the original sin of intellect. Malebranche (I v) traces the error of the senses to the Fall. Idolatry, literal and figurative, is traced to materialism again in 411; for materialism is the substitution of "some blind unthinking deputy" for God (<u>Princ</u>. 150), and what the representative idea is to the mind of the thinker, the idol is to the heart of the worshipper. On "divisibility," see 11n.; on substance see 80n.

18. There are many entries on extension; Berkeley had to study it closely, because of the popular association of space with matter, and because his argument required him to trace the connection between space and the secondary qualities and to establish the heterogeneity of visual and tactual space.

That extension is not without the mind is asserted also in 33, 37, 121, 249, 270, 290, 342, 801, 878, 882, the last three of these entries making the important provisos that extension is distinct from the mind, is not a property or mode of mind, and is independent of our mind; extension is a sensible quality, and visible extension, in particular, is colour, or the co-existence and continuity of colours, 78, 164-165, 242, 253, 318, 328, 362, 363a, 494, 711; it is composed of minimal points, visible and tangible, 78a, 287, 365, 440; any other extension is an abstract idea, 111a, 328, 365a, 440, TV 122ff., Princ. 116ff.; extension is not a simple idea, 105, 167; pure space is considered in 135, 290, 695, TV 126, Princ. 117; extension and matter are considered together in 37, 40, 269, 288a, 299, 325; on infinite divisibility, see 11n.; on the heterogeneity of visible and tangible extension, see 28n. Note that in some entries Berkeley uses "extension" as the equivalent of "magnitude."

19. "Those odd paradoxes, that the fire is not hot, nor the wall white" (Princ. 99, 1710 ed. only) are mentioned again in 392. Berkeley traces them to "a twofold abstraction," viz., abstraction of esse from percipi, and of primary from secondary qualities. His own teaching rests on the reality of the sensible world, and defends the solidarity of primary and secondary qualities and the inseparability of both from perception.

The term "immaterial hypothesis" (cf. 71) on the second page of the PC along with a summary (18-24) of its main tenets and arguments is noteworthy. Berkeley had reached immaterialism and had thought out its consequences some time before he began the PC; cf. "a long and scrupulous inquiry" (Princ. Pref.) and "the opinion of matter I have entertained some years" (letter of September 6, 1710, <u>Works</u> VIII 37). The word "hypothesis" may imply lack of full conviction -- in which case it points to the fact that Berkeley had not yet come on his intuitive New Principle, but was at the stage of his "first arguings" (see next note and 265).

20. This entry originally had the marginal letter P, index of the small group (about 35 in number) dealing with Primary and Secondary Qualities. This was Berkeley's first "method of arguing" (see previous note), viz., "after the same manner as modern philosophers prove certain sensible qualities to have no existence in Matter, or without the mind, the same thing may be likewise proved of all other sensible qualities whatsoever" (<u>Princ</u>. 14). In section 15 he remarks on the insufficiency of this line of proof. The "modern philosophers" are Locke and the Cartesians, especially Malebranche. Locke's account (II viii 9ff.) of the primary and secondary qualities and their ideas is not altogether clear or consistent; he confuses idea and quality, and gives the impression that the secondary qualities are in the mind, but he insists that "powers" to produce them in us are in the thing. Malebranche gives the name "sensible qualities" to what Locke calls "secondary"; Locke virtually places them in the mind; Malebranche goes further and makes them "modifications" of the mind. Bayle (<u>Pyrrho</u> and <u>Zeno</u>) says, with Berkeley, that the arguments which apply to the one group of qualities apply also to the other group.

21. 21a. For Berkeley, the supposition of length without breadth is absurd, as involving an insensible idea, i.e., an idea which is no idea; he admits that we can consider length and breadth separately, 254, 722, but to suppose that they really exist separately is to be guilty of false abstraction, 365a,

483; length without breadth is discussed further in 85, 342, 365; on infinite divisibility, see 11n.

22. 23. Anticipations of the New Principle, *esse est percipi*; *nec quid, nec quantum, nec quale*, also in 517, is a description of matter, founded on Aristotle, *Metaphysics* Bk. VII c. 3, quoted by Collier, *Clavis Universalis* II 9.

24. A hasty deduction from immaterialism, panpsychist in character. Berkeley's "second thoughts" are contained in later entries such as 437, 547, 563, 686a, 863, where, exactly as in the *Principles*, he teaches explicitly the existence of "other things" (ideas) which depend on mind, but are not mind, nor modes of mind.

25. For the development of Berkeley's views on the soul, see 14n.; the term "person" is freely used in the early part of the *PC*; in 713 he records his decision not to make much use of it, owing to its theological associations.

26. On infinite divisibility see 11n.; this argument is developed in *Princ.* 47, 123-124; Bayle (*Zeno*) has a similar argument.

27. Answered in the negative, *TV* 137. The "jocose problem" propounded by Molyneux in his letter to Locke of March 2, 1693 (*Some Familiar Letters between Mr Locke and Several of his Friends*, p. 37), was inserted by the latter in the second edition of the *Essay* (II ix 8).

    The Molyneux Problem supposes a man blind from birth able to distinguish by touch between a cube and a sphere of the same metal, and asks, "Suppose then the cube and sphere placed on a table, and the blind man to be made to see; query, Whether by his sight, before he touched them, he could now distinguish and tell which is the globe, which the cube?" Berkeley refers to the problem again in 32, 49, 58, 59, 62, 95, 97, 100, 121, 174, 294, 307, 454; he produces it with comments in TV 132, and refers to it in TV 41, 79, 137, Appendix (2nd ed.), Princ. 43, TVV 45 and 71, where he gives a résumé of the Chesselden case (for this and other cases of cure, see Fraser II p. 410ff. and Works I 275-276 and 276 n.).

Locke and Molyneux answered the query in the negative; Berkeley thought the man would not understand the question at all; Leibniz after a full discussion (Nouveaux Essais II ix 8) decided that if the man be informed that the two objects are cube and globe, he will know which is which; but that if he is not so informed, he will not at first connect either object with the cube and globe he has touched.

Locke uses the problem merely to illustrate mental interpretation of the data of sense; Berkeley gives it a much wider application, using it for a variety of purposes, but chiefly to establish by means of it the heterogeneity of visible and tangible ideas; see next note.

28. Locke taught that we see and touch the same thing, or, in his technical language, "We can receive...the ideas of our extension, figure, motion, and rest of bodies, both by seeing and feeling" (II v). Berkeley denied that we see and touch the same thing, and to establish the heterogeneity of visible and tangible ideas was a main aim of his Theory of Vision (I, 121-145; cf. TVV 41, "this main part and pillar thereof"). The heterogeneity is much discussed in the early part of the PC, but almost drops out of sight in the latter part; in the

Principles it appears only in sect. 44, where he deals with the Theory of Vision. The heterogeneity was an important interim argument; for if the visible idea is to act as sign of the tangible, the two must be two and not one; but once the full doctrine of things as "collections of ideas" is stated (Princ. 1), the question whether the types of constituent ideas are like or unlike, the same or different, loses much of its significance.

In the PC Berkeley is chiefly concerned with extension, visible and tangible, but he does not lose sight of figure and motion; his main argument for the heterogeneity is founded on the results of his analysis of the Molyneux Problem, 32, 49, 58-59, 95, 100, 174; but he attempts other lines of proof, 35, 49, 57, 61, 69-70, 103, 213, 226, 243, 295, 297, 328, 441; he applies the doctrine of heterogeneity to the minimal parts of the ideas, the **minimum visibile** and **tangibile**, 70, 441-442, 710, 869; he brings the other senses into comparison, 138, 241; and he tries to answer the obvious question, If the objects of sight and touch are so different in type, why do they commonly go by the same name? -- 28, 42-43, 54, 91, 114, 240; he says in 101 that the objects of geometry are tangible, not visible; and finally he turns his attention to the nature of the connection between the two types of object, and argues that it might have been otherwise, that it is a customary connection based on experience, and is not a necessary connection, 174, 181, 224-225, 246, 846.

29. The ancient problem of the relation of the diagonal of the square to the side is discussed also in 258, 263-264, 469; in spite of received opinion to the contrary, Berkeley argues that diagonal and side are commensurable in particular squares. Incommensurability, on which turn several of the mathematical

problems discussed in the PC, raises the question of the nature of point and line, and therefore of the infinite divisibility. Cheyne (Philosophical Principles of Natural Religion IV 7) calls the incommensurability "the most perfect and unavoidable proof" of the infinite divisibility. Berkeley denied both doctrines, holding that finite lines consist of finite parts, or minima; see Princ. 124-125.

30. Newton's doctrine of motion absolute and relative, outlined in his Principia, Schol. ad def. viii, is criticized by Berkeley in 316, 451, 455-456, Princ. 111-115, and in his letter to Johnson of March 24, 1730 (Works II 292); see also Mot. 16-17, 32. For Berkeley there is no motion other than relative. Newton's doctrines of fluxions, colour, and gravitation also are discussed in the PC.

31. Explained by 119, 319, and Locke II xvii 14; cf. TV 124, "figure is the termination of magnitude," and Anal. 31. The "compleat, positive ideas" (prima manu) refers to Locke's argument (loc. cit.) that we have no positive idea of infinity.

32. Because the tangible figures which he knew would not at first, Berkeley held, be suggested by visible figures; for the Molyneux Problem, see 27n. William Molyneux (1656-1698), of Huguenot family settled in Dublin, scientist, philosopher, and politician, friend and correspondent of Locke (see Some Familiar Letters between Mr Locke and Several of his Friends), promoter of the Dublin Philosophical Society, translated into English Descartes' Meditations (1680) and wrote Dioptrica Nova (1692, to which Berkeley's Theory of Vision on its technical side is much indebted), and The Case of Ireland, etc. (1698). His son, Samuel, who also rose to eminence, was Berkeley's

pupil in Trinity College, and to him the _Miscellanea Mathematica_ is dedicated.

33. 34. 35. 36. 37. 37a. Contain in outline most of Berkeley's teaching about space (see 18n.). Space is not "incompatible" with thought, i.e., the sharp contrast between the two, dear to the Cartesians, is unfounded. Space cannot exist without thought, yet cannot think; it is concrete not abstract, two-dimensional not solid; there is no "pure space" or vacuum, nor does space exist in matter; 96, 583; cf. _TV_ 122-127, _Princ._ 116-117; for the possibility of matter's thinking (34) see _Locke_ IV iii 6; for sensations "perfectly known," see _Princ._ 87; for the perception of planes and solids, see 106, and _TV_ 157-158; on the vacuum, see _TV_ 126, _Locke_ II xiii 21-23; on thought as active, see 153n. [Note the "ob:" in the marginalia of 36. This very odd abbreviation occurs only in this instance. -- Editor]

38. The answer to the query must be, "No"; for they are heterogeneous (see 28n. and _TV_ 137). In 54 the same question is raised about extension, and at first apparently answered in the affirmative; but subsequently the words "is proportional to tangible extension, also" were bracketed. Berkeley is on the question, "How do visible and tangible come to be called by the same name?" See 43 and _TV_ 139ff.

39. The succession of ideas, for Berkeley, constitutes time, and he was therefore interested in the variations in the rate of succession both in dreams and in waking life. See 4n.

40. "but etc.", i.e., but it is not so determined, for _ex_

hypothesi matter lies outside the mind, whereas size and figure are determined by the mind; see 65, 325, *Princ.* 11. Other hypothetical arguments against matter are to be found in 67 and 81 (if matter, then the infinite divisibility) and in 68, 269, 836 (if matter, how can beauty, proportion, and the sorts be explained?) and in 131 (if matter, then it affects us not). These arguments are for purposes of exposition, and do not necessarily imply any serious doubt in Berkeley's mind at this time about immaterialism. On extension, see 18n.

41. The "direct & brief demonstration" appears no doubt in *Princ.* 29, a passage clearly modelled on *Locke* IV xi 5 with the substitution of God for Locke's "brisk acting of some objects without me."

Locke's intricate theory of active and passive powers, according to which secondary qualities "are nothing in the objects themselves, but powers to produce various sensations in us by their primary qualities" (II viii 10) seems to have been taken over in a spiritualized form by Berkeley, the powers being located in Deity instead of in matter; but he outgrew part of the Lockian doctrine while filling the PC; for in the entries 52, 84, 155, 293, 293a, 298, 433, 461, 493, 621, we see him examining the notion of power, confining it to spirit, and finally equating it with the causal relation, and making God the cause of all ideas of sense.

42. Cf. 114. Hecht in his note on the entry says that the German Count is apparently E. W. von Tschirnhaus, whose *Medicina Mentis et Corporis* was published in 1687 at Amsterdam. The story was possibly about the "complication" of sense data, like those in *Locke* III iv 11, 12, intended to illustrate the heterogeneity of sight and touch.

43. Cf. 38n.; this question, which arises out of Berkeley's doctrine of the heterogeneity of sight and touch (see 28n.), is formally asked and answered in TV 139ff. The ultimate answer is that customary connection tends to make sign and thing signified indistinguishable.

44. As Locke does (III iv 4ff.), Berkeley at first takes definition seriously; he deals with definition of the soul again in 154, 178, of colour in 153, of extension in 178, 320, of idea in 507, of God in 845, and in general in 162, 562, 853. In his publications he says little about definition as such. On knowledge of the soul, see 14n. This scholastic approach to questions of psychology was only a passing phase.

45. Slow down the train of ideas, and apparent motion may become apparent rest. All motion is, therefore, perceived motion, relative to mind, and there is no way of detecting the supposed absolute rest and motion of supposed external bodies; see 30n.

46, 47. On likeness; against the representationist view that our ideas are pictures and likenesses of the material thing, and in particular against Locke's principle, "ideas of primary qualities are resemblances; of secondary, not" (II viii 15). Berkeley discusses the question further in 51, 81, 299, 484, 496, 551, 861-862, 885, Princ. 8-9, and sets out his position in formal propositions as part of the "demonstration" of the New Principle in 378 (props. 13-19).

48. Because time is the succession of ideas, "Each Person's time being measured to him by his own Ideas," 590; see 4n. and 9n.

49. Of these three arguments for the heterogeneity of the visible and tangible (see 28n.): the first, from the relativity of distance and size, is developed in TV 61; the second, from his own variety of the Molyneux problem (see 27n.) in TV 110; the third, from the original Molyneux problem, in TV 132-133.

50. 51. These are, in effect, the two heads of the argument against matter: (1) matter not being an idea cannot be perceived; (2) matter cannot be <u>like</u> what we perceive (see 46n.), for comparison can only be between ideas.

52. The active Being is God; on the "powers" theory, see 41n.

The problem of the reality of body becomes for the immaterialist the problem of the perceivable. This is one of the most carefully studied problems of the PC, and the discussion of it, continued in 79-80, 84, 98, 185, 185a, 228, 282, 288, 293, 293a, 298, 304, 305, 312, 408, 429, 446, 461, 472, 473, 474, 474a, 477, 477a, 493, 518, 535, 546, 546a, 550, 656, 777, 800, 801, 802, 807, shows that Berkeley's views fluctuated considerably during this period; the fluctuation amounts at times to flat contradiction, and the reader should note the number of recto statements, viz., 185, 293, 474, 477, 546, corrected on the verso (98 is on the verso and represents the later view).

The existence of body when not perceived by man is asserted throughout the series; but at first this existence is only the shadowy existence of "powers in the active Being." The "powers" theory, here accepted, is repeatedly criticized in later entries, and finally shelved (802); while Berkeley held it, the existence of the perceivable was to him "not actual" (185, 293a), and his assertion of the real existence of unperceived bodies seems to have been little more than a principle "to answer objections"

(312), to be understood in the conditional mood, viz., that if I think of them, they exist (472), all things being "entia rationis" (474). But on the page opposite the last-mentioned entry we meet the astounding correction, "according to my Doctrine all are not entia rationis" (474a). That is a change of view, not of terms; and on the verso of the next page Berkeley draws the vital distinction between matter, on the one hand, and "bodies & their quality," on the other hand, granting that the latter "exist indepen[den]tly of Our mind" (477a). He has come to realize that immaterialism is strengthened, not weakened, by the admission of sensible bodies, perceived by God when not perceived by man. That is his position in the latest entries of this series (800-807), where he distinguishes his view from the Cartesian, and asserts that "the things the effects themselves [i.e., not the powers] to really exist even wn not actually perceiv'd but still with relation to perception." That too is the position of the Principles; see sections 45-48, the main discussion of unperceived existence, where after arguing that annihilation, continual creation and intermittency are not absurdities, Berkeley states categorically that those doctrines do not follow from his principles, and warns the reader not to conclude from the esse est percipi that objects of sense "have no existence except only while they are perceived by us"; for the perceivable and identity, see Dials., Works II 247f. Cf. my "Berkeley's Doctrine of the Perceivable," Hermathena, No. LX, 1942.

53. 53a. Locke (II ii-vii) taught that simple ideas are the material of all our knowledge; some, e.g., colours, enter the mind by one sense only; some, e.g., space, figure, rest, motion, by more senses than one; some by reflection only, viz.,

perception, will, and their modes; some, viz., pleasure, pain, power, existence, unity, and succession, enter "by all the ways." This doctrine is much discussed in the early part of the PC and appears to be accepted; it drops out of sight towards the end, and does not reappear in the Principles. Simple ideas are mentioned twice in the Principles (13, 98) in connection with abstract ideas; see also Introd. to Princ. 22, "to see what ideas are included in any compound idea," where the Draft Introduction (Works II 143) for "ideas" has "simple ideas."

Berkeley analyses almost all Locke's examples of simple ideas: succession here and in 167, 460; extension in 105, 134, 167, 460; magnitude in 133; power in 134, 461, 493; colour in 134, 151-153, 484, 484a, 551, 562, 662; motion in 167, 450, 460; time in 167, 460; number in 167; existence in 408, 670-671; unity in 545; in several cases he shows that the supposed simple idea was in fact compound; but at the earlier stage he accepted the doctrine as a whole, and he planned to discuss it in a "preliminary discourse," 139, 570, and grounded upon it one of his "demonstrations" of the New Principle (378, 12-15); see also 179, 222, 280, 496, 526, 664, 760, 885.

The verso comment, no doubt a later addition, is clearly meant to qualify and correct the recto, and it points to Berkeley's doctrine of abstract ideas (see 318n.), developed while he was filling the PC, as the source of his dissatisfaction with Locke's doctrine of simple ideas; analysis had shown him that the simplest of the simple ideas, which enter "by all the Ways," existence, unity, and succession (545, 670-671, cf. Princ. 13) were not ultimate data, but abstractions from reality.

54. Cf. "The visible square contains in it several distinct parts, whereby to mark the several distinct corresponding parts

of a tangible square" (TV 142). Berkeley is trying to answer the objection, "If visible and tangible are heterogeneous (see 28n.), why are they commonly taken for the same?" For the bracketed words, see 38n.; on extension, see 18n. Fraser and Johnston misread "encreas'd" as "encreated."

55. An argument ad absurdum against external extension, because, for Berkeley, what is sensible is eo ipso an idea in the mind. The "or abstra[c]tible" is a later addition inserted sarcastically, no doubt, when he came on his doctrine of abstraction, and decided that non-sensible extension is an abstract idea.

56. "That the principles laid down by mathematicians are true . . . we do not deny" (Princ. 118). By "double sense" may be meant either the two objects, visible and tangible, or the two sorts of truth, theoretical truth, and truth for practice which is only approximate.

57. 57a. An idea such as extension (see 18n.) whose hedonic tone is low is readily located in matter, because it makes little call on our regard or activity; cf. 321, 692, TV 59; the mistake about the two senses, sight and touch (see 28n.) lends further support to matter, and (an after-thought) so does familiarity -- "the constant perception of 'em."

58. 59. For the blind man of the Molyneux problem, see 27n.; the man would not recognize distance or extension, Berkeley held, till experience had taught him to associate visible with tangible.

   Berkeley's doctrine of minimal ponts, one of the most prolific topics of the PC, is expounded at some length in TV 54, 79-83, but is only mentioned once in the Principles (132).

He probably intended to deal with it in his projected mathematical work, as part of his treatment of infinitesimals; and he would not wish to over-burden his exposition of immaterialism with controversial issues. His early essay <u>Of Infinites</u> (which was read before the Dublin Society, November 19, 1707) shows that his rejection of real qualities infinitely small had been thoroughly thought out.

Berkeley asserted the indivisible minimal point because he denied infinite divisibility; both the assertion and the denial are integral parts of his philosophy, fully stated. He does not deny matter on the ground that all is mind, but on the ground that the object of sense is sensible and composed of sensibles. If by going on dividing a given quantity, we could reach an insensible, the <u>esse est percipi</u> is violated, and matter cannot be refuted. Accordingly, Berkeley teaches that every sensible line is composed of a finite number of indivisible points, which differ from material atoms in that the points are possible objects of sense. The visible point he calls the <u>minimum visibile</u>, the tangible point the <u>minimum tangibile</u>, or when naming them together, the <u>minimum sensibile</u> (abbrev. <u>m</u>.<u>v</u>., <u>m</u>.<u>t</u>., and <u>m</u>.<u>s</u>.). Historically the doctrine was related to Cavalieri's mathematical theory of indivisibles (see 346n.); it has something in common with the quantum theory, and with the psychologists' theory of the least perceptible difference; it conflicts seriously, however, with the traditional geometry.

The <u>minimum</u>, for Berkeley, is a concrete, objective reality; the <u>m</u>.<u>v</u>. is measurable, and in entries 175, 296, it is clearly connected with Locke's sensible point (II xv 9) "which is ordinarily about a minute, and to the sharpest eyes seldom less than thirty seconds, of a circle whereof the eye is the centre."

<u>Minima</u> are defined as the "simplest, constituent parts or

elements" of visible and tangible extension, 70; their connection with extension is discussed in 78a, 88, 132, 273, 287, 295, 325, 365, 440-441, 445, 470, 516, 520, 530, 558; they measure magnitude, 256, 258, 469, 475, and are indivisible, 343, 346, 438-439, 462-464, 510; the m.v. is determined by the visual angle, 218, 296; it is "fixed," i.e., constant, 65, 66, 116, 169, 272, 277; m.v. and m.t. are compared, 710, 869; they are contrasted with mathematical points, 253, 344-345; they are difficult to imagine, 321. Berkeley raises several curious questions about them, showing himself convinced of their existence, but not clear about their nature. Are they extended (273)? Are they coloured (442, 489)? Could sight be enlarged by diminishing the point (175, 219)? Can superior spirits see more points (749, 835)? Can the points be compared with regard to evanescence (480)? Finally we must ask Berkeley whether his minima be the same as his "homogeneous particles" with which he was to solve objections from the Creation (60, 293).

60. 64. On "homoeomeries" written prima manu in both these entries, see Bacon, Nov. Org. I 63, and Bayle, Anaxagoras. Homogeneous particles are connected with the difficulty about Creation also in 293. This difficulty is discussed in the long account of Creation in the Three Dialogues, Works II 250ff., and in Berkeley's letter of Sept. 6, 1710 (Works VIII 37), and is mentioned below in 436, 723; for the Creation, see also 339, 830, 831; on minima, see previous note.

61. Probably this entry does not in the main represent Berkeley's own views, see 55, 67, 72; he is trying to see how his doctrine of the heterogeneity of sight and touch (see 28n.) would combine with the hypothesis of matter. Several entries on these pages revert to that hypothesis for argument's sake, viz., 64, 65, 67,

68, 74, and are used in the Principles (e.g., sect. 47) for answering objections. On extension, see 18n.

62. "a Blind at 1st," i.e., a blind man on first receiving sight (see 27n.). "in a point," i.e., not distant; "distance being a line directed endwise to the eye, it projects only one point in the fund of the eye," TV 2; cf. TV 41, PC 97, 835.

63. Glasses, i.e., the lenses used in microscope, telescope, and spectacles, usually opposed to the speculum or mirror. Molyneux's Dioptrics aims at showing "the properties of glasses."

Dioptrics furnished Berkeley with three problems: (1) the "Barrovian case" (TV 29-33) which led Tacquet to demolish the principles of his own Catoptrics, and led Barrow to to desiderate a fuller knowledge of "the manner of vision," and which Berkeley claims to have solved by his theory; (2) the Molyneux conjecture about the locus apparens of the object, discussed in TV 40, and dismissed; (3) the magnifying power of the microscope, discussed in TV 85-86. Other entries on glasses (mostly concerned with magnification) are: 94, 148, 182-183, 186-191, 197-199, 229, 232, 236-237, 249, 278, 324, 360, 366.

The invention of glasses drew attention to the relativity of visible magnitude, and so helped to refute the opinion of bodies outside the mind. On the other hand, the invention had also had the opposite effect, as Berkeley points out in 236-237 (cf. 94, 603), by making men assign the wrong cause of magnification and accept the infinite divisibility. Thus by showing the variability of sensible things glasses had promoted immaterialism, but by revealing the presence of unsuspected particles they had told against it.

65. 66. It is commonly supposed that matter is fixed while sense data vary. Berkeley here argues that the opposite is the case. The minimum visibile is fixed: take an m.v., and let there be in supposed relation to it a particle of material extension; then this particle will vary in size and shape as it approaches or recedes from the observer; but there will be no corresponding variation in the m.v. Therefore, the supposition of material extension is absurd.

Berkeley goes on to query the nerve of this argument. Is the m.v. fixed? He discusses the question in 116, 258, 272, 277, and gives the affirmative answer. "The minimum visibile is exactly equal in all beings whatsoever that are endowed with the visive faculty....Of these visible points we see at all times an equal number." (TV 80-83.)

67. Similarly in Princ. 47 in answer to the Fourth Objection Berkeley writes, "It follows there is an infinite number of parts in each particle of matter...." On infinite divisibility, see 11n. In this entry and the next he is arguing "upon the principles of others," see 40n.

68. "beauty & proportion" (see 269, 836; Princ. 109, 146; Maleb. I vi) imply the work of mind. Therefore matter, even if its existence be granted for the sake of argument, is not a sufficient explanation of the world.

69. 70. There is no proportion (in all cases, at any rate) or common measure between the visible and the tangible. Does that prove them heterogeneous (see 28n.)? Berkeley is in some

doubt about the answer. In 38 the question is raised with regard to motion; in 54 it is raised with regard to extension (see 18n.), and is at first decided in the affirmative, but subsequently the decisive words were bracketed. In 70 Berkeley answers in the negative. In TV 131 he accepts the absence of proportion is a good line of proof. On the punctum, see 59n.

71. Locke (II xxiii 23ff.) discusses the pressure of air and ether, and decides that neither is the adequate cause of cohesion. For Berkeley "the dispute ceases" because cohesion, like other physical facts, "depends entirely on the will of the Governing Spirit, who causes certain bodies to cleave together..." (Princ. 106, cf. Maleb. VI ii 9).

72. "Our idea we call extension," i.e., actually apprehended extension; note the correction of "of" to "we call" (see 115n.). Both the infinitely small particle and the infinitely great expanse involve, for Berkeley, the absurdity of unperceived existence. For the infinitely great and small, see Locke II xvii 4, 12; on infinite divisibility, see 11n.

73. Another reason against infinitely great extension (see previous note). This is the first mention of the optical angle, for which see also 150, 174, 182, 191, 195-198, 205-206, 218, 229, 233, 443, 603. That lines and angles are not the means whereby we judge distance, magnitude, and situation is taught in opposition to the geometrical opticians in TV passim. Berkeley asserts that such lines and angles are not perceived by sense, do not exist in nature, and that if they did exist and could be perceived, they would not explain the pheonomena of vision proper, as distinct from the behaviour

of rays of light and optical instruments; but he concedes a certain value to the conception of them, and occasionally, as here, he makes use of the conception; see TV 38, 78.

In the TV, though not clearly in the PC, he distinguishes two types of optical angle, the angle of binocular vision, and that of monocular. For the former we must imagine a triangle whose base is the distance between the two eyes, and whose sides are the optical axes which concur at the object making "the lateral angles" and "the angle of the optic axes" (TV 19); if the latter was obtuse, it was considered a sign of near distance, if acute, of far distance. Of it Malebranche (I ix) writes, "The first, the most universal, and sometimes the safest way we have, whereby to judge of the distance of objects, is the angle made by the rays of our eyes, whereof the object is the vertical point." For this angle Berkeley would substitute "the disposition of the eyes." For the angle of monocular vision we must suppose a triangle whose base is "the breadth of the pupil" (TV 21), the sides being formed by the diverging rays coming from the object to the pupil, the nearer object sending the more diverging rays. For the angle of monocular vision Berkeley would substitute "confused appearence." Both types are dealt with in Mol. pp. 113-114.

74. In close agreement with the argument of Princ. 18; cf. 359; for ideas and impressions on the brain, see Locke II viii 12 and Dials., Works II 208-210.

75. Berkeley here distinguishes between abstract unity, to which the notion of division does not apply, and the concrete unit, or one thing, which, on his theory, is divisible but not

infinitely divisible, being composed of indivisible points. According to Locke unity is the most simple of our ideas, and is suggested to the mind "by all the ways" (II vii 7 and xvi 1). Berkeley denies that unity is a simple idea; it is no idea, but a mere word, 545, 714, 746; mathematicians mistakenly suppose it to be infinitely divisible, 342; it is really an abstract idea, Princ. 13, 120. Cf. TV 109; on infinite divisibility, see 11n.

Isaac Barrow (1630-1677) was first Lucasian Professor of Mathematics at Cambridge. His works include Lectiones Opticae et Geometricae (1669) and Lectiones Mathematicae (1664-1666). He is often mentioned in the PC, viz., 170, 263, 334, 362, 384, 462, 501, 510 (in 564 other editors read "Barrow"; but "Bacon" is the true reading), and Berkeley seems to have read his works with care.

Berkeley was interested in: (1) the "Barrovian case," Lect. Opt. XVIII 13, stated as a problem in Mol. I prop. 31. 9, and discussed in TV 29-40; (2) Barrow's account of the abstract point as virtually "nothing", e.g., "A geometrical point is much better compared to a cypher, or arithmetical Nothing" (Math. Lect. III 6); (3) Barrow's arguments against indivisibles, his chapter Of the Divisibility of Magnitude (Math. Lect. IX) marshaling most of those arguments against indivisibles and for the infinite divisibility which are discussed in the PC.

76. These are Locke's words, quoted again in 534, and referred to in TV 48 as one of the reasons why we think we see and touch the same thing. On primary qualities, see 20n.

77. For "large numbers" cf. 217, Locke II xvi 6, Maleb. VI i 5. On number, see 104n.

78. 78a. Both parts of 78 give Locke's views; for the second part, see Locke, II iv 5, "the extension of body being nothing but the cohesion or continuity of solid, separable, movable parts; and the extension of space the continuity of unsolid, inseparable, and immovable parts." Berkeley does not endorse this view, and on the verso he tentatively advances his own view in terms of visible and tangible points, on which see 59n.

Solidity is discussed also in 105-106, 108, 114, 215, 533, 840; it is expressly equated with the third dimension or depth (105-106), and the point of all these entries is that solidity is a tangible, not a visible, quality. Hence the appositeness of Locke's illustration; the flint must be placed between his hands, not in front of his eyes. Solidity was distinctive of Locke's list of primary qualities, and in the form of resistance or impenetrability it still figures in the popular conception of material substance. Berkeley in his books follows for the most part the Cartesian formula, "extension, figure, motion," but he does not ignore solidity. In TV 45, 135 he argues that solidity is perceived by touch and not by sight; ibid. 154ff. he has a passage on mathematical solids; in Princ. 116 he deals with tactual resistance; solidity is equated with impenetrability in the account of Locke's doctrine (ibid. sect. 9); it is accepted as a real, sensible quality (sect. 37); and in section 11 (cf. sect. 67) the argument is advanced that solidity cannot be conceived without extension, and therefore cannot exist in an unthinking substance.

79. 80. Michel-Angelo Fardella (1650-1718) of Sicily, a Franciscan, physicist and philosopher, wrote Universae Philosophiae Systema (1691), Universae Usualis Mathematica Theoria (1691), Animae Humanae Natura (1698). Bayle (Zeno) says that Fardella in his Logic asserts the same doctrine as

Malebranche, viz., that the existence of the external world is known by revelation, and not by reason.

Berkeley himself says (686a) that Malebranche seems to doubt of the existence of bodies; he himself is quite sure of their existence, and he repeatedly declares that his Principle is the reverse of scepticism, because scepticism takes things to be distinct from ideas, while he identifies ideas of sense with things; see 304, 411, 491, 563, 606, 863, Princ. Title, Pref., and sects. 40, 87-89, etc. His assertion of body perceived by sense is as much a part of his philosophy as his denial of matter.

Note the correction of "without us" to "certainly"; Berkeley does not allow that body is external to mind, as matter is said to be; but towards the close of the PC (e.g., 882) and in Princ. 90 he admits externality in the senses there specified. The reference to Locke appears to couple him with the sceptics in respect of his "sensitive knowlege" (Book IV ii 14). On "combinations of powers" see 41n.; on the reality of body, see 52n.; on certainty and demonstration, see 163n.

The "unknown substratum" is spiritual substance. The PC entries on substance are mostly concerned with Locke's doctrine or they spring from it. Locke (I iv 18) says that we have no idea of substance "but only an uncertain supposition of we know not what...which we take to be the substratum or support of those ideas we do know." Locke also says (II xxiii 30) "the substance of spirit is unknown to us; and so is the substance of body equally unknown to us." Berkeley has these passages in view in 700-701; in 89 he mentions the well-known passage about the elephant and the tortoise; and in 179 he instances from Locke II xxvi 1 the looser use of the term "substance" for "a collection of simple ideas," i.e., sensible qualities.

Berkeley maintains substance in this loose sense in 512, 517, 700, 724; with regard to substance "in the philosophic sense" his course is not so clear; he rejects material substance, and maintains that there can be no extension without a thinking substance, 17, 270, 288a, 597, 622 (see also 413, 785); but he has great difficulty with thinking substance, and he is uncertain whether spirit is known, or is, as here, "an unknown substratum," see 194, 194a, 637, 672. In the Principles he speaks clearly on material substance, sects. 19, 37, etc.; on spiritual substance he is less clear, sects. 27, 36; broadly his position is that there are spiritual substances, and they may be known, but not as ideas are known.

81. Berkeley teaches that from the nature of the case there can be no likeness between a known idea and an unknown somewhat, see 46n.; here he adds the infinite divisibility (see 11n.) as a further point of contrast. This is an ad hominem argument reappearing in Princ. 47. Berkeley does not seriously entertain the hypothesis of matter.

82. A material cube should, by definition, have its edges without breadth, but an acute sense (cf. Princ. 47 and Locke II xxiii 12-13) would see their breadth.

83. This entry has been taken to be Berkeley's own opinion, paradoxically expressed, a corollary of the esse est percipere, asserting the intermittent existence of the subject to match that of the object. If he ever seriously held that view, he did not hold it for long; and in view of 590, "No broken Intervals of Death or Annihilation," and of his refusal (Princ. 48) to adopt the doctrines of annihilation and intermittency in

regard to the object, we should interpret the entry, I think, as either (1) an objection noted down for discussion, or, preferably, as (2) a reductio ad absurdum of the infinite divisibility of time, a doctrine which "lays one under an absolute necessity of thinking, either that he passes away innumerable ages without a thought, or else that he is annihilated every moment of his life" (Princ. 98, cf. Siris 312).

84. To be taken closely with 282; Berkeley is apparently asking whether the cause of the perceivable should be viewed as one or many; for the "powers" theory, see notes on 41 and 52.

85. For Berkeley length without breadth is an abstraction, supporting the notion of infinite divisibility (see 11n. and 21n.), of which one of the stock proofs was the intersection of lines in a point.

 The inseparability of colour and extension, urged also in 111, 121, 242, 253, 318, 362, 494, is used as an argument against matter in TV 43, Princ. 99, and against abstract ideas in Princ. Introd. 7.

 "Every position," i.e., of the observer; cf. 87, 120.

86. This query should be answered in the negative when kept in terms of idea, as in 557; but if expressed in terms of points, as in 558, it should be answered in the affirmative; see notes on 445-446.

87. 88. Locke (II xiii 4) says that men "settle in their minds the ideas of certain stated lengths, such as are an inch ..." Berkeley refers to this passage in the disputatio (see p. 473), and says, "Inches etc not settl'd stated lengths...";

-150-

but in TV 61 he writes, "Inches, feet, etc. are settled stated lengths," solving the apparent contradiction, as in 297, by showing that the visible inches, etc. vary with distance, while the determinate measures are tangible. For the minimum, see notes on 59 and 65.

[In 88 the "S" was erased immediately before it had dried and was, therefore, only a slip of the pen. -- Editor]

89. Locke here speaks of "the poor Indian philosopher," who would support the earth on an elephant, and the elephant on a tortoise. For substance, see 80n.

90. He may have in mind Locke's "empty, pure space" (II xvii 4) or Newton's "absolute space" (Princ. 116), or the divine, eternal space of Raphson and others; see 298, 825. The "absurditys" (sketched in Princ. 117) cease because the concept in question disappears.

91. Arguing, as in TV 62, that the connection between visible and tangible is a matter of custom, not of necessity (see 28n.); for if our sight were made more accute, our touch remaining as at present, the customary connection would not hold. For the supposition of microscopical eyes, see 97, 116, TV 85-86, Locke II xxiii 12, Maleb. I vi; on extension, see 18n.

92. Based on Psalm XC 4, and 2 Peter III 8. Berkeley rejects the notion of a succession of ideas in Deity, see 3n. and 4n. cf. Maleb. I viii, "God could so apply our mind to the parts of its duration, by giving us abundance of sensations in a very little time, as to make one hour appear as long as many ages."

93. If there is but one **colour only**, then what we call different colours are **degrees or shades** of it; see 526 and <u>Locke</u> II xviii 4.

94. "writers of Dioptricks," e.g., Descartes and Molyneux. Magnification was used **as an argument** for infinite divisibility (see 236-237, 324) and was therefore of interest to Berkeley in that **connection;** but he was chiefly concerned with it in connection with his **theory** of vision; other writers, he held, made **two mistakes:** they assume that the object under the microscope **is the same** as the object under the naked eye (236, 249), whereas "a microscope brings us, as it were, into a new **world**" where the accustomed connection between visible and tangible **does not** hold, <u>TV</u> 85-86; further they assume wrongly that **the glass alters** the appearance merely by altering the **visual angle.** In consequence they neglect the "confusion" **and the alteration** of the apparent distance, see 182-183, **189-191,** 197-199, 210, 229, 232, 271. The explanation by the **visual angle is** probably the "grand mistake" in view here -- **see 197 which** mentions p. 182 of Molyneux's book (<u>Dioptrica Nova</u>), where magnification is explained by the optical **angle.**

95. For the same argument, **see** <u>TV</u> 41, 79; on the Molyneux problem, see 27n.

96. Space without body **is, for** Berkeley, space without parts and distance between parts, **and therefore** self-contradictory, an abstract idea, "<u>pura</u> <u>privatio</u> <u>aut</u> <u>negatio</u>, <u>hoc est</u>, <u>merum nihil</u>," <u>Mot</u>. 53; cf. 583, <u>TV</u> 126.

97. On the Molyneux **problem, see 27n.** Berkeley proposes to

prove along two lines that the man would not see outness, but would see everything "in a point" (cf. 62n.). First, as argued in TV 85-86 (see also PC 91, 116), suppose macroscopic objects became microscopic, and that our eyes were "turned into the nature of microscopes," the ordinary connection between visible and tangible ceases, and their heterogeneity is demonstrated. Second, the radius of the visual sphere is "nothing at all to ye sight" (169), and therefore, Berkeley holds, the man would see everything in the flat, right up against his eye.

This is the first mention of the visual sphere, which we meet again in 122, 169, 214 (probably), 219, 256, 296, 475, 749. The Latin sphaera visualis (abbrev. S. V.) is used in 256; apparently it is the same as the "visual orb" of 204-205. The mention of the "30"" (296) clearly connects it with Locke's "sensible point" (II xv 9); cf. Reid, Inquiry VI ix, on the geometry of visibles. The Theory of Vision contains no mention of the visual sphere, although several of the entries about it have left their mark there (cf. 169 with TV 79). On the "spherae of the Retina" see 214n.

I have not met the term "visual sphere" used technically, in Barrow, Newton, or any other writer on optics consulted by Berkeley; but the term must mean either (1) the actual field of immediate vision, "those things that we take in at one propsect" (TV 83), or (2) the actual and the possible fields of vision from one point, i.e., what I do see from a given position, plus what I might see, if the eye were to make a complete revolution in every direction.

The visual sphere is stated to be a measure of intrinsic magnitude, 204-205, 256; its size is unaltered whether my vision be bounded by my hand or by the blue sky (169); its radius, i.e., the supposed distance of the object from the eye, is nil (97, 169) because vision in depth is, Berkeley holds, acquired, not original.

98. 99. I am inclined to think that there is no substantial connection of thought between the entries, that 98 is not a comment on 99, and that it is purely by accident that they face one another on verso and recto pages.

Entry 98 is on the problem of the unperceived perceivable, see 52n., 429, 472, and <u>Princ</u>. 3, 23, 45-48. Berkeley is considering and answering the objection that on his system "the objects of sense exist only when they are perceived."

Entry 99 turns on the distinction between motion and velocity formulated in 129-130. If, as he held, the speed of a moving body varies with the speed of the observer's train of ideas, a body impelled by the same force might have different velocities at the same time in relation to different observers. I might see it as fast; you might see it as slow; therefore it would <u>be</u> both fast and slow. Here Berkeley is content to deny the inference without giving his reasons. In the <u>De Motu</u> (e.g., 11, 17; cf. <u>Alc</u>. VII 6ff.) he argues that force, gravity, and similar terms do not denote so many distinct qualities, nor help us to understand the nature of motion. When therefore he allows the conception of physical force, he is arguing "upon the principles of others." His strict doctrine is that there are no physical forces, spirits being the only active beings. Hence in dealing with the difficulty propounded in this entry, Berkeley could have cut the knot, had he wished to do so, by declaring that the "same force" supposed to impel the body with varying velocities is an abstract idea, and therefore, nothing at all. On swift and slow, see <u>Dials</u>., <u>Works</u> II 190.

100. "blind," i.e., the blind man of the Molyneux problem, on which see 27n.; for the "powers" theory, see 41n.; on the

heterogeneity of sight and touch, see 28n.; on extension, see 18n.

101. In 443 Berkeley suggests that a particular sort of visible extension (cf. 400) may be the object of geometry; in TV 149-152, 160, he decides that visible extension and figures and abstract extension are not the object of geometry, suggesting, but not saying, that tangible extension is the object. In Princ. 123 he says that extension "considered as relative" is the object of geometry. The question arises from the problem of heterogeneity, on which, see 28n.; on extension," see 18n. For "motion" perhaps read "motions."

102. The PC contains 10 entries (with the distinctive marginal sign X3a) of which this is the first, dealing with the problem of the inverted retinal image, which Berkeley later called "the principal point in the whole optic theory" (TVV 52). This entry and 126 call attention to the problem; 148 and 278 deal with the experiment of inverted glasses, cf. Stratton's experiment (Stout, Manual of Psychology, 4th. ed., pp. 480-481); 224, 225, 226, 227, 246, 307 discuss the heterogeneity of visible and tangible with special reference to the arguments about erect and inverted contained in TV 88-119. Reid, Inquiry VI xi, has an account of this problem and of Berkeley's solution. The problem monopolizes the third main section of the Theory of Vision, that on Situation. Berkeley argues that the situation of objects is determined with respect to objects of the same sense only, and that the retinal images are not pictures of external objects.

103. I.e., apparent magnitude is not decided by visual

appearance alone; so TV 60 -- an argument for the heterogeneity of visible and tangible, see 28n.

104. Locke (II viii 9) **regards number** both as a primary quality of body and as the simple **idea produced** by that quality. Thus he places both the numerical quality and the source of the corresponding idea "without the mind." On number as the work of the mind, see also 110, 325, 759-766, TV 109-110, Princ. 12; other problems of number **are** discussed in 77, 123, 460, 648, 881.

105. 106. 108. A group **dealing with the** three dimensions of space in relation to **the senses by** which they are apprehended. Here, as in the Theory of Vision, Berkeley teaches that the direct object of vision **has two dimensions** only, and that of touch three dimensions; **the statement** that one dimension, length, is perceivable by hearing **does** not occur elsewhere; it must refer to the direct apprehension of long and short sounds, not to the indirect perception of distance by the ear as in TV 46. On **extension, see** 18n.; on simple ideas, see 53n. and 167; on solidity, see 78n. In 106 "nor" is, no doubt, a lapsus calami for "not." Fraser mistakenly reads "now," giving the forced explanation, "by the adult."

107. 109. On God (note **the marginal** letter G); "these," i.e., stones or trees, which **being purely** passive do not experience the misery of "unperformed **wills**" -- a phrase explained by Malebranche's words (VI ii 3), "'Tis the Author of our being that performs our desires...all the second causes, or divinities of the philosophers, are but unactive matter, and ineffective wills." Berkeley and Malebranch were agreed on the impotence of nature, and, in general, on man's absolute, entire, and immediate dependence upon God; see Princ. 29, 146ff.; on the

human will, see 131n.

There is little or no systematic discussion of Deity in the PC; the danger of making God extended is mentioned in 290, 298, 310, 391, 825; He is a being who thinks and wills, 109 610, 712-713, 812; He is the sole cause in nature, 433, 485, transcendent, 640-641, immanent, 827; we have no idea of Him, 782 (cf. 177); yet His existence is proved and His nature defined, 838, 845; see also 508, 675, 705, 813, 830, 831.

"subsist"; unthinking things, for Berkeley, exist, but do not subsist; i.e., they are not substances; they are entirely dependent and cannot act.

110. On number, see 104n.

111. 111a. Every colour being a coloured extent (see 85n.), has not extension as good a right as colour to be regarded as an immediate idea (a sense-datum)? The verso comment in effect rules out the question by making extension an abstract idea; 53 has a similar verso addition, where see note; on extension, see 18n.

112. 113. This paragraph (Locke II viii 8, also referred to in 326) contains the gist of Locke's doctrine of idea, quality, and power; Berkeley was particularly concerned with Locke's statement that he sometimes speaks of the ideas "as in the things themselves," which gives verbal support at least for his own account of things as "collections of ideas"; for his transference of the powers from body to the spirit, see notes on 41 and 52.

114. Berkeley is arguing that solidity, i.e., depth (see

-157-

78n.), is an object of touch and not of sight; on the German Count, see 42n.

115. This cryptic entry is fully explained by 581, 657, 657a, 658, 660. "Of" and "thing" are causes of mistake in so far as they voice and support the representationist theory of perception; for if we take the sense-datum as an idea <u>of</u> a thing, i.e., as a likeness of something not given to sense, the supposition of matter becomes inevitable. Berkeley's ideas of sense <u>are</u> the things of sense, and, strictly speaking, the only "ideas of" that he recognizes are the ideas formed by the imagination. The term "idea of" occurs a few times in the <u>Principles</u>, but all the cases can be explained; "ideas of light and colours" (sect. 1) is a quotation from Locke, see <u>TV</u> 130; there are cases of adjectival genitive, e.g., "ideas of sight"; in sections 10, 67, 84, 116, 138 the term occurs in objections or denials; in the remaining instances, i.e., 98, 112, 119, 140, 153 "idea" refers to ideas of the imagination or to abstract ideas, not to ideas of sense.

116. On the visible point, see 59n.; on microscopical eyes, see note on 91 and 97.

117. Berkeley is thinking of the axioms which assume infinite divisibility, and the propositions supposed to prove it, cf. 261, <u>Princ</u>. 125. He is in marked opposition to the geometry of his day -- see 247-248, 261, 276, 320, 384, 428, 509.

118. Locke answers, "No"; there is no necessary connection between time and motion, and if the sun were lighted up periodically, instead of moving, the purposes of measurement would be served as well as at present. Berkeley deals broadly

with the mutual relations of time, space, and motion in Princ. 110ff., but he does not deal with the particular topic of this entry, except in PC 12, where he says that the celestial revolutions measure both time and duration, the former immediately, the latter mediately.

119. For "these" perhaps read "those"; cf. notes on 31 and 319. A line is the termination of a surface, and a point is the termination of a line. These might be called "relative" conceptions because they explain the surface and the line in terms of something else. Euclid's conceptions are different: a line has length without breadth; a point has position without magnitude. These are "conceiv'd absolutely." Both conceptions alike, for Berkeley, are mathematical "nothings" and abstract ideas, and to both he opposes his sensible lines and points.

120. Repeated from 85, where see note.

12.. "Blind at 1st"; i.e., the blind man of the Molyneux Problem on first recovering his sight (see 27n.); on extension, see 18n.; on extension and colour, see 85n.

122. Such circles are equal, Berkeley holds, because they all contain an equal number of visible points; see 150n. and TV 79. He is considering the "field of vision" as spherical (see 97n.); all such fields are fixed, he holds, and do not vary in size with varying distance: whether I am looking on the palm of my hand or the open firmament, I see the same number of visible points. This is part of the proof that magnitude is judged, not seen.

123. Locke (II xvii 8) says that the idea of the infinity of

number is very clear, but that the actual idea of an infinite number is absurd; for when we frame the idea of any given number, "the mind rests and terminates in that idea; which is contrary to the idea of infinity." Leibniz (<u>Nouveaux Essais</u> II xvii 8, quoted by Hecht), commenting on this passage, is not satisfied with Locke's reason, and says that the true reason why we cannot have an idea of an infinite number is that the infinite cannot be a true whole. Berkeley does not tell us what he thought wrong in Locke's solution, and in his <u>Of Infinites</u> he gives high priase to this passage of the <u>Essay</u>. In general he objected to Locke's theory of number, as involving existence outside the mind; see 104n.

124. The marginal sign connects this entry with the later portion of the <u>Theory of Vision</u>, and no doubt the question refers to the opinion that "flat or plane figures are immediate objects of sight" (<u>TV</u> 157). Berkeley refutes this opinion, holding that flatness, like distance and magnitude, is not an immediate object of sight. Presumably he would hold the same view of the rightness (i.e., straightness) of a line.

125. Abbreviated duplicates of this entry and 126 occur together in 171 and 172. The horizontal moon and the inverted retinal image were, respectively (as indicated by the marginal signs here), the test problems of the second (magnitude) and the third (situation) divisions of the <u>Theory of Vision</u>.

Why does the moon on the horizon look larger than in the zenith? Descartes, Gassendi, Hobbes, Wallis, and Molyneux had each tried to explain the phenomenon; Berkeley refers to their attempts in his own discussion of the problem in

TV 67-78. He mentions the problem again in 140, 233, 302 (cf. 244), and sets forth his own explanation in terms of his theory of vision. His general aim is to show the insufficiency of lines and angles to explain the facts, and to substitute the faintness of the visible appearance.

126. On the inverted retinal image, see 102n.

127. The "question" concerned time, as shown by the marginal letter, and, no doubt, it turned on the text, "To-day shalt thou be with me in paradise" (Luke XXIII 43). Cf. Berkeley's notion "that the Resurrection follows the next moment to death." (Works II 293); on time, see 4n.

Mr. Deering was probably Daniel Dering (or Deering), cousin of Sir John Percival, and Commissioner of the Wine Licence in Dublin, who died in 1730. Dering's aunt is mentioned in 201, and several of the Dering family are mentioned in the Egmont Papers (Hist. MSS. Commission, see Rand, p. 57n. and Index; and Works VIII with index in IX). Through the Dering family Berkeley made the acquaintance of Sir John Percival, afterwards first Earl of Egmont, his life-long friend and correspondent. Percival's mother was Catherine, fourth daughter of Sir Edward Dering, Bart.

Percival was at his house in Capel Street, Dublin, apparently for the first time, on November 29, 1708 (see Egmont Papers, vol. 127, p. 195); about that time he met Berkeley, cf. "these few months that I have the honour to be known unto you" (TV Dedic.). Since the PC must have been more or less finished by the autumn of 1708, these references to the Dering family in the early part of it show that Berkeley made the acquaintance of the family some time before he met Percival.

128. Apparently a sarcastic comment on the notion of matter as "something we know not what," see 40n., and 364, "filling the world with a mite."

129. 130. On motion and velocity in relation to space, see 99n.

131. For the hypothesis of matter, see 40n.

The will is very fully discussed in the PC; some ten entries in notebook B, and almost seventy in A, deal with it. Berkeley is chiefly concerned to relate the will to our other faculties, and to deny that we know the will as we know ideas.

Other accounts of the will are critically considered, Locke's in 145a, 357, 423, 598, 611, 616, 624, 626-628, 630, 653-654, 797, 879, Hobbes' in 796-798, 806, 822, Descartes' in 798, Malebranche's in 107, King's in 142. The will is the only active power, in 131, 155, 712; it is considered in relation to our cognitive faculties in 166, 644-645, 674, 808, 815, 833; for the long debate on will and understanding, see 362a n. Will and volitions give Berkeley some trouble: at first he is inclined to regard the will as the unknown substratum of acts of will; later he denies the distinction, finally concluding that will is everywhere the same, and that whether it is to be called one or many is a question of words -- see 615, 615a, 621, 635, 714, 788. Will is identified with soul in 478a, 814, and with pure spirit in 828-829, 847, 848; it is the seat of personal identity 194a, and is the only causal power 499, 699. Concrete willing is coterminous with personal existence, but the abstraction "will" comes under the general condemnation of abstract ideas, 867, cf. Princ. 143. The divine will is touched on in 610, 712; see also 161, 629. Berkeley's chief negative contention is the denial that will can be the object of thought, i.e., he holds that we have no idea of the will, 657-659, 663, 665, 672, 684, 706, 756, 792, 828, 875, cf. Princ. 135ff.

132. 133. Denying infinite divisibility of concrete magnitude, spatial and temporal, while granting it of abstract magnitude -- see notes on 8, 11, 259. For ratio partium extra partes, see Locke II xiii 15; for magnitude visible and tangible, see 203n.; for minimal points, see 59n.

The reading "not all divisible" (Fraser and Johnston) in 133 makes nonsense of the entry; I have restored "not at all divisible"; for the MS. has a mark of insertion between "not" and "all," and a blot or erasure immediately above it. As restored the reading agrees with the interlinear addition in 132. It is true that the entry as a whole is scarcely consistent with the first part of 132, but then 132 is not consistent with itself, thanks to the addition "or not at all perhaps." No doubt Berkeley's views on the point were at the time in a fluid state; he was feeling his way into his doctrine of abstraction, and gradually came to recognize that the coexistence and succession to which he is conceding infinite divisibility are abstract ideas, and therefore, in his final doctrine, nonexistent.

134. Locke (II xv 9) says that space and duration include parts, that indeed it is their nature to consists of parts, and yet that they count among the simple ideas, because their parts are all the same kind; Berkeley, arguing that simple ideas should be simple, queries the claim of space, colour, and power to come under this category and claims to be the first to raise the question. For his later position about simple ideas, see 53n. "hardly separated," i.e., sharply distinguished. Relations (see 540n.) are of course involved

in the notion of parts. "Nor" perhaps read "or."

135. Berkeley opposes the notion of infinite space, partly as the supposed background of external, absolute space, and partly as a supposed attribute of God; see 290, 417-418, 695, TV 126, Princ. 116-117. Even if we imagine it, he here argues, we are imagining it only in relation to a moving body, and the space traversed by the body may quite as well be supposed annihilated as persisting; on space, see 18n.

136. Therefore we cannot see matter, nor touch it -- the argument against matter from the immediacy of the object of sense.

137. 138. Locke (II xiii 25) says that there is no idea of extension in taste and smell. "Why not?" asks Berkeley. He may be querying Locke's facts (for there is a feeling of volume in both taste and smell); but more probably he is accepting Locke's facts, and asking the reason why, arguing, in effect, that the heterogeneity of smell and taste ought to carry with it heterogeneity of sight and touch (see 28n.); cf. 240-241, 497, TV 45, 145; for "blue & red" see TV 131.

139. The first open reference to authorship in the PC; for the projected books, see 508n. The Principles appears to have been planned before the Theory of Vision (see Princ. 43). The Introduction to the Principles is here in view, but not the Introduction as we have it now; for as he worked, Berkeley's interest in simple ideas waned (see 53n.) and was more or less replaced by his doctrine of abstract ideas -- the subject of the existing Introduction.

140. On the problem of the horizontal moon, see 125n. Hecht is wrong in charging Berkeley with inconsistency about the size of its visible extension; both in the PC and in TV (70, 74) Berkeley insists that the horizontal _visible_ moon is not greater than in the zenith; indeed, following Malebranche, he says that on the horizon it is rather less; the _tangible_ moon in his account is thought greater on the horizon; on the optical angle, see 73n. Johnston omits "equal" before "angles."

141. 142. The beginning of a series of entries on ethical questions which occupies the next few pages, and is mainly concerned with Locke's doctrine of liberty, indifference, and uneasiness, and King's related doctrine of _potentia_.

"A.B." is William King, Archbishop of Dublin (1650-1729), author of _De Origine Mali_ (1702). I was led to this identification, here and in 159, by observing that Berkeley had written "A. B. of Cashel" on a page of the Chapman MS. (Trinity College, Dublin); I then found that several of these entries refer to passages in the _De Origine_. Potentia was, for King, an important concept, applying both to the divine _arbitrium_ and to man's freedom of choice; King intended it to express indifference and the will's delight in its own election.

Leibniz, who reviewed the _De Origine_, said that King's Deity would be so "indifferent" that He would not care whether the world was made well or not. On indifference, see 143n.; on will, see 131n.

143. According to Locke's complicated theory of action (II xxi 71) some present uneasiness accompanied by desire determines the will, together with "an indifferency of the operative powers" which remains even after the determination of the will.

Berkeley was critical of this theory, 141n., 149, 158-159, 166, 610-613, 624, 743; in his sermon on Life and Immortality (January 11, 1708) written while he was filling the PC, he writes, "I know a late incomparable philosopher will have the present uneasiness the mind feels, which ordinarily is not proportinate to the goodness of the object, to determine the will"; but he could not conceive a rational agent indifferent to pleasure and pain, and he regarded indifference as leading to "inconsistency and mutability in acting [which] though it be an imperfection is looked on as a mark of freedom" (Princ. 57, cf. Alc. VII 17). Descartes calls indifference "the lowest degree of liberty" (Med. IV), and Malebranche (I i) denies the freedom of indifference nad places liberty in the mind's power of turning towards agreeable objects. Cf. 145n.

144. Berkeley accepts nature as an order of reality directly dependent on the will of God, 312, 838; in consequence he recognizes laws of nature which control sensation and which have a beneficient tendency, here and in 843; these laws are the general principles of divine action; our knowledge of them is imperfect, partly because of the limitations of our minds, but also because the laws themselves, being the effects of will, may be changed, 221, 734, 884, see Princ. 30, 62, 106-107, 146, 153. On Berkeley's hedonism, see 541n.

145. 145a. 146. Berkeley does not accept the conception of the prescient "Calculator," but is using it, as the verso comment shows, as an argument against Locke's doctrine of uneasiness. Locke (II xxi 71) says, "That which in the train of our voluntary actions determines the will to any change of operation, is some present uneasiness...." Berkeley thought this doctrine incompatible with the spontaneity of finite

spirits. He argues that there can be will without uneasiness and uneasiness without will, 611, 613, 624, 628, 707; uneasiness is for him an idea, and therefore inactive, 653; he suggests that complacency, and not uneasiness, precedes volition, 630. God and blessed spirits will; yet they have no uneasiness, 610; there is no uneasiness in heaven, and, for Locke, there can be no will there, 357, 423, also 166, 598, 743, 833, 857. "Billard balls," see Locke II xxi 4; on liberty, see 149n.; on will, see 131n., cf. 143n.

147. "the difficulty" is probably "the Barrovian case" (see 75n., TV 29-40), the test problem for Berkeley's new theory of distance. Barrow had pointed out that the received theory could not account for the confused appearance of an object placed in a certain position relative to the retina, and Berkeley is speculating here as to the effect on the judgement if this confusedness disappeared, the object remaining in statu quo; would the object look smaller or nearer? Similarly Molyneux (Dioptrics, p. 119, quoted in TV 40), making reference to this problem, writes of "an object placed as in this 9th section."

148. This experiment, described more fully in 278, appears to be the same in principle as Stratton's experiment, which (see Stout, Manual of Psychology, 4th. edition, pp. 480-481), refutes the suggestion that one direction is felt as upward, because we have to move the eye-ball upward, and proves that the distinctions between up and down, and between right and left, belong primarily to touch, and are for the eye acquired meanings, thus largely confirming Berkeley's theory.

Berkeley does not refer to the "inverting glass" in his books. Molyneux (Dioptrics, p. 212) speaks of "my frequent use of inverting telescopes" as reducing "the disagreeableness of the <u>inverted</u> Prospect," but he does not go all the way with Hook, who had said that "use and custom" alone make us judge objects erect. On the inverted retinal image, see 102n.

149. The duplicate of this entry (see folio 164 verso, inverted) adds the reference to <u>Locke</u> II xxi 71. Berkeley's point is that we do right or wrong in virtue of the act of will; but on Locke's theory this act comes first, and the free choice as to whether or not to give effect to this act comes subsequently; thus virtue and vice would be excluded from the area of freedom, and Locke's liberty of the "operative faculties" would not touch the heart of the problem; it would be psychological freedom without moral freedom, see 156n. For a discussion of human liberty, see <u>Alc</u>. VII 16ff.

150. In his discussion, in 528, of equality as congruence Berkeley says that if sight is to judge congruence, then all lines seen under the same angle are equal, which the mathematicians will not acknowledge. In this entry Berkeley is arguing that tangible magnitude is judged and not seen, and judged by other signs than optical angles (see 73n.), because one's thumb can hide a tower ("an easy experiment"), and "whatever object intercepts the view of another hath an equal number of visible points with it, <u>TV</u> 79. On congruence, see 515n.

151. 152. 153. A group of entries dealing with Locke's teaching on colour; for Locke colours are simple ideas (II iii 1) and therefore indefinable (III iv 4). Berkeley seems to have experimented a good deal in colour analysis along the lines of Newton's <u>Optics</u>, and he does not accept colours,

or most colours, as simple ideas; see 242, 489, 502-504, 526, 551, 562, 662, 664; on simple ideas, see 53n.; on sounds compared to sights, see 220; on definition, see 44n.

Sensible things are described as "thoughts" also in 164, 181, 226, 228, 280, 282, 286, 293, 299, and perhaps in 194, 220, and TV 41; in the latter portion of the PC and in the Theory of Vision (mostly) and in the Principles (entirely) "idea" is substituted. They were "thoughts" for Berkeley, because thought of; but when he had considered the question of terminology from other angles, he decided to confine "thought" to the subject (see 37a, 437a) and gave up using it of the object.

154. On the nature of the soul, see 14n. The question about our knowledge of the soul, raised in 25 and glanced at in 44, here receives a first answer, viz., that the soul is a complex idea, that it is known and may be defined. This answer is modified in 178, criticized and rejected in 230; from that time on it became a fixed point with Berkely that there is no idea of active spirit. Other questions remained: How are the soul and mind to be classed? Are they passive? Are they active? Are they one with their "contents" (ideas), or with the active being which has the ideas? After a long debate (see especially 576ff.) Berkeley decides that they are active, and he identifies them with "this perceiving active being [which] I call mind, spirit, soul, or my self" (Princ. 2). On definition, see 44n. In the second edition of the Principles (1734) Berkeley, without any alteration of doctrine, so far alters his terminology as to admit that we may be said to have a "notion" of spirit (sect. 27, 89, etc.).

155. On powers, active and passive, see 41n.; on will, see 131n., and cf. Maleb., **Excursus** on Second Causes, "All the efforts that my mind can make can discover no other force, efficacy, or power, than in the will of the infinitely perfect Being."

156. 157. Is Berkeley here stating his own views for the time being, or merely those of others? It is not clear which. The "tis true" appears to make the views his own; but in that case the entries would conflict with 149 (on which see note) and would involve Berkeley in a virtual denial of human freedom.

Locke placed freedom in the operative faculties, and made the will itself determined by feeling ("uneasiness"). This freedom is veiled determinism; it is not the freedom of spontaneous will, but merely the freedom of putting into effect the determined volition.

Entry 157 may refer to King ("A.B.," see 159n.) or to the occasionalists. Malebranche taught that we **will** (e.g.) to move our arm, and we know what will happen as a result of our will; but we do not know **how** to move our arm; and in point of fact we do **not** move it, but God moves it when we **will**.

158. 159. Berkeley reminds himself that awareness of voluntary action does not imply the doctrine of indifference taught by Locke and King. He has King especially in view here; on "the potentia of A.B.," see 141n. King (**De Origine Mali** V v 5) says, in language similar to that of 157, "**Omnes vero sibi actiones voluntatis suae imputant**, & **sive bonas, sive malas pro suis proprie** & **vere habent**," and he infers that men partake in the universal **potentia**.

For Berkeley, will is not blind, either in God or in man, and therefore the freedom of the will does not involve indifference (see 143n.), i.e., action without motive, action detached from desire. Desire as a faculty may be called indifferent; desire does not desire; but the concrete ego that desires is certainly not indifferent in respect of what it desires and wills.

160. Locke (II xxi 38) argues that the will is determined not be greater good but by uneasiness (see 145n.), "because all who allow the joys of heaven possible, pursue them not."

161. The "I will will them" in the previous entry reminds Berkeley of the will to will, and the will to will to will -- a theoretical difficulty (stated in Locke II xxi 25) here called "the progression of wills in infinitum."

162. 163. Ethics is considered in relation to mathematics in 239, 336, 697, 755, 853. Berkeley endorses Locke's dictum, "morality capable of demonstration" (III xi 16, IV iii 18), but he finds mathematical method hard to apply in ethics, and still harder in metaphysics (239) owing to the ambiguity of words. On definition, see 44n.; with "prejudices" cf. 239, TV 138.

"demonstrate the truth"; demonstration with its subjective counterpart, certainty (see 693n.), figures largely in the PC. Demonstration was the cry of the hour; Clark had just published his Demonstration of the Being and Attributes of God (1705-1706); Newton in his Optics (1704) writes, "My design in this book is not to explain the properties of light by hypotheses, but to propose and prove them by reason and experiments." Defoe in his Consolidator (1705, p. 59) has

-171-

an amusing skit on this prevailing fashion. Berkeley shared
the general confidence in reason. He is to write on
demonstration in his Introduction (212); he elaborates a
demonstration more geometrico of his New Principle (378-379);
he writes "Wt I say is Demonstration, perfect Demonstration"
(551), and again, "I shall Demonstrate all my Doctrines" (586);
and he repeatedly asserts, as here, that ethics and metaphysics
have as good a claim to certainty as has mathematics. But
towards the end of the PC a change is noticeable; he becomes
critical of Locke on demonstration and certainty; for Locke
makes demonstration depend on abstract ideas (586); Locke
rates sensitive knowledge scarcely higher than opinion, and
Berkeley in 466 had opposed sense to reason and demonstration;
now (740) he decides that "We must wth the Mob place certainty
in the senses," yet remaining certain that there is a God and
a future judgement (776, 813); demonstration becomes verbal
(734, 804), and finally he writes, "I must not pretend to
promise much of Demonstration, I must Cancell all passages that
look like that Sort of Pride, that raising of Expectation in
my Readers" (858); see also 80, 336, 363, 376, 426, 468, 532,
562, 584, 693, 697-698, 705, 719, 728-732, 739. Claims to
demonstration occur in his books; e.g., TV 90, 95, 121, 154,
Princ. 61; but demonstration is not stressed in the Principles,
and sections 96, 107, tone down his previous claims and limit
their scope.

164. 165. The second entry limits the assertion to visible
extension (see 18n.), but otherwise the two entries amount to
the same thing, viz., that space seen is an expanse of
homogeneous points of colour in the mind (cf. 365n.). Hecht
is wrong in taking 165 as a concession to popular opinion in
substantial conflict with 164. "Thoughts" must be understood

as non-mental things thought of; for Berkeley's use of the term "thoughts" for sensible things at this period, and for his subsequent change to "idea," see 153n.

166. The first sentence states King's theory of moral action, which is much indebted to Locke's account (II xxi). Berkeley proceeds to criticize it on the grounds that moral action demands moral choice of the good as good. For uneasiness and the identification of "A.B." with King, see notes on 141-142, 145. On will, see 131n.

167. There is a fuller analysis of the same simple ideas in 460, see 53n.; extension is analyzed also in 105, motion in 184, time in 4, number in 104.

168. Berkeley was interested in these mathematical problems because of their bearing on the alleged infinite divisibility of matter, see Princ. 123-132, and his essay Of Infinites; for the angle of contact, see 309n., 381; for fluxions, i.e., the infinitesimal calculus, see 333. The calculus had its origin, in part, in the problem of drawing tangents to curved lines.

169. For the hand that may hide the firmament, see TV 79; on the visual sphere, see 97n.; on minimal points, see 59n.

170. 171. 172. Here are juxtaposed the three problems which Berkeley used as tests of the three parts respectively of his theory of vision, the Barrovian case (see 75n. and TV 29ff.), the test for distance, the horizontal moon (see 125n. and TV 67ff.), for magnitude, and the inverted retinal image (see 102n. and TV 88ff.) for situation. On the purblind,

see 199n., TV 37, and Mol., p. 108.

173. Marked N (Natural Philosophy) in the margin, this entry is probably considering an account of the laws of nature as the experience "that such and such ideas are attended with such other ideas, in the ordinary course of things," Princ 30; cf. TV 147.

174. These two methods of judging magnitude are stated as Wallis' opinion in TV 76, and in the following sections Berkeley explains the extent to which he accepts them, using the blind man of the Molyneux problem (see 27n.) as part of his argument; on the optical angle, see 73n.; on the connection between visible and tangible, see 28n. "Extension" in this entry means magnitude; see 18n.

175. Berkeley speculates on the possibility of enlarging the sight also in 219, 749, 835, TV 83-87, and concludes that the enlargement in theory a perfection, would in practice be impossible, because it would destroy the usual connection between visible and tangible; on magnification, see 94n.

Locke (II xv 9) says that the sensible point (see 59n.) is "to the sharpest eyes seldom less than thirty seconds." Molyneux (Dioptrics, pp. 229, 243) speaks to the same effect, adding "armed with a telescope it may discern an angle less than a second."

176. 176a. On terms metaphorically applied to mental operations, see 544, Princ. 144 "terms borrowed from sensible ideas," and Locke III i 5. For metaphors as the dress of ideas, see 737, Princ. Introd. 24. As we have no ideas of the operations of our minds (see 490n.), we have to use

metaphors, Berkeley holds, when speaking of them.

177. 177a. Locke (II xxiii 33, 35) makes the two statements about God, which Berkeley cannot reconcile. In 782 Berkeley calls the idea of God "impossible," idea being passive and spirit active.

Hecht's note, attributing an error to Berkeley, is based on the misreading "complex and uncompounded." There is no error in the text. Berkeley first wrote "complex and compounded," and then inserted "or" over the "&," and Hecht or Lorenz mistook the "or" for "un." On God, see 107n. "His" (after "essence"), a slip for "is."

The quotation on the verso from Le Clerc (Logic I viii 5) occurs twice more in the PC in 348 (Latin) and 812 (English); the sentiment is frequent in Le Clerc, and would impress Berkeley by its resemblance to his own panentheism and to Malebranche's doctrine of Seeing all things in God. It is difficult to reconcile with the traditional doctrine of the divine simplicity, and no doubt Berkeley meant the note to be a comment on the recto "simple & uncompounded."

Jean Le Clerc (1657-1736), philosopher and man of letters, is often mentioned in Locke's correspondence; Molyneux writes to Locke, "I take Mons. Le Clerc to be one of the greatest scholars in Europe...but, I fear, an ecclesiastical preferment will be very difficult to be obtain'd for him" (Some Familiar Letters between Mr Locke and several of his Friends, p. 186). He edited the Bibliotheque Choisie, in which (vol. 22, 1711) the New Theory of Vision was reviewed. Two draft letters by Berkeley to Le Clerc, commenting critically on the review, was in MS. 39304 (British Museum). Le Clerc was a prolific writer. His works include Logica sive Ars Ratiocinandi (dedicated to Boyle) with Ontologia et Pneumatologia (dedicated to Locke), 1692; **Physica**, 1696; Eloge de fue Mr Locke, 1705; Opera Philosophica, 1698.

178. The imperfections of language and the relation of words to ideas are carefully studied in the latter part of the PC, and the study is reflected in TV 120 and Princ. Introd. 18-25. Berkeley's general aim is to indorse Locke's attack upon jargon and his plea for a measure of wordless thought, while rejecting Locke's principle (III xi 8) that all significant words stand for ideas. This principle was at first accepted by Berkeley; it was an "axiom," and it heads the list of the nineteen propositions which form the Demonstration of the New Principle (378); but when he found that it entailed the doctrine of abstract ideas, he suspected it, and when he observed that words have emotive uses as well as cognitive, he rejected it. "He that knows names do not always stand for ideas, will spare himself the labour of looking for ideas, where there are none to be had." Princ. Introd. 24, cf. Alc. VII 8ff.

The principal topics discussed are: words such as thing, substance, existence, a source of difficulty and error, 223, 513, 537, 544, 553, 581, 596, 608, 627, 636, 702; the Solitary Man and language, 566, 607, 727; words and ideas, 356, 494, 591, 595, 661; the practice of wordless thought, 600, 696, 736; the due use of words, 750.

On the soul, see 14n.; on the definition of the soul, see 154n.; on definition in general, see 44n.; on extension, see 18n.

179. No doubt the word "collection" caught Berkeley's attention, for he defines **thing** as "a collection of ideas" (Princ. 1), thus leaving no room in it for matter. On

substance, see 80n.; on simple ideas, see 53n.

180. The orbicular lattice is apparently "the micrometer, or lattice of fine hairs, strained before the eye-glass in a telescope for measuring the diameter of objects"; see Mol., pp. 138, 250.

If "strait lines" means straight lines, as sometimes in Pardies' Geometry (see 432n.), Berkeley is probably dealing with the apparent curvature of straight lines, e.g., the oar bent in water. But he usually calls straight lines "right lines," and therefore "strait" here may have its other meaning "narrow," in which case he must be proposing a microscopic examination of a narrow line, in connection with the subject of length without breadth, see 85n.

181. The query is answered in the affirmative with regard to the faintness and magnitude of the moon in TV 72, "there being no necessary, but only an experimental, connexion between those two things."

The denial of necessary connection (see 195, 206, 227, 233, 246, 256, 794, TV passim, Princ. 31, Maleb. II ii 3) is part of the general case against universal mechanism, and is applied in particular to the customary connections between the visible and the tangible, and between the various sensations by which we judge distance, magnitude, and situation. On "thoughts," see 153n.

[The "P" is the beginning of a capital "B." -- Editor.]

182. 183. Molyneux and Wallis explained the alteration of apparent magnitude by the alteration of the optic angle, either by itself or in conjunction with alteration of

distance, appealing in proof to the alterations made by optical glasses. Berkeley discounts the direct influence of the angle (see 73n.), distinguishes visible magnitude from tangible, and says that the latter is not seen, but is judged, and judged by means of things immediately perceived, e.g., confusion, faintness, etc. The group of notes on the speculum is not directly represented in the Theory of Vision.

On magnification, see 94n.; on glasses, see 63n.; "blind" means the blind man of the Molyneux Problem, see 27n.

184. For Locke (II viii 9) motion is a primary quality which produces simple ideas in us. Berkeley here denies its simplicity on the ground that the perception of it involves a succession of ideas; see notes on 167 and 450.

185. 185a. An important pair of entries disclosing the trend of Berkeley's thought. The recto merely concedes existence to the perceivable as a matter of tactics, but implies that it does not exist. The verso, a later comment, asserts its real existence, as in 802 and the Principles.

"persons not thinking," see 83n. If the percipient does not exist when he is not perceiving, scepticism about the soul is inevitable. Berkeley passed through the sceptical phase when he was writing the PC (see 577ff.), and when he realized the danger, he corrected his first thoughts, and set his face against scepticism with regard both to subject and to object. On the perceivable and the reality of body, see 52n.

186. 187. 188. 189. 190. 191. Exercises in dioptrics and catoptrics, examining the effects of distance, confusion, and visual angles upon visible magnitude -- see 94n., and

182n.; on glasses, see 63n.; on the optical angle, see 73n. Molyneux (Dioptrics, pp. 173, 203-204) discusses inversion and the convex lens.

192. 192a. 194. 194a. On identity. There is a discussion of identity in the Three Dialogues, Works II 247ff., where Berkeley distinguishes "the abstracted idea of identity" from concrete sameness, "where no distinction or variety is perceived." He does not deal with it in the Principles, but the PC shows that he had given it a good deal of thought.

He discusses personal identity in 194a, 200-202, the identity of things in 568, and both types, perhaps, in 192, 194, 681. He wants to allow identity to persons, but he does not know where to place it; he cannot, with Locke, place it in consciousness, and the verso entry 194a which places it in the will (see 131n.) probably belongs to the later stage represented by 681. The identity of things for him consists in perfect likeness (i.e., as written on the verso opposite 192 and erased, "where there is no difference intrinsical or extrinsical of a moment"). When he was writing the earlier part of the PC he seems to have held the intermittent existence both of things and of persons, and at that stage identity must have been to him little more than an abstract conception; but later on he rejected intermittency, annihilation, and perpetual creation (Princ. 45-48), and accepted the continuity of the will, thus securing practical sameness both to the finite spirit and to sensible things.

Johnson's letter of February 5, 1730 (see Works II 288ff.), asks Berkeley some pertinent questions about the identity of the self. On substance, see 80n.; on "thoughts," see 153n. The "finite substances" of 194 is used broadly to include unthinking things, though technically they are not substances for Berkeley. The passage clearly refers to Locke's long chapter on identity (II xxvii), especially to section 2, where Locke considers the identity of three sorts of substances, and of identity determined by "time and place of beginning to exist"; see also notes on 200 and 681.

193. In criticism of Locke (II xxiii 19) who makes "spirits capable of motion"; cf. 822, and the query, "Whether is a spirit movd wth absolute or relative motion or wth both?" (See MS. fol. 164v.).

195. 196. An outline of the negative part of the argument about magnitude ("extension"); cf. **TV** 52, "Neither angles nor distance being perceivable by sight..."; on the optic angle, see 73n.; on "no necessary connexion," see 181n.

197. 198. Exclusive regard to the optic angle (see 73n.) to the neglect of the confusion, faintness, etc., was, Berkeley held, the fundamental mistake in other theories of apparent magnitude, see 94n. The passage cited from Molyneux's Dioptrics explains magnification in terms of angles; on Molyneux, see 32n.; on glasses, see 63n.; "but to no purpose" seems to mean that even if it were proved that magnification occurs without alteration of the angle, Berkeley would not be able to make use of the fact.

199. According to 189 the convex speculum diminishes; if it does not diminish proportionately in the case of the purblind (i.e., the near-sighted), that would indicate that magnitude is not judged by the angle alone.

200. 201. 202. On personal identity and consciousness.

Berkeley's reference to an entry as a section should be noted; it shows that he regarded the PC as a systematic composition, not as a string of jottings; he comments on his own work again in 252, 448a.

Identity in general is discussed in 192, on which see note; here Locke's doctrine (II xxvii 9ff.) that personal identity consists in consciousness, not substance, is under review. Locke writes, "consciousness always accompanies thinking...and as far as this consciousness can be extended backwards to any past action or thought, so far reaches the identity of that person." Locke admits interruptions of consciousness, which open the door for the possibility of a change of substance; and he certainly would accept a "natural potential consciousness" (see his words in section 10, "as far an any intelligent being can repeat the idea of any past action..."), and he says that Socrates and the present mayor of Queenborough are the same person, if they agree in consciousness.

"praeternatural potential consciousness" is taken by G. A. Johnston to mean existence in the mind of God; but this explanation does not, I think, fit the context; for Berkeley is thinking of human consciousness, cf. "all persons might be the Same"; "praeternatural" does not mean "supernatural," but "abnormal." The reference is probably to questions about pre-existence, e.g., Locke II xxvii 14, "I once met with one who was persuaded his had been the soul of Socrates." No doubt the "story of Mr. Deering's Aunt" was of this character. On the Dering family, see 127n.

Berkeley was familiar with the term "consciousness"; he uses it again in 578, 681; but he never, I think, uses it for mind in his books; his doctrine of existence "in the mind" takes a wrong turn if "in consciousness" be substituted.

In Locke's <u>Essay</u> "consciousness" often means self-consciousness.

203. 204. 205. 206. 208. A group dealing with magnitude, the second main division of the <u>Theory of Vision</u>. Magnitude, or extension as he often calls it, seems to have given Berkeley more trouble than distance, and in this group he is concerned with his main crux, viz., Is there such a thing as visible magnitude per se? If so, what part does it play in our customary judgements of size? He is clear (203, cf. 213) on the distinction between visible and tangible magnitude, and he recognizes that external measures, inches, etc., have no application to visible magnitude, apart from experience. He then turns (204) to visible magnitude per se, "the pictures" as he calls it, and his first conclusion is that visible magnitude is only proportional to other objects in the field (sphere or orb) of vision; and that (205) since this field is itself indeterminate it cannot yield any absolute standard of size. It follows that the true media of size-judgements are faintness, confusion, and other immediate data (see <u>TV</u> 77), including the muscular straining or relaxation represented by great and small angles; and as usual he insists that the connection of these things with magnitude is arbitrary. In 208, however, he seems to attempt a new approach to the same question; for he is not satisfied that there is any ratio between the act of perception and distinctness and confusion; for instance, it takes as much effort to see a part distinctly as its whole indistinctly; and the implication is that visual magnitude does play its part, and that distinctness, etc., are not the only bases of our size-judgements. On straining, see 210, <u>TV</u> 27, 77; on the visual orb and sphere, see 97n.; on necessary connection, see 181n.; on optical angles, see 73n. In 206

for "angle" (before "faitness") perhaps read "angles."

207. Berkeley insists that his aim is practical, see Princ. 134, 143, Introd. 22, and Title-page; he even speaks (751) of "banishing Metaphisics, &c & recalling Men to Common Sense"; for the benefit proposed to optics, see 726, to geometry, see 384, 428, Princ. 123, 131.

209. "To avoid giving handle," to the mathematicians 633-634, to Churchmen, 715; as regards his language Berkeley's aim was to avoid both the "Lofty & Platonic" and the "Subtil, Scholastic" styles (300), and to be plain and simple; in the Draft Introduction to the Principles (Works II 144-145) he says, "I shall throughout endeavour to express myself in the clearest, plainest, and most familiar manner."

210. Attempting to prove the insufficiency of the optical angle to explain our judgements of magnitude; see notes on 182, 198. For alterations in the convexity of the crystalline (eye-ball), both those due to age and those produced by experiment, see 218, 255, 271, 296, Maleb. I vi and ix, Mol. pp. 103-104; on magnification, see 94n.

211. "pictures in the fund," i.e., the retinal image, discussed in TV 88-119; see 102n. The Theory of Vision Vindicated, 48-61, explains more clearly Berkeley's meaning; in this later work he distinguishes two senses of the term "picture"; there are the pictures on the retina, truly visible, modes of light and colour, the proper and immediate objects of sight; and there are the the tangible figures, projected by tangible rays upon the tangible retina; these latter are often called "pictures," but being tangible they are not properly objects of sight,

and they ought rather to be called "images." In this entry Berkeley is considering, not the situation of objects, but their size, and he decides that retinal pictures can be no measure of absolute size; for we can imagine ourselves seeing the pictures on another person's retina, and they, of course, like other visible objects, will vary in size according to their distance from the observing eye. See _TV_ 116ff. for the same point made about situation.

212. "Introduction," i.e., to the _Principles_, which was the parent book, the _Theory of Vision_ being an offshoot from it (_Princ_. 43). A discussion of demonstration would be out of place in an Introduction to the _Theory of Vision_, and the words "the design of the whole" apply naturally to the _Principles_ as originally planned (see 508n.). There is no intimation elsewhere of any intention to write an Introduction to the _Theory of Vision_, while the Introduction to the _Principles_ receives much attention in the _PC_. It has a marginal letter (I), which was originally prefixed to no less than 85 entries, but in 27 cases the "I" has been stroked out, clearly owing to changes in the design of the Introduction. Of these changes the most important was the abandonment of the intended discussion of demonstration (see 163n.). Abstract ideas displaced it, and from 586, which originally was marked "I" and declares Berkeley's intention to treat of demonstration in the Introduction, we may infer that the dependence of Locke's doctrine of demonstration upon abstract ideas led to the change.

213. On the two sorts of magnitude, see 203n.; on the optical angle, see 73n.

214. The question concerns the nature of our judgements of size; and from 205 it would seem that the sphere of the retina is another name for the visual sphere, on which see 97n.

215. 216. If our first impressions about distance, depth, and inequality be proved erroneous, why should we trust our first impressions about size? The fact is, Berkeley suggests, that we see sights which suggest size, just as we hear words which suggest thoughts. On solids, see 78n.; for the comparison of sights and sounds, see 151-152; "thoughts by the ear," cf. 220 and TV 50, which gives 216 almost verbatim. On extension in the sense of magnitude, see 18n.

217. On large numbers, see 77n. For "form'd" Johnston reads "found"; Fraser omits the entry.

218. 219. Dealing with arguments used by Gassendi and Malebranche. Gassendi (TV Appendix, 2nd edition) said that an enlargement of the pupil augmented the retinal image, using this "false principle" to explain the size of the horizontal moon. Malebranche (I vi; cf. PC 255, 257) said that the short-sighted have their crystallines more convex and see the objects smaller; and he argued that since we are not sure that any two men have eyes exactly alike, we we cannot know that there are two men in the world who see a body the same size. Berkeley opposes this stress on the "conformation of the Eye"; he says that the minimum visibile with the visual angle subtended by it determines, or principally determines, visible magnitude, and that since we can experiment ("try the Angle") we can find out whether two men see the same thing of different sizes.

    He then (219) turns to the other relativity argument,

-185-

dealt with by Malebranche (ib.) and referred to by Locke (II xxiii 12), viz., that if we had superhuman acuteness of vision ("if a man could see seconds"), we should see things much bigger than we do, and he argues that the minimum visibile (see 59n.), as well as the visual sphere (see 97n.), is therefore a standard of visible size. These two sorts of "purely Visible magnitude" are not to be confused with the "Two sorts of bigness" which differ toto coelo (213), viz., visible and tangible magnitude. For the enlargement of sight, see 175n.; on the optical angle, see 73n.

220. The substance of this entry appears in TV 66; the supposition is intended to illustrate the closeness of the connections established by experience, and particularly the fusing of visible and tangible magnitude; on "heard thoughts," see 216n.

221. On adequate ideas, see Locke II xxxi. Locke classifies ideas according as they are adequate or inadequate; for Berkeley all ideas of sense, being realities in the mind, are adequate; for they "are perfectly known; there being nothing in them which is not perceived" (Princ. 87); but the laws of nature (see 144n.), i.e., the regular connections of these ideas, are not perfectly known to us, not only because of our limitations, but also because they, being effects of God's will, may be changed at any time.

222. Because, for Berkeley, sensible things are collections of ideas (see 112n.), he sets primary and secondary qualities on the same level (see 20n.), and he usually places both

types in the mind, but he is prepared, as here, to place them outside the human mind, having regard to their external origin and their distinctness from mind; see Princ. 90. On simple ideas, see 53n.

223. On knowledge without words and the defects of language, see 178n.

224. 225, 226. 227. Questions on the visible and the tangible, all arising from the problem of the inverted retinal image, and all bearing the distinctive marginal sign of that section of the Theory of Vision (see 102n.). How would the blind man of the Molyneux Problem (see 27n.), on receiving sight, collate the immediate data of sight and touch when he perceives a man erect on the earth? Would the sight of the man's head be at all like the touch of it? Would there be any apprehension of number by sight? Would he connect the oneness of the visible head with the oneness of the tangible head, or the twoness of the visible legs with the twoness of the tangible legs? Berkeley answers these questions in TV 100ff.

These entries, read along with the Theory of Vision, are perfectly plain, without it they would be a riddle. Could any one in his senses compose de novo the cryptic 224, and solemnly write it out in a notebook? Yet as a comment on an existing composition it is perfectly plain and intelligible. I think, therefore, that a somewhat new explanation of the close correspondence between some, or least, of the entries and publications is required (e.g., between 226 and 227 and TV 103, 106), and I suggest that Berkeley must have had a draft composition before him when he started to fill these notebooks. This composition may well have included, not only a discussion of vision, but a discussion of time (see 4n.) and of infinitesimals (cf. the essay Of Infinites) and an outline of his first conception of the argument for immaterialism ("my first arguings," 265).

If this conjecture be sound, we must modify the received conception of the function of the PC; the PC, instead of being a commentary on Berkeley's reading, put together for purposes of his writing, must have been in part a commentary on his writing, put together for purposes of rewriting. The suggestion is intrinsically probable, especially in respect of the first notebook (B), and it would help to explain the existence of the elaborate system of marginal signs and letters; for some such system of cross-referneces between the draft composition and the notebook would be essential.

On the connection of ideas, see 181n. and TV 51; on the heterogeneity of sight and touch, see 28n.; on the early use of "thoughts" for "ideas," see 153n.; this (226) is a very good instance of the change, because the corresponding passage in TV 103 has "ideas."

228. Up to this stage (cf. 293) Berkeley credited body with powers to raise thoughts; therefore "things" in this entry must be confined to unthinking things. The entry is a summary account under three heads of non-spiritual reality, an attempt to combine immaterialism with Locke's doctrine of active and passive powers. Later (see notes on 41, 52, 153) Berkeley decided to confine "thought" to the active spirit, adopted "idea" for the sensible object, dropped the "powers" theory, and thus reached the summary of reality, found throughout the Principles, viz., spirit and ideas, a summary which has not place for matter. Note the substitution of "cause" for "occasion."

229. On magnification, see 94n.; on the optical angle, see 73n.

230. Malebranche holds that there is an idea of the soul, known to God; but when he is speaking precisely, as in III ii 7, he denies that we know the soul by idea; "we know her not by her idea...we know her only by conscience...we know nothing of our soul, but what we feel pass within us." Berkeley's mature doctrine of self-knowledge (see *Princ*. 135ff.) is similar to that of Malebranche; for both thinkers it is a case of "knowledge without ideas" and in *Mot*. 21 Berkeley uses Malebranche's term for it "*conscientia quadam interna*."

This is the first mention of Father Nicholas Malebranche (1638-1715), whose main work *De la Recherche de la Vérité* (1674-1675) was well known to Berkeley (see his *De Ludo Algebraico*, 1707), and is often referred to in the *PC* (in criticism, for the most part), see 255, 257, 265, 288, 358, 388, 424, 548, 686, 686a, 800, 818, 888. For its influence on Berkeley's philosophy, see my *Berkeley and Malebranche* (1934, reprinted 1967).

231. Berkeley makes this comparison both under "distance" and under "figure" (magnitude), *TV* 9, 23, 65; the sudden transitions of thought, he holds, make us overlook the immediate objects, and fancy that the mediated object is immediately given. Note the addition "or Distance" as in 220a.

232. On magnification, see 94n.

233. On the problem of the horizontal moon, see 125n.; Berkeley thinks that the optical angle (see 73n.) and the inferred distance are not sufficient explanations of the phenomenon, and wishes to refer it to faintness of appearance.

234. The term "corpuscularian" was used broadly to cover what we should now call materialsm and mechanism, and, more narrowly, for the atomism of Epicurus and Gassendi. In <u>Princ</u>. 50 we find "the whole corpuscular philosophy," i.e., the physics of the day, and <u>ib</u>. 25 "corpuscles" occurs in the description of Locke's theory of sensible qualities. His theory of the dependence of the secondary qualities upon the minute parts or corpuscles of the primary, probably derived from Boyle, is described by Locke himself as "the corpuscularian hypothesis" (IV iii 16; cf. <u>Siris</u> 232), and as the only other entry (533) to use the term mentions the passage from Locke, there can be little doubt that this entry has Locke in view.

Clearly then "the Essences of the Corpuscularians" are the real and nominal essences which Locke sets forth in III vi 2ff. The "real essence" is the "something we know not what," depicted and ridiculed in <u>Princ</u>. 101; it conflicts with Berkeley's view that all real things are in the mind, and therefore perfectly known. The "nominal essence" is made by the mind; it is the abstract idea to which the name of the sort is annexed; all general knowledge, says Locke (IV vi 13) "consists barely in the contemplation of our own abstract ideas." The abstract idea (see 318n.) became the focus of Berkeley's attack on Locke, and this entry may mark the first turning of his attention to the subject; for real essence, cf. 44, 536.

235. "Perfect Circles &c," probably a reference to the theory, attributed to Plato, of mathematical objects which conform exactly to the definitions, and are viewed as archetypes of sensible figures. Perfect circles are mentioned by Bacon, <u>Nov. Org</u>. I xlv. Abstract ideas of circles, etc., are denied in 238.

236. 237. Berkeley here considers two errors which have promoted belief in infinite divisibility (see 11n. and cf. 342); external existence and infinite divisibility are discussed in Princ. 125ff., and the mistake about magnification is touched on in TV 85 (see 94n.). "They who knew not Glasses," see 63n.

238. See 235n. and, on abstract ideas in general, 318n.

239. On demonstration in general, see 163n., in ethics, see 669n.

240. 241, 242. 243. Notes on the comparative distinctness of the data of various senses, and on the connection between this distinctness and extension (see 18n.). Tangible data are, Berkeley holds, the most vivid; next come the visible. Visible and tangible are heterogeneous (see 28n.), but they both suggest extension. King (De Origine Mali, I ii 14) says that if we had only the three senses, sound, smell, and taste, we should not even imagine there was such a thing as space. Time is connected with the distinctness of sense-data in 647, and in TV 145 sights and sounds are contrasted in respect of distinctness. On taste and smell, see 137n.; on colour and extension, see 85n.; for experiments in green, yellow, and blue, see 489, 502-505, 526.

244. An objection to Berkeley's solution of the problem of the horizontal moon (see 125n.), stated and answered in TV 71, 72.

245. 249. 250. 251. 252. A group dealing with the quadrature of the circle, see also 360n., 395, 457-458, 510-511. Strictly speaking, there are two kindred problems: (a) to square the

circle i.e., to find a **square equal** in area to that of a given circle; and (b) to "rectify peripheries," i.e., to find a straight line equal to the circumference. Berkeley was interested in both problems, and distinguishes them in 457; but he fails to distinguish them in 249, 510-511, and perhaps some other entries.

These problems had in Berkeley's day acquired celebrity owing to the Hobbes-Wallis controversy. Berkeley's interest in them lay in their connection with infinite divisibility. He held that any given sensible line must be composed of sensible points, which are indivisible <u>minima</u> (see 59n.), and is not, therefore, composed of elements too small to be sensed. Similarly the area of a figure is to be measured by the number of sensible points it contains. If then you know the number of points in a given curve, you can in practice find a straight line equal to it; and in practice any given circle can be squared provided that the number of points it contains is a perfect square (cf. 458, 469).

For the magnifying glass objection, see 94n. In 249, note "therefore there is no difference" -- a hint of the New Principle, <u>esse</u> <u>est</u> <u>percipi</u> (see 265n.). In 251 "in Squaring or other Curves" is probably short for "in squaring the circle or dealing with other curves."

246. This entry has the marginal sign peculiar to those dealing with the inverted retinal image (see 102n.); "smooth & round" refers, no doubt, to the globe in the Molyneux Problem (see 27n.), which in <u>TV</u> 94ff. is considered in connection with the retinal image. On "no necessary connexion," see 181n.

247. 248. It was commonly held that geometry supplied formal

proof of the infinite divisibility, but Berkeley maintained that this was a mistaken notion, due to a confusion between concrete sensible extension, such as this inch (cf. 260-261, 341, 341a) and some much larger abstract extension supposed to be represented by the inch; see 11n. and *Princ.* 123-128.

"Determined" or "determinate" were the terms adopted by Locke (see his Ep. to the Reader) in his fourth edition in place of "clear and distinct."

253. "A meer line," i.e., abstract length without breadth (see 21n.); on points see 59n., 259n.; on colour and extension, see 85n., *Princ.* Introd. 7.

254. In his publications Berkeley from the first insisted (e.g., *Princ.* Introd. 10) on the distinction between the legitimate process of abstraction, which consists in considering separately *separable* parts, and the illegitimate process of framing abstract ideas. Here he appears to admit that we can consider separately *inseparable* parts, such as length without breadth (see 21n., 318n., *Princ.* Introd. 16, 2nd ed.).

255. 257. These remarks on Malebranche's (see 230n.) doctrine of sense-relativity are explained in the note on 218.

256. This entry, too, probably refers to Malebranche, who says (I ix) that the size of the retinal image is the third medium by which we judge distance; it receives point from the problem of *TV* 70-73 as to why faintness which ordinarily magnifies visible magnitude does not always do so.

"greatest pictures," i.e., the largest retinal images, measured by occupancy of the visual sphere (S.V., see 97n.), or by the number of *minima visibilia* (M.V., see 59n.).

258. On the incommensurability, see 29n.; on M.V., see 59n.

259. If I deny that surfaces consist of lines, I should also deny that lines consist of points. Now if lines do not consist of points, then the sophism, argued by Leibniz in the dialogue he wrote for Spinoza (A. E. Taylor, The Parmenides of Plato, p. 46n.) falls. This sophism consists in proving the side and the diagonal of a square to be of equal length, by drawing perpendiculars from the side so as to cut the diagonal; thus there appears to be a point-for-point correspondence between side and diagonal, i.e., the numbers of points in both are equal, and the lines are proved equal though known to be unequal. The sophism proceeds on the assumption that lines literally consist of abstract, mathematical points. Cf. the difficulties about concentric circles (315n.).

Berkeley carefully distinguishes mathematical points from sensible points; the former are abstractions or "nothings"; the latter are the minima (see 59n.) into which, he holds, real lines and surfaces may be resolved; see 132, 253, 267, 447, 516, TV 112.

260.261. For the inch representing the mile, see 247n., and cf. "There is no such thing as the ten-thousandth part of an inch," Princ. 127 (in the draft of this section -- British Museum MS. 39304 -- Berkeley first wrote "a thousandth part," as in this entry). On geometry, see 117n.; on infinite divisibility, see 11n. "demonstrable" is a slip for "demonstrate."

262. Since we do not see distance directly, we cannot see directly the motion of an object moving in the optic axis, i.e., straight away from us. Other motions are admitted to be

directly visible, but they are heterogeneous, Berkeley insists, from tangible motions, see 28n. and TV 137; for the optic axis, see 400, 443; for motion in the optic axis, see Maleb. I ix and diagram ib.; for motion including succession, see 167, 184.

263. 264. On incommensurability, here explicitly connected with infinite divisibility (see 11n.), see 29n.; on Barrow, see 75n.; "indivisibility" is a slip for "divisibility."

265. A somewhat tantalizing, yet illuminating entry, in which Berkeley expresses dissatisfaction with his two main sources, Locke and Malebranche, and with his own "first arguings." Locke and Malebranche had brought him a certain distance towards immaterialism, but not far enough; they had established the relativity of the secondary qualities (note the marginal letter P, for primary and secondary qualities), but that argument is insufficient, as Berkeley points out in Princ. 15.

What, then, were his "first arguings," and why does he refer to them here? I should hazard a reply as follows:

These "arguings" may well have been on paper, as were Locke's "arguings." If they were only "in his head," he would hardly have made this objective reference to them. I suggest, supporting the suggestion by my note on 224, that Berkeley had written out a first attempt at an argument for immaterialism, starting with the conception of time as a sensation in the mind, basing his argument largely on the subjectivity of the secondary qualities, and drawing on Locke's theory and on Malebranche's study of perceptual relativity. Dissatisfied with those lines of reasoning and feeling the need for an ad hoc study of vision (Princ. 43), he began the PC in order to clear up difficult and doubtful

points, and in the hope of feeling his way to a really
decisive argument against matter. He found that argument,
the New Principle, and found it, I think, about the time when
he wrote this entry; for the sense of discovery is marked in
these pages -- see 266, 270, 285, and especially 279. From
now on the New Principle becomes the spearhead of his attack
on matter, superseding his former argument from primary and
secondary qualities. On Malebranche, see 230n.

266. "distrustful," prima manu "sceptical"; this interesting
little reminiscence may be compared with his remark, "I have
always thought and judged for myself" (Def. 19). Berkeley
has no doubt about the novelty of his doctrines.

267. Cf. 276. On Berkeley's theory of minima (see 59n.) a
line cannot be bisected with absolute accuracy, if it consists
of an odd number of points. The words "ad infinitum,"
bracketed in the MS., are irrelevant.

268. The "Pictures," i.e., the retinal images, which, Berkeley
holds, are properly tangible, not visible, see 211n.

269. Malebranche (see 230n.) says (I vi) that we do not see
the true magnitude of things, but the relation or proportion
they bear to our bodies. Berkeley here argues that if the
things were outside the mind, we could have no knowledge of
them at all, not even of their relation to us; for the hypothesis
of matter, see 61n.; on extension, see 18n.

270. Obvious truth, cf. "obvious tho' Amazing truth" (279),
and for the same epithet Princ. 6, 149; this truth is Berkeley's
New Principle, the esse est percipi, his "intuitive" disproof

of matter; on extension, see 18n.; on thinking substance, see 80n.

271. That the mind makes the species or "sorts" (see 288, 289, 836n., Locke III iii 13) was one of Berkeley's indirect arguments against matter. "by turning Men's Eyes into magnifyers or diminishers" means, I think, considering the increase or decrease of apparent size which an alteration of the eye might produce. It might then be argued that since the particular size seen depends on the mind, the general or sort to which that particular size belongs must be no less dependent on the mind. Berkeley may especially have in view those marked qualitative changes (changes in kind or species) to which magnification gives rise, e.g., in a drop of water. On magnification, see 94n.

272. 273. 277. On Berkeley's doctrine of minima, see 59n.; 272 and 277 are attempts to prove the equality of all minima visibilia, using the argument that minima have no parts, as in TV 80; 273 asks whether these elements of extension are themselves extended. Berkeley does not answer his own question; but the answer required by his teaching would seem to be "Yes," with the provisos that (1) the extension of the minimum visibile differs in kind from that of the minimum tangibile, (2) both types of extension are sensible, not material.

   [Note the correct reading "everts" in 272. Other editors have read "diverts." -- Editor]

274. 275. The pictures are the retinal images, on which see 211n.

276. For the problem of bisection, see 267n.

278. For "inverting perspectives," see 148n.; on the inverted retinal image, see 102n.

279. This entry has an intimate personal quality, and, like others in this part of the PC, is marked by a sense of discovery; for about this time, probably, Berkeley came on his New Principle, the *esse est percipi*; this suggestion is confirmed by the words which Berkeley wrote at the end of the entry, and erased. On "obvious truth," see 270n.; "stupid inadvertency," cf. "the stupidity and inattention of men," Princ. 149, where the divine omnipresence, the necessary background of the New Principle, is spoken of as a truth "near and obvious." In the erasure the words "our" and "think" are not quite certain.

280. These are alternative forms of the New Principle, all yielding the conclusion that there is no matter. These arguments are formally set out as a "demonstration" in 378. On simple and complex ideas, see 53n.; on "thoughts," see 153n.

281. Berkeley is considering the orthodoxy of his views; for his concern about arguments from scripture, see 404-405, 686, 720, Princ. 82, Works VIII 29, 37-38.

Malebranche taught that light and colours are "modifications of the soul"; his views were widely shared in England; the subjectivity of secondary qualities in its mild Lockian form was freely taught by orthodox divines. Archbishop King in his famous sermon on Predestination (May 15, 1709) says, "I think it is agreed by most that write of Natural Philosophy that light and colours are nothing but the effects of certain bodies and motions on our sense of seeing, and there are no such things at all in nature, but only in our minds."

282. For the development of Berkeley's views on the existence of body unperceived, see notes on 41 and 52; on "thoughts," see 153n. This entry belongs to the early stage, as is shown by the erasure of "really."

283. 284. Studies in the apparent magnitude of plane surfaces; for "successive, curious inspection" and the two kinds of visible extension, see 400n.

285. Berkeley's Principle is here so named for the first time. Malebranche (VI ii 1) holds out the prospect of finding "an infallible principle" to those who follow his rules of method; Berkeley praises those rules highly in his <u>De Ludo Algebraico</u>; they may, or may not, have influenced his work; but it is certain that he regarded his New Principle as a decisive discovery. It is the climax of notebook B and the starting-point of A; it is named in 291, 304, 402, 407, 410-411, and it is the "obvious tho' Amazing truth" of 270, 279-280; it is set forth with a "demonstration" in 378-380, being there formulated in the words "that neither our Ideas nor anything like our ideas can possibly be in an unperceiving thing." The Principle is Berkeley's direct disproof of matter from the nature of existence, the <u>esse</u> <u>est</u> <u>percipi</u>, and it is by him contrasted with his "first arguings" (265).

"Ignorance" means either Socratic ignorance, or native common-sense as opposed to "learned dust"; cf. 405, <u>Princ</u>. Introd. 17. Hecht misunderstands this entry, misled, no doubt, by Lorenz's conjecture "disaver" for "discover"; the MS. has "Discover." Berkeley is not charging his opponents with ignorance, but is claiming it for himself, as a naive realist will take a pride in his naivete, or like the Baconian seeking entrance into the kingdom of man "as a little child"

(Nov. Org. I 68). The entry may well be a reference to the "ignorance" commended ironically by Bayle in his article Pyrrho as one of the great defences against scepticism.

286. On thoughts, see 153n.; on soul or mind, see 14n. "yt is all a case," i.e., both types of thoughts come under the New Principle.

287. 288. 288a. 289. 290. A group which summarizes the results of his study of extension (see 18n.): (1) extension is composed of sensible minima (see 59n.), which imply a perceiving substance; (2) there is no extension apart from sensible quality, e.g., colour, which implies relation to the mind, cf. Princ. 10 -- this "great argument" (288a) subsequently becomes of secondary importance; (3) extended things have their sorts, which are the work of the mind -- this argument later is dropped. The Draft Introduction had a paragraph on the sorts (Works II 128-129), which has completely disappeared in the revised Introduction; (4) if there is external space, there is infinite space, a conception which implies either extended Deity, or an anti-God, see Princ. 117. From 288 we see that at this stage Berkeley held the intermittent existence of sensible things, see 52n. On the sorts, see 836, Locke III iii 13; on God, see 107n.; on infinite space, see 135n.; on Malebranche, see 230n., 265; on the hypothesis of matter, see 61n.; on substance, see 80n.

291. Arguments ad absurdum for the Principle (see 285n.) are implied in Princ. 3, e.g., the unsmelled smell.

292. The finiteness of our minds was, for Berkeley, an "excuse" with which geometers and natural philosophers cloaked the

contradictions in their theories, see 323, 350, 350a, 747, 859-860. In the Draft Introduction (note the marginal letter "I") the three opening paragraphs (Works II 121-122) attack this "excuse," the passage being divided later between Introd. 2,3, and Princ. 101. "Geometers," e.g., Keill and Cheyne, both of whom have recourse to the "excuse."

293. 293a. Creation and perception were connected in Berkeley's mind (see 60n.); he saw that the objection, Where on your theory were created things during the Mosaic "days" prior to the creation of man? is parallel to the objection, Where are my books when I am out of my study?

Entry 293a should not be taken as Berkeley's full and final account of the perceivable (see notes on 41 and 52), but it agrees with Princ. 3 in holding that the existence of the table which I am not seeing means that "if I was in my study I might perceive it"; the passage from the Principles adds, however, the important words, "or that some other spirit actually does perceive it." That God perceives things when we do not is the keystone of Berkeley's full, final theory of the perceivable, as it appears in 802 and Princ. 45-48; on "thoughts," see 153n.

294. This query is answered in the negative by Locke (I iv 20), by Malebranche (I xiii), and by Clarke (Demonstration of the Being and Attributes of God, Prop. X). On the blind man of the Molyneux Problem, see 27n.

295. The third "demonstration" of the heterogeneity of sight and touch, TV 131, cf. above 28n.; on minimal points, see 59n.; on extension, see 18n.

296. 296a. Molyneux (_Dioptrics_, pp. 103-104), states this problem and leaves it to others to determine. Berkeley has not, I think, recorded his proposed method for solving it. V.S. is the visual sphere (see 97n.); M.V. is the _minimum visibile_ (see 59n). From thirty seconds to a minute is the size assigned by Locke (II xv 9) to his "sensible point." The verso addition, which was not noticed by Fraser or Johnston, contains part of Berkeley's own explanation of judgements of magnitude (see _TV_ 56). On near vision, see _TV_ 3ff.; on the crystalline and fund, see 210n. and _TV_ 34.

297. On this distinction, see 87n.

298. The same charge is made against Hobbes and Spinoza, 825, 827. Locke, More, and Raphson lay themselves open to the charge by their opposition to inextensionism, the doctrine of those who hold that there is no extension in addition to matter.

Locke in II xiii 27 and xv 2-4 has guarded references to the divine immensity, and Query IX (see MS. fol. 102), "God space...," shows that Berkeley had noticed these passages.

Henry More (1614-1687) Cambridge Platonist, author of _Encheiridion Metaphysicum_ (1671), maintained against Descartes the existence of real and infinite space as a substance distinct from matter.

Joseph Raphson, F.R.S., in his _De Spatio Reali seu Ente Infinito_ (1697, chap. V) virtually deifies space, calling it "_actus purus, incorporeum, immutabile_, aeternum, omni-continens, omnipenetrans, attributum_ (viz., _immensitas_) primae causae." Raphson is named also in 827, and is referred to in Berkeley's letter to Johnson of March 24, 1730 (_Works_ II 292), as a mathematician who "pretends to find out fifteen of the incommunicable attributes of God in space." On powers, see notes on 41 and 52.

299. This entry opposes the doctrine that ideas are <u>like</u> matter (see 46n.), and corresponds fairly closely with <u>Princ</u>. 8; on "thought" see 153n.; "Contradiction," cf. 573, 579, <u>Princ</u>. 24, 54; on extension, see 18n.

300. Cf. <u>Draft Introduction</u> (<u>Works</u> II 144-145), "I shall throughout endeavour to express myself in the clearest, plainest, and most familiar manner, abstaining from [all flourish and pomp of words, <u>prima manu</u>]..." Berkeley well describes his own clear style, modelled perhaps on Locke's; for his care about his language, see 209n. "Lofty & Platonic," e.g., More and Norris. Johnston says, "Berkeley himself was later in <u>Siris</u> to use 'the lofty and Platonic strain.'" That comment might be challenged; for the style of <u>Siris</u> is almost entirely plain and level even when lofty, Platonic things are under discussion.

301. Matter, as non-percipient, cannot be the substance of ideas; for perception as passive reception, see 756. Berkeley's full theory stresses the activity of percipient mind and its distinctness from passive ideas; see 672a, 673, <u>Princ</u>. 2, 89.

302. 302a. 303. On the problem of the horizontal moon, see 125n.; dimness due to the atmosphere is Berkeley's main explanation; but he gives subsidiary explanations, e.g., the turn of the eye, straining, upper and lower situation (see <u>TV</u> 77), all of which in particular cases may affect our judgements of distance, and so of magnitude. <u>TV</u> 71 mentions the magnifying effect of mist, but not of dusk; these cases are the same in principle as that of the horizontal moon.

304. 305. The reverse of the Principle is more than a <u>denial</u> of the Principle. The reverse of the Principle is that the <u>esse</u> of sensible things is <u>non-percipi</u>, that their being or existence is to be unperceived (see 285n.); the sceptical tendencies of that doctrine are obvious. Aware that he himself might be charged with scepticism (see 79n.) Berkeley adds an assertion of his belief in reality and the course of nature (see 52n.), i.e. in a world not produced by the human mind, nor dependent thereon for its conservation and character.

306. 308. 309. Mathematical problems bearing on the infinite divisibility (see 11n.); surds, cf. 469, 482; doubling the cube -- take a cube with side of length x, where x is a rational number; its volume is x^3. Take a cube of twice its volume, $2x^3$; the length of the side of this new cube is $\sqrt[3]{2x^3}$, i.e. $x\sqrt[3]{2}$ which is a surd or incommensurable number.

"Angles of Contact," Berkeley's point is that we cannot speak of <u>the</u> angle between a curve and a straight line, because by its very nature a curve is continually changing its direction; see 168n., 381.

Charles Hayes (1678-1760), author of <u>Treatise of Fluxions</u> (1704), "the first English work explaining Newton's method of infinitesimals" (<u>Dict. Nat. Biogr.</u>).

John Keill, F.R.S. (1671-1721) lectured on physics and geometry at Oxford, and later became Professor of Astronomy; he was the "first who taught natural philosophy by experiments in a mathematical manner" (quoted <u>Dict. Nat. Biogr.</u>). He wrote <u>An Examination of Dr. Burnet's Theory of the Earth</u> (1698), <u>Introductio ad Veram Physicam</u> (1702), and several papers on fluxions in <u>Philosophical Transactions</u>. He drew up for the Royal Society the <u>Commercium Epistolicum</u>, which claimed priority for Newton against Leibniz in the discovery of the calculus. Berkeley has in mind <u>Lectiones</u> IV, V of the <u>Introductio</u>.

[Note the correct reading "2d order." Other editors read 3d order. -- Editor]

307. This entry is on the verso, but is not a comment on a recto entry. The test of the blind man (see 27n.) is an attempt to isolate the immediate data of sight; Berkeley applies it in each of the three main divisions of the <u>Theory</u> <u>of</u> <u>Vision</u>, viz., to distance (41ff.), to magnitude (79), to situation (92ff.). Here, as shown by the marginal sign, it has special reference to situation and the problem of the inverted retinal image (see 102n.)

310. E.g., St. Patrick's exposition of Trinitarianism, in the legend, by aid of the shamrock leaf; on God, see 107n.

311. Berkeley discusses the variation of size with distance in <u>TV</u> 44; he does not rest his immaterialism on the variation of the primary qualities, and in <u>Princ</u>. 15 he points out the limitations of "this method of arguing [which] does not so much prove that there is no extension or colour in an outward object, as that we do not know by sense which is the true extension or colour of the object." His point here is that <u>all</u> our judgements of size, both of "distant" objects and those "near us" are determined by human use and convenience.

312. Berkeley answers objections to immaterialism in <u>Princ</u>. 34-84, using these principles, 1, 2, and 4 in sections 34, 62, and 61 respectively. The fourth principle is used again in the case of identity in <u>Dials</u>., **Works II 248**, and it recurs almost verbatim in Berkeley's letter to Johnson of November 25, 1729

(Works II 281), where he speaks of a theological consideration as "beside the question; for such I hold all points to be which bear equally hard on both sides of it." The third principle combines Locke's two principles, (a) no knowledge without ideas, and (b) all significant words stand for ideas. Berkeley at first held them both, and sets them forth at the head of his formal "demonstration" (378, where see note), but he subsequently abandoned both; see 178n., 730. On the reality of body, see 52n.; on the laws and the course of nature, see 144n. and 305.

313. ἀκρίβεια, accuracy, or exactness, cf. 330, 449; Berkeley claimed demonstration for his doctrines, but he opposed the mathematicians' claim to accuracy; partly on general grounds, for "It is beneath the dignity of the mind to affect an exactness ..." (Princ. 109); and in particular because his doctrine of sensible points required him to neglect very small differences, e.g., in bisecting lines consisting of an odd number of points, or in squaring the circle (see 249n.). N.B. "Darling of the Age"; cf. Mol., Adm. to the Reader, where it is said that dioptrics "cannot be delivered with that ἀκρίβεια geometrica" because rays of light are material lines and glasses have thickness. In the Analyst (19) Berkeley makes the point that the doctrine of infinitesimals compels mathematicians to neglect very small differences, and therefore to forgo their boasted ἀκρίβεια.

314. On infinite divisibility, see 11n.; on extension, see 18n.

315. The "Difficulties about Concentric Circles" are set forth by Barrow (Math. Lect. IX) as an argument against indivisible points and for infinite divisibility. They are

considered at length by Bayle in his article Zeno. If we consider circles as literally composed of indivisible points (ex hypothesi of equal "magnitude"), and then construct a geometrical figure showing a one-one correspondence between the points of two concentric circles, we reach the absurdity that concentric circles are equal. Cf. the sophism of the side and the diagonal (259n.).

Concentric circles are mentioned also in 122, but the two entries are dealing with different topics; in 122 Berkeley is on a problem of vision, visible magnitude.

316. This is the well-known scholium on absolute and relative motion, see 30n. The "Mr" is curious, for Newton was knighted on April 15, 1705 (Berkeley gives him his title in 374 and in his essay Of Infinites, read before the Dublin Society November 19, 1707); it should not, however, be regarded as evidence that the entry was written before that date. The evidence to the contrary is overwhelming; and as one would expect, the notes not being intended for publication, Berkeley is not careful in such details. Indeed he usually writes "Newton."

317. Berkeley is not a sensationalist, for he believed in reason and spirit; but he is far from being, as is generally supposed, against the senses; on the contrary, he gives them "all the stress and assurance imaginable," Princ. 40. In the PC he teaches that it is foolish to despise them, 317, 373, 539; that sense must be used about the sensibles, 466; that without sensation there is no knowledge, 539, 779; he places certainty in the senses, 731a, 740, recalls men to commonsense, 751, and vindicates the senses against Descartes' teaching, 794. If mathematicians would trust their senses

and would take sensible things as wholly sensible, they would reject, he held, the doctrine of infinite divisibility, "the source from whence do spring all those amusing geometrical paradoxes which have such a direct repugnancy to the plain commonsense of mankind" (Princ. 123).

318. Almost certainly one entry; other editors print as two. Johnston's text is seriously at fault here; for he reads "It is not" for "is it not" and with Fraser he erroneously inserts "abstract" before "general ideas." Curiously, both he and Fraser make the same erroneous insertion again in 497, 555, 591, 666, and they both erroneously insert "concrete" in 497.

This is one of the first entries to attack general ideas, more precisely styled "abstract general ideas," and usually abbreviated to "abstract ideas." Berkeley here attacks them on the ground that all ideas are from without, and are particulars; at the same time he concedes, as he always did from the very first (see Princ. Introd. 10), the mind's power of abstracting in the sense of "considering asunder."

The source of Berkeley's doctrine of abstraction cannot be determined precisely; Browne, The Procedure, Extent and Limits of Human Understanding (1728) has a chapter on abstraction (pp. 186ff.) which has several points in common with Berkeley's doctrine. He may have taken them from Berkeley, but it is quite possible that Berkeley learned them from him, for he was Provost when Berkeley was an undergraduate. Bacon (see 564), and Hobbes, and Malebranche had attacked vigorously certain types of abstraction, and no doubt they influenced Berkeley, and put him on his guard against abuses of abstraction; but the PC shows that there were as well two specific lines of approach to his doctrine, viz., simple ideas and mathematical problems; 53a clearly connects it with Locke's doctrine of simple ideas (see note there), and 85 and 238 (on abstract lengths, points, and circles) speak of mathematical abstractions, and Locke's "absurd triangle" (see 687n.) eventually became the focus of his attack, his "killing blow."

The second notebook (A) contains many references to the doctrine, viz., 401, 496, 497, 524, 552, 561, 564, 566, 586, 591, 594, 602, 666, 687, 688, 703, 727, 772, 779, 809, 811, 865, 867, 871, 873; and in that series several close parallels with his published works may be found. It seems that when he began to write the PC Berkeley had only vague views on abstraction, or none at all; but certainly before he finished it his doctrine had taken full and final shape. The attack on abstract ideas makes a brief, unheralded appearance in TV 122-125, as if it had only recently been reached; it monopolizes the Introduction to the Principles, and throughout the whole series of Berkeley's publications it dominates his epistemology, remaining unwithdrawn and in full force to the end of his life; see my Berkeley and Malebranche, chaps. vii, viii, and my article in Mind, vol. xlvi, N.S., No. 181, on "The Unity of the Berkeleian Philosophy," p. 51.

All ideas come from without, i.e., ideas of sense; qua ideas, they are in the mind, but their source is external to man, so Princ. 29, 90; all ideas particular, see 497, 666, Princ. Introd. 15, Locke III iii 1; on colour and extension, see 85n.

319. On the distinction between a mathematical and a sensible termination, see 31n. Locke (II xvii 14) writes, "he that perceives the end of his pen is black or white, will be apt to think that the end is something more than a pure negation." Locke's argument "concludes nothing here," because his pen is not "a mathematical line."

320. On geometers, see 117n.; Keill (e.g., Introductio, p. 20) often attacks the "ἀγεωμέτροι philosophers"; on the definition of extension, see Locke II xiii 15, and cf. 44n. and 164n.

321. "We regard the objects that environ us in proportion as they are adapted to benefit or injure our own bodies, and thereby produce in our minds the sensations of pleasure or pain" (TV 59). Cf. Maleb. I vi and x; on minima, see 59n.

322. Keill (see 308n.) in his Introductio, p. 33, tries to answer the atomist's objection that "if all quantity is divisible in infinitum, every smallest part will equal the greatest"; see 11n.

323. For this "excuse" see 292n.; Johnston reads "infinites" and explains as infinitesimals. As a reading his is possible, but it is inferior to "infinity." The non-comprehension of infinity was a commonplace with the physicists of the day (e.g., Cheyne), and is referred to repeatedly in the PC, and is discussed in Princ. Introd. 2.

324. M is apparently "moment," Newton's term for differential; see 333, 389, Anal. 4, Def. 28; dd would then be differential of the second order, see Anal. 8; on disregarding small quantities, see Anal. 23. On magnification, see 94n.

325. If you admit that size and number are the work of the mind, you must also admit, says Berkeley, that there is no matter; for matter ex hypothesi being outside the mind, could have neither size nor number of points, and would therefore not be matter. Cf. 40n.; on the subjectivity of number, see

104n.; on extension, see 18n.

326. The same passage in Locke on idea, quality, and power, is referred to in 112, where see note.

327. This comparison is developed in 409, 449, 492, 642.

328. I.e., extension (see 18n.) is an abstraction from the concrete mass of visible and tangible sense-data; see 85n.

329. Berkeley claims to have simplified mathematics, see 385, 414, TV 160, Princ. 123, 134; for the scale cf. 332 and Mol. p. 19, "this is easily done by scale and compass." A problem of sub-tangent and abscisse is discussed in Anal. 21.

330. On mathematical accuracy, see 313n. If the accuracy be confined to the conceptions of the mathematicians, e.g., in the niceties of the calculus, and if nothing objective correspond to those conceptions, then it is labour lost, argues Berkeley, to strive for accuracy.

331. "As oft as you talk of finite quantities inconsiderable in practice, Sir Isaac disowns your apology; Cave, saith he, intellexeris finitas" (Def. 26). Newton is inconsistent, Berkeley argues, (ib. 25), in falling back on the method of approximations in practice, while claiming rigorous accuracy for his method of fluxions, and laying down that in rebus mathematicis errores quam minimi non sunt contemnendi.

332. Probably some concrete problem involving a mathematical progression is in Berkeley's mind, and he suggests solving it by use of the scale, see 329n.

333. For Newton infinitesimals were velocities of nascent or evanescent increments, hence called fluxions (see 168n.); for Leibniz they were differences, i.e., infinitely small increments or decrements. Berkeley rejects both conceptions as involving quantities less than the <u>minimum sensibile</u>, and therefore without the mind; see his <u>Of Infinites</u>, <u>Princ</u>. 132, and <u>Anal</u>. 3-6, where both theories are considered. On M, see 324n.

334. "hang together," part of the thesis of the <u>Analyst</u> (20ff.) is to show how, by a compensation of errors, mathematicians "deduce true propositions from false principles." Berkeley complains of "that nice and extream subtilty, which renders the study of <u>mathematics</u> so very difficult and tedious," <u>Princ</u>. 123; on Barrow, see 75n. (the reference is to his <u>Lect. Math</u>. V).

335. 336. Mathematics are made easier (see 329n.), Berkeley holds, if we are content with approximate correctness (which is all that we can obtain), and do not insist on absolutely rigorous proofs. On certainty and demonstration in ethics, see notes on 163 and 669.

337. 338. The opening of the attack on infinitesimals as "nothings," and on mathematicians as "nihilarians," i.e., supporters of the infinitely divisible mathematical point, which, Berkeley argues, is a "nothing"; he sets in contrast to it his own indivisible, sensible point in 438-439; see also 343-345, 372, 384, 394, 399, 449, 462-464, 471, 488, 633, <u>Princ</u>. 130, and <u>Anal</u>. 35 where he calls evanescent increments "ghosts of departed quantities." In his <u>Of Infinites</u> he appeals to Wallis's <u>Arithemetic of Infinites</u> in proof "that an

infinitesimal even of the first degree is merely nothing."
"begets a Contradiction," such as an "Unperceivable perception"
(347), or a minimum visibile composed of invisibles (464).

339. Creation (see 60n.) is "when things, before imperceptible
to creatures, are, by a decree of God, perceptible to them"
(Dials., Works II 252).

340. A departure from the received view of the constant ratio
between circumference and diameter, cf. 457, 481; the departure
is required by Berkeley's method of rectifying particular
circles (see 245n.).

341. 341a. 342. 342a. 343. After an argument against infinite
divisibility which agrees closely with Princ. 126-128 (see
notes on 11, 247, 260) Berkeley summarizes the case which
occupies so much of the notebook B. The infinite divisibility
involves (1) unperceived existence, (2) the real existence of
abstract lines, etc., see 21n., (3) a unit which is no unit,
viz., a divisible minimum sensibile. This third argument
works round to the first, as is shown in 343; for ultimately
Berkeley's opposition to infinite divisibility depends on his
opposition to unperceived existence and the "something we
know not what."

344. 345. The signum is the mathematicians' point (337n.),
which Berkeley compares with his own sensible minimum (see
59n.), finding the latter much easier to conceive.

346. Bonaventura Cavalieri (1598-1647), Professor of Mathematics
at Bologna, wrote Geometria Indivisibilibus Continuorum nova
quadam ratione Promota (1635) and Exercitationes Geometricae

Sex (1647). In the latter work he expounds his methods, prior and posterior, and defends his geometry of indivisibles from the attacks of Guldinus. He imagines the continuum to be composed of an infinite number of ultimate elements or molecules, which he calls indivisibles, and he is generally thought to have held that bodies are composed of an infinity of juxtaposed surfaces and surfaces of lines. Berkeley agreed with Cavalieri as to the existence of indivisibles, but differed from him as to the number of indivisibles in a finite line. Berkeley held that the number is finite, which apparently Cavalieri denied.

347. Such as matter, or an infinitely divisible finite line, see 337n.

348. On Le Clerc and his doctrine of the divine immensity, see 177a n.

349. Berkeley was a keen controversialist; some sixteen objections are formally stated and answered in Princ. 34-84.

350. 350a. Berkeley distinguishes the status of Trinitarian dogma (see 310 and 584) from that of transubstantiation (cf. 720, Princ. 124); the former rests on implicit faith, the latter on the "excuse" -- the finiteness of our minds -- see 292n.

351-358. These entries are duplicated in the other notebook as follows:

    351 corresponds to 415
    352   "   416
    353   "   420

354 (355)	"	421
356	"	422
357	"	423
358	"	424

This is the only duplication of a series in the PC; whatever its reason, it seems to prove that notebook A was begun before notebook B was finished, and that for a time the two were filling together. Entries 351-356 have affinities with the essay Of Infinites, and possibly Berkeley transferred them into both notebooks from that manuscript.

351. The parallel, 415, puts it more clearly, viz., since the integer is supposed infinite, its infinitesimal part may be imagined big, as truly as little. On straining the imagination, see 321, Anal. 4. "intesimals," a slip for "infinitesimals."

352. Cf. 416. "There is in effect no such thing as parts infinitely small, or an infinite number of parts contained in any finite quantity" (Princ. 131).

353. Cf. 420. Some mathematicians held that a line might be infinitely divisible, and yet might not consist of an infinite number of points. Berkeley takes the commonsense view that a thing consists of those parts into which it can be divided, see 438.

354. 354a. 355. 356. Cf. 421 and 422. These two Lockian principles, no knowledge without ideas (IV i 1), and all significant words stand for ideas (III xi 8), are used in the essay Of Infinites. Berkeley here uses the former to prove that we cannot argue about infinitesimals; see 178n.,

312n. He subsequently abandoned both principles.

357. Cf. 423 and 610. On the will, see 131n.; for Berkeley's criticism of Locke's doctrine of uneasiness, see 145n.

358. Cf. 424. Berkeley was dissatisfied with the Cartesian problematical idealism -- see 265n. On Malebranche, see 230n.

Pierre Bayle (1647-1706), Professor at Rotterdam, pioneer of the French Enlightenment, author of the influential <u>Dictionnaire Historique et Critique</u> (1695-1697), a copy of which was sold at the auction of the Berkeleys' library [see R. I. Aaron, <u>Mind</u> XLI (N.S.), p. 465]. Berkeley names Bayle as an atheist in his <u>Theory of Vision Vindicated</u> 6, but probably several of the articles in the dictionary, especially those on Pyrrho and Zeno, influenced him when he was writing the <u>PC</u>. Entry 26, for instance, relates the infinite divisibility to external extension exactly as the <u>Zeno</u> article does.

Bayle was one of the few who attacked infinite divisibility, and he criticizes severely the principles of mathematics and the doctrine of infinitesimals. Dealing with geometrical problems, such as the ratio of the side to the diagonal of the square, and the equality of concentric circles (see 315n.), Bayle says that these do not prove the infinite divisibility, but only make it appear "that extension doth not exist anywhere but in our minds." In the <u>Zeno</u> and <u>Pyrrho</u> articles he anticipates Berkeley's assimilation of the primary and secondary qualities; he quotes from Malebranche's "Illustration" on bodies, which Berkeley knew well (and to which this entry probably refers) remarking, "I was obliged to prove that there are stronger objections than those of Malebranche" (<u>Zeno</u>).

359. Cf. "our senses...do not inform us that things exist without the mind," Princ. 18; "not to be Blam'd" -- ironical; perhaps Berkeley is thinking of the "blame" which Malebranche heaps on the senses.

360. Refers to the squaring of the circle (see 245n. and 511); a paraboloeid is one of "Those Curve lines that you can Rectify Geometrically"; a microscope would show that the equality of curve and straight line is only approximate; and since on his method of sensible points Berkeley can get a straight line equal to the circumference approximately, he claims that his squaring of the circle is "as good and exact as the best."

Curves are discussed also in 515-516, 519, 527, 575; for the attempt to equate right line with curve raises the questions of the nature of equality, of superposition, and of distance (TV 155), and supports Berkeley's view, he holds, that equality of lines consists in an equality of the number of sensible points. On the microscope, see 63n.

361. Against the argument that gravity is proportional to matter. Berkeley says that this argument is circular, indirectly in Princ. 103, directly in Dials. (Works II 241-242), and in his letter to Johnson of November 25, 1729 (Works II 279-280), and again, with great force, in Siris 319, "The modern demonstration of that tenet...a vain circle, concluding in truth no more than this -- that gravity is proportionable to weight, that is, to itself." The entry is repeated in 618. On attraction, see 403, 486. In Siris 231-254 Berkeley gives a full discussion of the metaphysical aspect of gravity, relating it to his philosophy of passive idea and active spirit, doing full justice to the greatness of Newton and the relative truth in the Newtonian theory, but remaining firm in

his early philosophy.

362. 362a. 363. 363a. A group dealing with extension, colour, and existence in the mind. The last three have the marginal letter P, which shows that Berkeley is considering his first argument, from the inseparability of the primary and secondary qualities (265n.), side by side with his second argument, the New Principle, a "demonstration" of which he is on the point of giving, viz., 378; on **Barrow, see** 75n.; on extension and colour, see notes on 18 and 85, Princ. 10, 73.

The question of colour and the mind promotes an important development in Berkeley's thought about the mind -- that contained in 362a. At first he was inclined, with Malebranche, to make colour a modification of the mind, and at that stage mind, for him, was more or less passive and identical with its contents; but in the latter part of the PC and in the Principles, as here, he takes mind for "the Active thing wch I call I, my self." In this sense mind is entirely distinct from colour and other objects, which exist in the mind by way of idea only, and not by way of mode (Princ. 49), and therefore could be spoken of, as here, as without the mind in regard to origin.

The reference to the understanding, which except for this verso entry is not mentioned in notebook B, marks the entry as transitional. The understanding is studied closely in the latter part of notebook A. Distinguished from the mind in the entry, the understanding is joined to the will and identified with the mind in 713. One with its ideas and therefore passive in 587, 614, 681, it becomes an aspect of the active spirit in 848, 854, and is distinguished from its objects. It is mentioned in a general way in 544, 579, 656, 665, and in connection with error in 816. But Berkeley studied it chiefly in connection with the will. At first understanding and will differ toto coelo, 643; they are distinct, 681, 708; they are united, 614a, 713, 812 (in God), 841-842, 848, cf. 820-821; they are identical, 854; and, finally, 871, they are nothing at all, because they are abstract ideas. These changes are not so violent and arbitrary as they appear at first sight; they are for the most part changes of terminology, consequent on the rise to prominence in Berkeley's mind of the sharp contrast between active and passive, and the passing of his early panpsychism into the dualism of the Principles, with its ultimate distinction between spirit and idea.

364-376. These entries occupy a pair of pages facing each other; Johnston assumes that Berkeley wrote one or two entries on the verso page and then one or two on the page opposite, and he numbers accordingly; but 365 with its important verso comment 365a (the two are connected by asterisks) proves that Berkeley followed his usual custom of filling the recto and leaving the verso blank for subsequent comments, and that later he found that he needed the verso space for a continuation of his attack on mathematicians. I have numbered accordingly.

364. This is one of the "amusing geometrical paradoxes" (Princ. 123) which follow from the infinite divisibility (see 11n.); on Keill, see 308n.; the reference is to his Introductio, p. 47ff.

365. 365a. Berkeley's earlier and later accounts of extension (see 18n.); the two are not necessarily inconsistent; for he believed in visible and tangible extension, composed of visible and tangible points, even after he had rejected abstract extension. On length without breadth, see 21n.; on minimal points, see 59n.; on abstraction, see 318n.

366. Probably a reference to the Barrovian case (<u>TV</u> 29ff.) in which, Berkeley argues, geometrical explanations of vision break down; on focal length, see <u>TV</u> 40; on glasses, see 63n.

367. George Cheyne, F.R.S. (1671-1743), a learned London doctor, wrote <u>Fluxionum Methodus Inversa</u> (1703) and <u>Philosophical Principles of Natural Religion</u> (1705). Berkeley refers to the former work in 459 and in his essay <u>Of Infinites</u>. Cheyne lays much stress on the infinite divisibility, and in the physiological part of the latter work he repeatedly mentions "vessels" -- apparently a general term for veins, arteries, etc. -- e.g., lacteal vessels, lymphatic vessels, capillary vessels, blood vessels. I suggest therefore that this puzzling little entry is meant as a <u>reductio ad absurdum</u> of infinite divisibility; Berkeley is arguing, half in jest, that if there are material vessels, there must be an infinite number of them in the human body.

The entry is duplicated in 387; the duplication, whatever its reason, helps to refute Johnston's pointless transposition of these concluding pages of notebook B to the end of notebook A; for by so doing he is compelled to number these duplicates 388 and 931, thus separating by half the length of the <u>PC</u> two entries which in the MS. are only two pages apart.

368. 370. 371. 372. 373. 374. 375. 376. A series of rather irresponsible remarks about mathematicians; with these connect 381-386 and 392-395. One naturally asks why Berkeley, a trained student of mathematics, whose first publication was a work on mathematics, who speaks in the Preface of that work of "<u>suavissimum matheseos studium</u>," came to speak of mathematicians in these unflattering terms. The answer is that the mathematicians he read, Barrow, Keill, Hayes, Cheyne,

Raphson, and Newton, were more or less identified with one or other of certain tenets to which he strongly objected -- materialism, extensionism, abstract ideas, infinite divisibility, and irreligion. In addition Berkeley thought that mathematics was showing a bias against sense and common sense, wasting time on trifles, encouraging paradoxes, and supporting perverse explanations of vision ("What a noble piece of geometry is manifested in the fabrick of the eye, and the manner of vision!" Cheyne, Philos. Princ. of Natural Religion, p. 260).

Nor was Berkeley singular in holding such views. Bayle (Zeno) attacks mathematicians, and Le Clerc's review (Bibliothèque Choisie, vol. 22, p. 88) of Berkeley's Theory of Vision speaks in approval of its attack on mathematics. On nihilarians, see 337n.; on the geometry of indivisibles, see 346n.; on truth and certainty, see notes on 163 and 554, and Locke IV vi.

"Praeclarum ingeninum non potest esse magnus mathematicus" -- Scaligerana (Cologne, 1695), p. 95. Joseph Scaliger (1540-1609), French scholar and chronologist, son of Julius Caesar Scaliger, is speaking in the context of Christopher Clavius, a Jesuit geometrician. Clavius was employed by Gregory XIII on the reformation of the Calendar. Scaliger's chief works were De Emendatione Temporum (1583) and Thesaurus Temporum (1606). In his edition of Manilus' Astronomicon (1579) he rails frequently against the ignorance and presumption of contemporary mathematicians with regard to ancient astronomy and chronology. "Sir Isaac," cf. 316n. and 383.

369. For Berkeley's technical use of "thing" and "idea," see 644, 685, 689, 757, 807-808, 872. There are, for him, two entirely distinct types of being, thinking things and things thought; he usually calls them spirits and ideas (Princ. 89).

He has three chief concerns about this technique. (1) He must justify his use of "idea" in place of "thing" for the object of sense. His reasons are that "thing" is too wide (see 644, <u>Princ</u>. 39), that "idea" is in vogue, that "idea" preserves the thing's relation to mind, and safeguards immediacy and the distinction between active subject and passive object. (2) To insist that spirits are not ideas and cannot be represented by ideas, see 490n., 808. (3) To oppose representationism; if "thing" be used of the object of sense, it is to be used of the object itself, and not of a supposed external archetype thereof. See 115n., 689.

377. 378. 378a. 379. 380. The "demonstration" of the Principle, forecast in 363, and the doctrinal climax of notebook B. It consists of nineteen connected propositions, formally stated and numbered by Berkeley; these with the summary (379, 380) occupy two folios (recto) of the manuscript, the verso being left blank except for 377, an abbreviated statement of the Principle, which heads the first verso, and for 378a just beneath it, a note on the use to be made of the demonstration.

The nineteen propositions fall into three groups, 1-9, 10-15, 16-19, which I will call A, B, and C, respectively. A proves that no idea is in matter; B and C prove in two ways that nothing like an idea is in matter.

A (1-9) proceeds as follows; all words signify ideas, and all knowledge is about ideas; ideas from without are sensations; ideas from within are thoughts; neither sensations nor thoughts are in matter; therefore no idea is in matter. This argument corresponds in outline to that of <u>Princ</u>. 1-7; the first two propositions, however, represent positions abandoned by Berkeley before he published the <u>Principles</u>; on the first (all words stand for ideas), see 178n. and 356n.; on the second (all knowledge is about ideas), see Princ. 135ff., where knowledge without ideas (except "in a large sense") is asserted with regard to spirits, cf. 312n.

B (10-15) argues that whatever has ideas must perceive them, perception being passive reception of ideas; that ideas are either simple or compounded of simple ideas; that if there is to be resemblance between two complex ideas, they must have a simple idea of the same sort in common (cf. 484, 496). Therefore, there is nothing like an idea in matter.

C (16-19) argues that likeness involves comparison, that comparison is viewing two ideas together, and that the mind can compare only its own ideas. Therefore, there is nothing like an idea in matter.

The common conclusion of B and C and the nerve of the argument of C appear in Princ. 8, and form a standing part of Berkeley's argument for immaterialism; the involved argument of B, based on Locke's doctrine of simple ideas (see 53n.), has disappeared.

Combining the two conclusions, of A, and of B and C, we have the full formulation of the Principle, as given in 379, viz., neither our ideas nor anything like them can possible be in an unperceiving thing, i.e., in matter. On demonstration, see 163n.; on comparison and likeness, see 464n.; on arguments a priori and a posteriori, see Princ. 21.

381. 382. 383. 383a. 384. 385. 386. Further attacks on mathematicians, see 368n.; on the definition of angle, see 432n.; on the angle of contact, see 168n.; on infinite divisibility, see 11n. "The Algebra of pure intelligences" must mean, I think, the sense symbolism which yields that enlarged capacity of the mind which pure spirits are supposed to possess; cf. TV 153. Sir Kenelme Digby speaks of one real

moment giving happiness "multiplied beyond the Arthmetick of intelligences" (Man's Soul, 1657, p. 142). Algebra, extravagantly praised in the De Ludo Algebraico, is spoken of in more sober terms in the PC, see 697, 758, 767, 770, 880, and is not discussed in the Principles. "Newton's propositions," cf. 374. On Barrow, see 75n.; in his Lect. Math. I, he writes "from this assertion of the composition out of indivisibles the whole of geometry is altogether subverted and destroyed;" but his argument is ad hominem and ironical; for he adds, "The poles of the world will sooner be removed out of their place, and the fabric of nature destroyed, than the foundations of geometry fail." On geometry, see 117n.; on "the nothings," see 337n.; on Berkeley's claim to simplify mathematics, see 329n.

387. Duplicate of 367, where see note.

388. Newton (Optics I p. 90) says, "the rays to speak properly are not coloured. In them there is nothing else than a certain power and disposition to stir up a sensation of this or that colour." I have not found the statement which Berkeley here attributes to him.

Malebranche (see 230n.) discusses the materia subtilis of Descartes' vortex theory in VI ii 4; see also his Discourse upon Light and Colours (Taylor's tr. 2nd ed., 1700), where he says that light and colours consist in the vibrations of pressure produced by the subtle matter on the retina.

389. Jacques de Billy (1602-1679), French mathematician; his chief work was Nova Geometriae Clavis Algebra (1643). The only other mathematician of the name mentioned in the Nouvelle Biographie is Erar Billy (or Bile) (1610-c. 1645),

professor of theology and mathematics at Caen.

There is nothing to show whether $\frac{1}{m}$ is an infinitely great or infinitely small quantity. If the stress falls on the "visible," then the symbol probably means something infinitely small, and therefore imperceptible; but if the stress falls on the "finite," the symbol means something infinitely great, which the Billys represent by a finite visible line, thereby sliding into the belief in infinite divisibility (see Princ. 127).

390. According to Baronius, Marsilius Ficinus (1433-1499) and Michel Mercatius, Italian Platonists, agreed that whichever died first would appear to the other and confirm belief in the future life. One day when Mercatius was engaged in philosophical mediation he heard a galloping horse, and saw a white phantom in broad daylight; then he heard the voice of Ficinus saying, "Michel, Michel, it is true." He sent for news of Ficinus, and learned that he had just died. On Ficinus, see Siris 206ff.

Berkeley finds the story credible because on his account of time (see 4n.) the series of ideas is time, and therefore a soul who willed to appear a friend the moment after death could do so; see his remarks on death and the resurrection which "follows the next mement to death" in his first and second letters to Johnson (Works II 282, 293). The same motif probably underlies the question about the thief and paradise; see 127n.

391. Reviewing the results of his philosophy. Berkeley repeatedly urges that immaterialism simplifies the tasks of speculation and of the sciences without the loss of any reality (cf. 518). Princ. 35 does not contain the references to mathematicians, but otherwise it corresponds closely to

this entry. "insensible sensations," e.g., lines without breadth, extensions without colour; on extended deity, see 107n.; on the reality of the body, see 52n.

392. 393. 394. 395. Another group of remarks on mathematicians (see 368n.). The "we Irishmen," three (four, including 398) times repeated, is striking, but we need not read a political reference into the words. Berkeley certainly always regarded himself as an Irishman, and Newton was, to him, "a philosopher of a neighbouring nation" (<u>Princ</u>. 110, 1st ed.); but when he writes "we Irishmen," he simply means "we ordinary folk, shrewd judges of fact and commonsense"; the words are not voicing aggressive nationalism, but appealing to fact against fanciful speculations. If an Englishman wrote in a similar diary "we Englishmen," his words would simply mean "the man in the street," and that is all, I think, that Berkeley meant. On the wall and the fire, see 19n.; on squaring the circle, see 245n.; on infinite divisibility, see 11n.; on the mathematical point as "nothing," see 337n.

396. 397. 398. A group of entries of biographical interest, wrongly interpreted by commentators, and made into a reason for abandoning the MS. order of this part of the <u>PC</u>.

First, who is "P"? and what is "ye treatise"? P is the Earl of Pembroke who was Lord Lieutenant of Ireland from April 1707 to November 1708. Fraser and Hecht agree in this identification; the conclusive reason for it [see my article in <u>Hermanthena</u>, Vol. XXI (1931) p. 161n.] is that "ye treatise" is not one of Berkeley's books, as commentators have assumed, but is Locke's <u>Essay</u>, which is dedicated to Pembroke, the dedication opening with the words, "This treatise which is grown up under your Lordship's eye."

Berkeley is expressing gratitude to Pembroke for his patronage of Locke's Essay, and for an approving word, spoken no doubt at some College meeting, of his own "harangue," perhaps his essay on the Cave of Dunmore, or his Of Infinites. Berkeley was subsequently to dedicate his own Principles to Pembroke, but that treatise could not possibly be said to have grown up under Pembroke's eye (even if any considerable portion of it were written while Pembroke was in Ireland, which is extremely unlikely), for Pembroke was the first man in Ireland, the King's representative, and Berkeley was a very junior Junior Fellow, "an obscure person, who has not the honour to be known to your Lordship" (Princ. Dedication).

Johnston and Rossi explain "P" as Sir John Percival, afterwards Earl of Egmont, Berkeley's friend and correspondent, to whom the Theory of Vision is dedicated; but that Dedication speaks of "these few months that I have the honour to be known unto you." Those words published in 1709 would be quite inconsistent with "that grew up under his Eye"; besides, it is almost certain that the greater part of the PC was written before Berkeley met Percival. Percival, a young Oxford graduate, came over to the south of Ireland in May 1708 (Rand, p. 3); I found evidence in the Egmont Papers (Hist. MSS. Commission) that he was in Dublin on November 19 of that year, but he was not there much earlier, and this entry must have been written about the early spring of 1708, if my dating of the manuscript is correct, and if the manuscript order of the entries was approximately the order of writing.

Johnston and Hecht reject the manuscript order here; they transpose these entries and those that go with them, viz., in all 378-399, the contents of the last eight pages of notebook B, to the end of the whole work, and print their texts accordingly; they have to suppose that Berkeley left these eight pages blank at first, went ahead and filled notebook A, and then, weeks or months later, came back and filled these eight pages. Their argument is very largely conjectural and cannot stand against the positive evidence that these pages were filled, approximately at any rate, in the manuscript order. Here I will only deal with the one point which at first sight gives a certain plausibility to this conjectural transposition, viz., that these pages look like a <u>finale</u> to the whole work, that in 396-398 Berkeley is clearly contemplating publishing a work of his own, and must therefore be presumed to have already done all the preliminary work of the whole <u>PC</u>.

I reply that these entries do not prove that Berkeley was on the eve of publication when he wrote them; they do not prove that he was contemplating immediate publication. He was certainly letting his mind go ahead to the day when his work would see the light; but even the "I publish not this..." (398) may merely be a literary experiment in writing a preface, and the words look like an echo of Locke's Epistle to the Reader, "I pretend not to publish this Essay...." But, granting for the sake of argument that publication was imminent when these entries were made, do we know that the publication was the publication of the <u>Principles</u>? The answer is, "No." The book-to-be might equally well have been the <u>Theory of Vision</u> (Johnston on his identifcation of "P" with Percival ought to make it so), or some third work drafted, but never published (see 224n.). Johnston thinks that the phrase "ye treatise" points to the <u>Principles</u>, the <u>Theory of Vision</u> being an "Essay"; but there is nothing in that argument; for, as I have shown above, the treatise in question is Locke's and not Berkeley's. There is, therefore, no ground whatever for taking the entries 396-398 as the _finale_ of the whole PC, and of course the humdrum 399, which concludes that page and notebook B, is a pretty strong indication that no _finale_ was in view.

399. "Nihilarians," i.e., the mathematicians whose point was a "nothing" (see 337n.). Up to the present Berkeley has been hitting out at both materialism and mathematics, but now perhaps he begins to think it imprudent to provoke too many adversaries at once. Certainly by the time he penned 633 he has modified his tone, and while he is still determined to oppose the infinite divisibility and the mathematicians who held it, he will do so "wth the utmost civility & respect. not to stile them Nihilarians, &c."

Folio 3. The index of marginal letters. This index on the opening page of notebook A is in Berkeley's handwriting; the page also contains his initials, "G: B: Coll: Trin: Dub: alum:" and his son's name (probably signature) "George Berkeley A.B. ex Aede Xti."

The dividing line appears to indicate the distinction between the topics of _Principles_, Part I, and those of the other projected part or parts.

The whole index was in a sense an afterthought -- hence its position in the manuscript. When Berkeley began to fill notebook B, he could not have known that there would be a notebook A. Not knowing whither the argument would lead, he could not have foreseen the need for a second notebook and an index.

The notebooks are one twofold work, hinging on the New Principle. All the subjects indexed, _with one important exception_, appear in both notebooks, and the two central subjects, viz., matter and the primary and secondary qualities, are distributed evenly between them. The one exception is E for Existence. There are twenty nine entries, marked E, in notebook A, and none at all in notebook B. This is a key fact, which throws a flood of light on Berkeley's original enterprise and on Berkeleian interpretation today. When he began notebook B, Berkeley took existence for granted, as most of us do. When he was two-thirds of the way through it, he was brought hard up against "the nature & meaning & import of Existence" (PC 491). His discovery of the New Principle followed. The New Principle was a new principle of existence, which supplied a new basis for his immaterialism and the master motive of his doctrinal revision of 1708-1709. Notebook B virtually closes with a "demonstration" of that principle, and though the demonstration was more or less dropped, the principle itself continued to exert a decisive influence on the development of Berkeley's thought.

Turn now to some details in the index and the apparatus indexed. First, when did Berkeley insert the marginal letters and signs? The margins were clearly left ready for them ab initio; but my guess is that Berkeley took his time about filling them, and had no settled practice. In a few cases the blots show that the marginal signs and letters were inserted along with the entries; but for the most part the indications are the other way. Generally the entries were written first and the marginal signs and letters later, sometimes (I think) weeks or months later. Some letters and signs were provisional and temporary. We can see that Berkeley changed some of them, as he worked; and their meanings were by no means hard and fast. The meaning of the plus sign was particularly fluid (see below).

The index is clear, so far as it goes; but Berkeley has

not explained S̶ (S erased), nor the arithmetical symbols, X and +. There are forty two entries in notebook B marked S. Doctrinally they are an important group. They range from no. 18 to no. 325, and there they stop abruptly; there are none in notebook A. They do not fall naturally under the S of the index, which means Soul or Spirit. A large majority of them mention extension or deal with it. Accordingly in the table in my diplomatic edition I **suggested** "? Space" as the meaning of the erased S, assuming **that Berkeley** troubled to **make** these forty two erasures, because the second notebook was not in prospect, and in it he wished to use the letter S with a new meaning, viz., Soul or Spirit. I still think that is a reasonable hypothesis; but be it right or wrong, nothing of importance turns on it today, so far as I can see.

As regards the arithmetical symbols, they may have formed the first beginnings of a system in notebook B, which Berkeley later merged with the letter system, and did not trouble to explain.

From the margins of 676 and 853 we can see that <u>at that time</u> Berkeley was using X to signify mathematics in general as one of the three branches of higher learning, coordinate with moral philosophy and natural philosophy. Quite arbitrarily, it would seem, Berkeley also used X in combination with the numbers 1, 2, 3, and 3a (usually set in one of the angles) to signify the original parts of his <u>Essay on Vision</u>. X with 1 refers to distance, with 2 to mangitude, with 3 to the heterogeneity of sight and touch, and with 3a to the problem of the inverted retinal image. This usage is quite certain. It extends from the first page of notebook B to the last page but one of notebook A, and how to square it with the use of the X to signify mathematics I do **not see**. It is hard to think of the theory of vision as a branch of mathematics. I should add that entry 869 combines X with 1, 2, and 3, and is actually represented in all three divisions of the Essay on Vision (sections 49, 54, and 144). This fact illustrates the closeness of the connection between the notebooks and the publications, and has a bearing on the question of the dates. There is room for a further study of this sign (X).

The plus sign (+) is an attractive theme, but presents many difficulties. It was extremely useful to Berkeley, and it can be useful to us, provided we do not seek to credit it with one cut and dried meaning. It was in effect a negative sign, and its general purpose can be gathered from its distribution in the notebooks. "There are nine on the first page, and none at all on the last twenty-four pages. There are one hundred and twenty-three, or so, in notebook B, and only some sixty-five in notebook A, and practically all those in A come in the first half. After no. 664 there are only two, and one of the two (no. 741) is non-doctrinal, and after no. 741 there are none at all. At the start of the work there was much to check and re-check, much to alter and re-shape, much to hold in suspence, much to disapprove and re-appraise, much to reject. For all such cases the plus sign was needed; but as the weeks slipped by the notebooks filled, the need for the plus sign grew less and less; mistakes were ironed out; faults were corrected, doubts resolved, and finality asymptotically achieved [A. A. Luce, "Another Look at Berkeley's Notebooks," Hermathena, CX (1970), 5-23].

The above facts about the distribution of the sign are a clear indication of its meaning, or rather its meanings. It meant doubt, hesitation, indecision, suspense of judgement, further study, often followed by decision and final rejection. It was an elastic negative sign in the nature of a star or query. Clearly, if it is to be of any use to us today, it must be studied with patience, and interpreted with sympathy, knowledge, and understanding of the author's position.

Some fourteen entries have no marginal letter or sign. Of these nos. 113, 266, 560, 634, 715, and 789 are personal or trivial (but interesting); nos. 537 and 642 are on the meaning of words; nos. 620 and 751 give rules for writing; no. 811 is on Locke and the Cartesians; and no. 406 simply lets off steam.

The following table shows the distribution of letters and signs between the two notebooks:[1]

	Letter or Sign	Notebook B	Notebook A
I	Introduction	3	55
Ɨ	Introduction	1	26
M	Matter	59	67
P	Primary and Secondary Qualities	19	19
E	Existence	0	29
T	Time	10	3
S	Soul -- Spirit	16	121
Ꞩ	? Space ?	42	0
G	God	5	15
Mo	Moral Philosophy	5	43
N	Natural Philosophy	8	26
X		207	116
+		127	64

---

[1]. Editor's note: The tabulation in the chart is slightly different from Luce's of his 1944 edition due to different readings of the marginal signs and different principles of counting, e.g., counting <u>all</u> the marginal signs even where there are two of the same before the same entry ("X" and "✶").

-233-

400. The distinction (suggested perhaps in 208) between two kinds of visible extension, vague expansion and clearly defined space, is first drawn in 283-284; the latter kind may be the object of geometry (443), and, containing the idea of succession, is "of Mathematical Consideration" (460). In TV 145 the movements of head and eye, involved in the successive direction of the optic axis, are mentioned as helping to confuse visible and tangible extension.

401. "No general Ideas" subsequently became "no abstract ideas," see 318n.; Berkeley's criticism of the abstractions of mathematics, lines without breadth, infinitely divisible points etc. culminated in his attack on Locke's typical abstract idea, his absurd trangle (IV vii 9) "neither oblique nor rectangle, neither equilateral, equicrural, nor scalenon; but all and none of these at once"; see 687 and Princ. Introd. 13. On "ye Introduction," see 212n.

402. Note the juxtaposition of Berkeley's three main principles at the start of the new notebook, "No general Ideas" in the previous entry, "The Principle," i.e., the esse est percipi (see 285 n.) in this, and spiritual causation in the next.

Bayle (Rodon) says that the divine preservation or conservation, taken as continual creation, was a doctrine very common among Spanish and Irish Schoolmen, who taught that creatures, not having in themselves the cause of their existence, continue to exist only by the co-operation of God's will, which, having created, does not cease to create. This doctrine is Augustinian, and was reaffirmed by Descartes. Berkeley speaks of it sympathetically in Princ. 46, but does not endorse it. At any earlier stage he had held, I think, that the objects of our senses pass into nothingness when we are not sensing them; but later he altered his opinion, and decided (Princ. 48) that it does not follow from his principles "that bodies are annihilated and created every moment, or exist not at all during the intervals between our perception of them."

403. Physical causes, as coexisting ideas, are identified with occasions in 754. Berkeley's doctrine of cause, derived mainly from that of Malebranche, appears to have been fixed before he began the PC; it is not much discussed here, but the main tenets, developed in Princ. 25-26, 64, are that (1) God is the cause of all natural things, (2) there are no unthinking second causes, (3) an idea, being passive, cannot be a true cause, but may be called the cause of another idea, being related to it as a sign to thing signfied. These tenets or the makings of them may be found in the entries 433, 461, 485, 499, 780, 831, 850, 855-856. The ordinary usage of the term "cause" is conceded in 504, 562, 783, and reference is made to Spinoza's cause in 827, 831. On attraction, see 361n.; coexistence, for Berkeley, designates the field of natural philosophy -- see 164, 677, 754, 853; he does not mean by it the simultaneous, but the continuous, and he usually thinks of it as a succession, e.g., Princ. 26.

404. 405. On scripture, see 281n.; we are not to gather that Berkeley seriously doubted the Copernican theory; he speaks as if he accepted it in Princ. 51, Dials., Works II 238; he is in a general way appealing, as he often does, to commonsense against "learned dust," see 285n., 552, 703, 772, 867, Princ. 34, 51, Introd. 10. For his philosophy as truth "shared between the vulgar and the philosophers," see Dials., Works II 262. The term "mob," derived from mobile

-235-

vulgus, had been vigorously attacked by Swift: "I have done my utmost for some years past to stop the progress of "Mobb" and "Banter," but have been plainly borne down by numbers" (<u>Tatler</u>, No. 230); it was only a recent acquisition, coming into vogue soon after the Restoration.

406. Berkeley is taking the measure of the support and opposition he expects; for the reception accorded to the <u>Principles</u> in London, see <u>Rand</u>, p. 80, "A physician...argued you must needs be mad....A Bishop pitied you." "Hypothetical Gentlemen," i.e., those who substitute hypotheses for experiment, cf. "speculative gentlemen," <u>Draft</u> <u>Introd</u>. (<u>Works</u> II 132). "Experimental Philosophers," i.e., physicists, cf. 498. Newton in his <u>Optics</u> makes the same contrast, "My design in this book is not to explain the properties of light by hypotheses, but to propose and prove them by reason and experiments."

407. Probably read "Principle" for "Principles" (Fraser and Johnston); on Berkeley's Principle, see 285n.; by Newton's Principle is meant his law of gravitation, which, Berkeley repeatedly argues, is a <u>petitio</u> <u>principii</u>; see 361n.; on demonstration, see 163n.

408. The first entry with the marginal letter E (existence); that existence means either to perceive or to be perceived is Berkeley's New Principle, discovered apparently in the course of the studies represented in notebook B, and used as the starting-point of notebook A (see note on fol. 3). Existence is not a simple idea (see 53n.), again in 670-671, but an abstract idea, coined by the Schools, 552, 725, 772, 811; existence is not conceivable without perception, 429, 597, 646, <u>Princ</u>. 3; but the term need not be restricted to

sense-perception, 472-473; Berkeley does not take away existence, but declares the meaning of the term, 593; he begs his readers to examine for themselves the meaning of the term, 491, 604.

The new view of existence at once brings under discussion the nature of the perceivable and the reality of body, on which see 52n.

409. Schoolmen compared with mathematicians, cf. 327n.

410. "Intellectual beings," i.e., intelligences, unbodied spirits, beings higher than man, lower than God, cf. 663, 723, TV 153, Princ. 81, Locke IV iii 6, 17, 27; on the Principle, see 285n.

411. An expansion of 304, developed in Princ. 92-96 and Introd. 1. On scepticism, see 79n. Idolatry is traced to materialism also in 17, where see note.

412. 413. Berkeley is apparently examining the Hebrew and the Greek verbs "to be" for light on the meaning of existence. היה "to be," is by some grammarians connected with חיה, "to live"; hence vixit. Johnston and Hecht both explain היה as Jehovah; this is a mistake in grammar and in interpretation; for the sacred tetragrammaton is יהוה, and Berkeley is very far from identifying God with existence; besides, if he had had Deity in mind in these entries, he would have marked them G, not E. On substance, see 80n.

414. For Berkeley's claim to have simplified mathematics, see 329n.

415-424. This series duplicates 351-358, where see general and particular notes. If the figures 1754 1755 1755 at the head of folio 7 are dates, presumably they were added after Berkeley's death, which occurred in 1753.

417. 418. 419. These are not contained in the other series, but being on infinites they arise out of the context; they contain several echoes of Berkeley's essay, Of Infinites, e.g., "quovis dato [not lato] majus," and "quavis data minor"; he argues that a line or figure imagined, like one seen, or assigned, or given, is necessarily finite, and therefore is not to be treated as infinite; on the imagination, see 531n.; on infinite space, see 135n.

424a. This entry, the verso comment on 424, is not represented in the other series; Berkeley distinguishes his views on the reality of body from the Cartesian idealism, see 52n. and 265n.

425. 426. Eculid is no more infallible than Aristotle; his abstract lines, for instance, suppose existence without the mind (117) and give rise to sophisms (see 259n.); on demonstration, see 163n.

427. 427a. Asserting direct perception; we see the horse itself, not a mental copy of it, as representationists allege. The words "& nothing more" are not said in depreciation of "idea," but in denial of matter; i.e., what we sense is the object, the only object, and there is nothing more to it, such as matter. The verso puts the same thing in other words, stressing the immediacy of the object, which on that very account Berkeley names "idea," see Princ. 38.

428. On the benefit to geometry, see 207n.

429. 429a. The first appearance of the Latin form of the Principle, see <u>Princ</u>. 3. Note the verso addition "or velle i.e. agere" which, though it adds nothing essential to "percipere," is meant to underline the active side of percipience. <u>Percipere</u> and <u>percipi</u> are, respectively, Berkeley's two "heterogeneous" heads of reality, active spirit and passive idea. The horse in the stable and the books in the study are his stock examples of the unperceived perceivable, see 52n., 472. On existence, see 408n.

430. 431. Gravitation, the tides, and crystallization are among the physical phenomena in which Berkeley finds confirmation of his doctrine; see <u>Princ</u>. 101ff. "Hyps" is no doubt, the plural of "Hyp," an old abbreviation of "hypochondria"; see Oxf. Eng. Dict., and cf. "Heav'n send thou hast not got the hyps" (Swift). Hecht translates <u>Trübsinn</u>, i.e., melancholy. Depression, moods, "blues," etc. are still regarded as "unaccountable things"; they come and go suddenly, and they are psychological in character as well as physiological. How do they "confirm" Berkeley's doctrine? Is it because they appear to negate mechanical causation (cf. 435)? Or is it because, like dreams, they emphasize the subjective aspect of experience? The latter explanation has the merit of taking "my Doctrine" in the more pointed way for Berkeley's personal and peculiar doctrine.

432. Ignatius Gaston Pardies (1636-1673), French geometrician, author of <u>Eléments de Géométrie et de Trigonometrie</u> (Paris, 1671); the English translation by John Harris, F.R.S., went through several editions. It defines angle as follows: "When

two lines meet in a point, the Aperture, Distance, or Inclination between them is called an angle"; cf. 381.

433. Sensible things, for Berkeley, are collections of ideas; ideas are passive, and have no caual power. God (see 107n.) is therefore the one true cause of natural events (see 403n.); on powers, see 41n.

434. Astronomy is not mentioned elsewhere in the PC; for "usefull & practical Mathematiques," see 471, 509, Princ. 131.

435. Malebranche deals with memory in II i 5, and rests his explanation on traces in the brain. Locke barely mentions the brain in his vivid account of memory (II x). Berkeley has a short passage on traces in the brain in Dials., Works II 208-209, where he shows that the trace theory has to presuppose "that primary idea or brain itself" which "being a sensible thing exists only in the mind."

436. On this difficulty about creation, see 60n.

437. 437a. The two kinds of reality again (see 429n.), spirit and ideas, active and passive. Contrast Berkeley's earlier view, "Nothing properly but persons i.e., conscious things do exist" (24), and note the verso addition, which is needed because in the early part of the PC he makes thought passive, see 228n.

438. 439. 440. 441. 442. A further discussion of sensible minima (see 59n.) versus insensible or mathematical points, "nothings" as he pleasantly calls them (see 337n.). He may have had in mind Locke's grain of wheat, divided and subdivided

"till the parts become insensible" (II viii 9). Berkeley presses his argument both ways; sensible things cannot be made up of matter, and matter cannot be made up of sensible things; abstract extension is an abstract idea (see 318n.), i.e., nothing; and the process we call "abstracting" is simply a considering a particular sensible length, or number of points, apart from its sort, i.e., in its representative capacity, cf. Princ. Introd. 10.

At this period Berkeley was, no doubt, writing or rewriting the Theory of Vision, and here he reminds himself not to speak of the minimum sensibile (m.s.) until he has made clear the distinction between visibile (m.v.) and tangibile (m.t.), see 28n. He speaks of minima in TV 54, 80-83, but says comparatively little about them, considering the amount of attention he devotes to them in the PC. The note on the verso, "this belongs to Geometry," probably refers the entry to the section dealing with the object of geometry (TV 149ff.). The curious question as to the colour of a minimum (cf. the question, recently asked, Has an electron a colour?) must be answered in the affirmative; for the m.v. is, by definition, "a proper and immediate object of sight," see 489, TV 81. On extension, see 18n.

443. On the two sorts of visible extension and the optic axis, see 400n.

444. For Malebranche a pain in the finger is a modification of the soul which men erroneously, by both a natural and a voluntary judgement (Bk. I xiv), locate in the finger. Berkeley rejects this separation; for him finger and its pain go together; for both are in the mind; not that either

or both of them are mental, or mental copies of material things, but they are what we see and feel them to be; there is no finger other than the finger we see and touch; there is no pain other than the pain felt; therefore the pain felt must be in the finger which, as perceived, is in my mind.

445. 446. Berkeley considers the term "consist of" in the light of the esse est percipi. What is the meaning of saying a line consists of points? I can think of the line without ever thinking of its points; therefore, on Berkeley's theory, there should be no points in it. "No," replies Berkeley; that interpretation of the Principle ignores the perceivable (see 52n.); for figures, points, etc., which I may perceive in the circle "are actually in it, i.e., are perceivable in it"; see 86n.

447. Explained by TV 112, where we are told that things can be compared in respect of distance only if they exist after the same manner; we can compare the distance between two visible points, or that between two tangible points, but not that between a visible point and a tangible point. "intermediate ideas" is apparently not used technically here, as it is in 697-698, 729. Locke IV xii 14.

448. 448a. Edmund Halley (1656-1742), F.R.S., Astronomer Royal, Savilian Professor of Geometry at Oxford. Halley is said to be the "infidel mathematician" to whom the Analyst is addressed; but see Rigaud, Defence of Halley against the charge of Religious Infidelity (1844). Query 1 at the end of the Analyst asks, Whether the object of geometry be not the proportions of assignable extensions? And whether there be any need of considering quantities either infinitely great

or infintely small? See also other queries *ibid*.

The erasure and the verso comment thereon are proofs of the care Berkeley bestowed on the PC; it was much more to him than a collection of casual jottings; for here, as often elsewhere, he takes the trouble to correct an entry, and even to correct his correction. He made the erasure, I presume, because the words might suggest that his ideas of sense were copies of reality; he was afraid of the term "idea of," see 115n., 660.

449. For the passages in which the comparison between Schoolmen and mathematicians is developed, see 327n.; "nothing at all," apparently a reference to his attack on the mathematical point as a "nothing," see 337n. "Mean" (Fraser and Johnston) is not in the text.

450. 450a. 451. Motion is among the simple ideas (see 53n.) in which Locke hoped to find the bases of knowledge; he says little, however, about its simplicity. Berkeley queried its simplicity; motion is definable and therefore complex (Query 14, MS. fol. 102); it includes succession, 167; it is not perceived at once, 184. His second thoughts here restore it to the category of simple ideas; his third thoughts, on the verso, in effect destroy the catagory; for he refuses to abstract motion from the thing moved, and virtually says that the simple idea of motion is an abstract idea.

Locke discusses scholastic definitions of motion in III iv 8, 9; he offers no formal definition of his own, but he writes, "motion being nothing but change of distance between any two things" (II xiii 14).

Newton (*Principia*, Schol. ad def. viii) says, "*tempus, spatium, locum et motum ut omnibus notissima non definio*";

but a little later he writes, "<u>Motus absolutus est translatio corporis de loco absoluto in locum absolutum, relativus de relativo in relativum</u>." Berkeley mentions Newton's two sorts of motion in 30, and discusses them in <u>Princ</u>. 111ff.

452. From the <u>Principia</u>, p. 7; Newton is speaking of pure or absolute space, arguing that its parts are immovable, cf. <u>Locke</u> II xiii 13, 14. Berkeley refers to the immovability of Newtonian space in <u>Princ</u>. 111; he rejects pure space and absolute space. His apparently inconsequential remark about number means, I think, that the only sense in which the parts of space are immovable is that the number of sensible points in a given line or area remains constant through all local changes.

453. Descartes' theory of vortices and globules is discussed by Locke, III iv 10, IV ii 11, 12, and by Malebranche in <u>Recherche</u>, VI ii 4, and in <u>Treatise concerning Light and Colours</u>. Berkeley is apparently debating his question (see 442n.) whether visible <u>minima</u> are coloured. Newton certainly speaks of rays of light as coloured, but when he does so, he says, he is speaking popularly; he holds that in the rays colours are nothing but a disposition to propagate this or that motion to the <u>sensorium</u> (<u>Optics</u>, Bk. I, p. 90).

454. The marginal sign suggests that Berkeley is considering judgements of distance; the man born blind (see 27n.), who, not having seen colour, could imagine only a space of touch (see 28n.) is, for him, proof that our ordinary judgements of distance by vision are not primitive, and do not assure us of the existence of external space (see 18n.).

455. 456. In both these entries, as in 451 and 452, Berkeley is considering Newton's Scholium on Def. viii. In the passage quoted Newton is arguing that relative quantities are not the quantities themselves those names they bear, but the sensible measures thereof -- the measures being commonly used instead of the quantities measured. In the other entry Berkeley is criticizing Newton's experiment of the water in the rotating vessel -- see his own Princ. 113-114. Newton used the experiment to illustrate his distinction between absolute and relative motion.

457. 458. On squaring the circle (see 245n.); D is the diameter, and P the circumference (periphery); on Berkeley's theory there is no fixed number (π) such that for every circle the circumference = π X diameter -- see 340 and 481. "to rectify perhipheries" means to find a straight line equal to the circumference. To square the circle arithmetically means to find its area in terms of the numbers of points it contains, which Berkeley claimed to be able to do in the case of particular circles.

459. Cheyne's argument, referred to in Berkeley's Of Infinites, is that abstract geometry depends on the possibility of infinites, great and small; on Cheyne, see 367n.

460. On succession as the basis of Locke's simple ideas, see 53n.; on number, see 104n.; on time, see 4n.; on the two kinds of visible extension, see 400n.

461. Locke's simple idea of power (see notes on 41 and 52) is resolved into the relation of cause and effect (see 403n.). Berkeley here adopts the occasionalist theory of causation

with regard to the animate as well as the inanimate cause, identifying physical cause with pure sequence. On relation, see 540n.

462. 463. On Barrow, see 75n. This passage form his <u>Lectiones Acad. Contab.</u> I 16 (delivered 1665, pub. 1684; Lect. IX, p. 153 in Kirby's tr.) uses several mathematical arguments against indivisibles including the following. Take a circle with a radius in length 3 points; in this circle by using the proposition of Archimedes we get the absurdity of an arc equal to its chord. Now the circumference of this circle equals $\pi \times 6$, which is less than 24; and Barrow's argument is invalid, Berkeley points out, because Archimedes' proof applies only to circles of more than 24 points in circumference. Barrow then takes a circle of radius 5 points, and offers a similar argument <u>ad absurdum</u>. Berkeley's argument would not apply to this case; hence he suggests a new line of attack, viz., that Archimedes' proposition itself (the radius equal to the side of the hexagon) may have to assume the infinite divisibility (see 11n.); on points, see 59n.; on Archimedes' proposition, see 510.

464. A further study in the meaning of composition, see 445n. Visibles cannot, Berkeley argues, be composed of invisibles; the supposed invisibles are "nothings" and self-contradictory, see 337n.; on the m.v., see 59n.

465. Read "receiv'd," not "reviv'd" (Fraser and Johnston). In the Preface to the <u>Principles</u> Berkeley defends himself against the charges of "novelty and singularity." "I do not pin my faith..." cf. "I have always thought and judged for myself" (<u>Def</u>. 19.).

466. Berkeley was no sensationalist; for he is careful to limit the scope of this maxim, saying in effect, "use your senses about things sensible, and your reason about things rational"; he has in view the mathematical reasoning which would make sensible lines infinitely divisible, by confusing an assertion about the subject "I can go on dividing" with an assertion about the object "It is divisible." On "nothing" see 337n.; on the senses, see 317n.; on demonstration, see 163n. "nonsense" seems to be a sly touch of humour, the insensible being non-sense; he has a similar double entente in his words, "if what you mean by the word matter be only the unknown support of unknown qualities, it's no matter whether there is such a thing or no" (Princ. 77), anticipating Byron's pleasantry to the effect that if Berkeley said there is no matter, it's no matter what Berkeley said.

467. He is thinking of Locke (see 567n.). Note the erased words "free & unprejudic'd search after"; Malebranche's Recherche was commonly known in England as the Search.

468. Expanded in 532; on certainty, see 163n.

469. 470. For the denial of incommensurables, see 29n.; on points, see 59n.

471. "Nihilarians," see 337n.; on "usefull & practical Mathematiques," see 207n.

472. 473. Berkeley is considering the perceivable (see 52n.) in the light of the esse est percipi, and answering the objection, still commonly urged, that his doctrine removes the distinction between fact and fancy. "by reason of yt

very question," these words must be read carefully and in the light of the clear, explicit statement of 473. Berkeley does not say that if you ask a question about anything, it thereupon springs into sensible existence, and, as the context shows, he is very far from holding any such absurdity. What he, in effect, says is that if you ask a question about anything at all, that thing thereby has its <u>appropriate</u> type of existence, all types being equally "in the mind," though in other respects very different from one another. There is no confusion here between fact and fancy; on the contrary the distinction is most carefully preserved. Images are images, says Berkeley, and not sense-data; but images, equally with sense-data, are "in the mind," and therefore if you think you can imagine matter outside the mind, you are self-deceived; see <u>Princ</u>. 23, 34; on "books in the study," see 429n.; on existence, see 408n.; on the imagination, see 531n.

I agree with Fraser in reading "discours'd." Johnston reads "discuss'd." But Berkeley could hardly write "discuss'd <u>of</u>," and on comparison on the word in the MS. with "discuss'd" in 569, there can be no doubt that the word here is "discours'd."

474. 474a. Here the verso flatly contradicts the recto with regard to the scolastic distinction between <u>ens rationis</u> and <u>ens reale</u>; so also 535, 546, 546a. At first Berkeley was a panpsychist (see 24), and understood existence in the mind as mental existence; but in the latter part of the <u>PC</u>, as in the <u>Principles</u>, he is a dualist, accepting sensible things ("ideas") as entirely distinct from mind, though dependent thereon; see 304n.

475. 475a. What is an infinite idea? Answer suggested: (1) a mental process which can go on indefinitely, e.g., vision

round the visual sphere, see 97n., (2) an extension consisting of innumerable points, (3) an idea too big to be comprehended at once. The first answer, subjective infinity, Berkeley accepts; the other two he rejects, the second on the ground that numbers, however great, can be counted and named, the third on the ground that an idea e vi termini is comprehensible. He draws similar distinctions in his essay Of Infinites; on points, see 59n.

476. 477. 477a. Matter in the Cartesian philosophy is, Berkeley argues (as in Princ. 22, 53), purposeless and pointless. "according to their own confession" may refer to Malebranche's well-known Illustration (excursus), mentioned in 800, On the difficulty of proving the existence of bodies. There Malebranche confesses, in effect, that everything could go on as it does, if there were no matter, that the evidence for matter is slight, almost negligible, resting entirely on a point of religious faith, not on reason. The verso addition is important (477a); note its distinction between matter and bodies, its unequivocal recognition of the reality of bodies (see 52n.), and its distinction between the divine mind and the human, implicit in the initial capital of "Our." The same capital letter, with the same implication, occurs in 801, cf. 838. All things always depend on the mind of God, but they are independent of the mind of man when they are not being actually perceived by him; this is Berkeley's revised and final doctrine of the perceivable. For the word "compages," see Princ. 22.

478. 478a. A question of high importance, not only for its own sake, but for its bearing on Berkeley's doctrine of existence in the mind. Soul (or mind; the two terms because

synonymous; but at first when he is attending to the nature of the ego he calls it "soul" for the most part) is a subject on which Berkeley modified his views while he was writing the PC. The question for him was partly one of terminology, and even when he speaks as Hume spoke, he was not really thinking as Hume thought; true, at the earlier state he identifies soul with its ideas, and calls mind "a congeries of Perceptions" (580); but that does not necessarily mean that he accepted the passing thought as "the only thinker"; for behind his soul or mind stood the person or spirit or active principle, see 14n.; on will, see 131n.

"as it is distinct from Ideas," i.e., in so far as it is distinct from its ideas.

479. Berkeley must be referring, I think, to the final paragraph of the sixth Mediation (cf. 794) where Descartes writes of "that general uncertainty as to sleep, which I could not distinguish from waking." Berkeley's solution would be, no doubt, that of commonsense with respect to the subject, and with regard to the object would consist in his distinction between ideas of sense and ideas of the imagination (Princ. 29-33).

480. "minima or near minima," i.e., minima in their pure, uncompounded state. The notion of evanescence, no doubt taken from the theory of fluxions, is only here applied to minima (see 59n.). Berkeley appears to be considering a possible objection to his theory of minima. viz., let there be two minima, i.e., two areas each containing only one point, and therefore, on Berkeley's theory, of equal size. Now suppose them to "evanesce," i.e., to decrease in size gradually. One might vanish before the other, and would

therefore be proved to be smaller, "So that one sensible [note the reading] may be greater than another tho it exceeds it not by one point."

Berkeley's reply, presumably, would be to traverse the conception of an evanescent <u>minimum</u>. Grant a <u>minimum</u> in his sense, and the smallest decrease in it would make it vanish.

[Note the correct reading "near minima." Other editors have read "meer minima." -- Editor.]

481. 482. Cf. 340n. and 457. Berkeley is here denying that a circle is a polygon with an infinite number of sides -- an assumption sometimes made in proving that all circles are similar figures.

John Wallis (1616-1703), Savilian Professor of Geometry at Oxford, author of <u>Arithmetica Infinitorum</u> (1655) -- a landmark in the history of the calculus, mentioned in Berkeley's essay <u>Of Infinites</u>. For this "harangue," see his <u>Arithmetica</u>, prop. 165. See 834n. for the controversy with Hobbes, which touches most of the mathematical problems debated in the <u>PC</u>.

483. Berkeley regarded geometrical abstractions such as length without breadth (see 21n.) as the main source of the doctrine of infinite divisibility. On "general" (figure), later called "abstract general" and abbreviated "abstract," see 318n.

484. 484a. Studies in <u>resemblance</u>, of importance to Berkeley because of Locke's dictum, "Ideas of primary qualities are resemblances; of secondary, not" (II viii 15). The point is whether an idea in our minds can be <u>like</u> something outside our minds, viz., matter. Berkeley's broad conclusion here

that "nothing can be like an idea but an idea" forms an important part of the demonstration of the New Principle in 378, where see note.

From Locke's account of complex ideas as made out of simple ones it would seem to follow that simple ideas held in common must be the basis of comparison and likeness. Berkeley is here debating that issue, and on the verso he expresses himself dissatisfied with the provisional conclusion of the recto. The same point appears in 378, props. 13-14, and 496. When Berkeley gave up Locke's doctrine of simple ideas (see 53n.), he gave up, of course, this line of argument, and it is not found in his publications; but the principle that matter cannot be <u>like</u> an idea remained an important part of his argument for immaterialism (see 46n. and <u>Princ</u>. 8). On extension, see 18n.

485. "No sharing," cf. "Hath Nature no share...," <u>Princ</u>. 150. On "second Causes," i.e., unthinking second causes, see 403n. and <u>Princ</u>. 32; on Nature and God, see 107n. and 794.

486. E.g., "<u>Si lapis vi gravitatis suae deorsum ad terram cadat, terra vicissim ad lapidem assurget</u>," Keill, <u>Introd. ad veram Physicam</u>, p. 125, cf. <u>Mot</u>. 12; on attraction, see 361n.

487. 488. Christian Huygens (1629-1695), mathematician, physicist, and astronomer; friend and correspondent of Leibniz, who said that Huygens "ought to be named immediately after Descartes and Galileo." Locke (Ep. to the Reader) couples him with Newton as "masters." His greatest work was <u>Horologium Oscillatorium</u> (1673), in which he sought an exact measure of time for astronomical and nautical calculations, trying to

correct minute variations in the swing of the pendulum, and thus to reduce its movements to geometrical exactitude. His theorem is given as, "<u>tempus unius oscillationis minimae est ad tempus descensus perpendicularis ex dimidia penduli altitudine ut circumferentia circuli ad diametrum, hoc est ut</u> 355 <u>ad</u> 113," <u>ib</u>. p. 155. On the same page he uses the symbols ' ' ' ' ' ' for small measurements of time. From these minute durations Berkeley went on, no doubt, to consider the infinitesimals of time (see 8n.), proposing to neglect them as "nothings," see notes on 337 and 590. By "attained to by my Doctrine" Berkeley means presumably, "consistent with immaterialism and my doctrine of indivisibles."

489. On colour and the <u>minimum</u>, see 442n.; on colour composition, see 151n.; on the minimum, see 59n.

490. Locke classes ideas of the operations of our minds with ideas of reflection. Berkeley seems to have been disposed at first to adopt Locke's classification (see 571); but later he decided that ideas were passive, and that accordingly there can be no ideas of operations, see 176a, 523, 663, <u>Princ</u>. 27, 135ff. He refuses the term "idea" to the mind and its operations, but, strictly speaking, he does not "confine" it to things sensible; but he applies it freely to objects of the imagination, which, though they have a basis in sense, are framed by the mind and are not properly described as "sensible." In the second edition of the <u>Principles</u> (1734) he inserted several paragraphs which authorize the use of the term "notion" for mind and its operations.

491. Zeno's antinomies of motion are a case in point. On the meaing of existence, see 408n.; on scepticism, see 79n.; on

the New Principle as a cure for scepticism, see 304n.

492. "One may often meet with very clear and coherent discourses that amount yet to nothing," Locke IV viii 9; cf. 574; for strictures on the Schoolmen, see Princ. Introd. 17, and for the comparison between them and mathematicians, see 327n.

493. On power, see notes on 41 and 52; on simple idea, see 53n.; on cause, see 403n.

494. 495. Berkeley here questions Locke's principle that all significant words stand for ideas, see 178n. He denies that we can imagine colour without extension; but he grants that we can consider one without the other (318). On colour and extension, see 85n.; on extension, see 18n.

Locke (III ix) deals with the "double use of words." Berkeley repeats his criticism of "recording" in 565, but seems to withdraw it in 607; the Draft Introduction to the Principles (Works II 134) discusses both "recording" and "communicating"; the published Introduction (18ff.) omits the reference to "recording."

496. 497. On simple and abstract ideas see notes on 53 and 318; on the comparison of simple ideas see notes on 378 (14) and 484. Extension is seen and touched, but is not tasted or heard (see notes on 137 and 240); that is Berkeley's reason for holding that it is easier to form abstract (not abstract general) ideas of tastes and sounds. Colours are essentially located; but tastes and sounds are not.

498. On experimental philosophy, see 406n.

499. 499a. Distinguishing cause (see 403n.) from occasion (see 228n., 754, 855-856). According to 856 occasions are causes that do nothing. In **Princ**. 69ff. Berkeley examines what is meant by "occasion"; it is to him simply matter in disguise; he is therefore not an occasionalist, but he shares with the occasionalists belief in the omnicausality of God and the rejection of unthinking second causes.

Since for him existence is simply to perceive or be perceived, "a Being wch wills" is a pleonastic phrase. Hence the verso comment.

"some other Cause," the first appearance of his causal argument for the existence of God, see **Princ**. 26, 29.

500. The sides of the two squares would have to be in the ratio of 1 to $\sqrt{2}$, a special case of the problem of incommensurability.

501. On Barrow and Barrovian Case, see 75n.

502. 503. 504. 505. Remarks on the composition of colour, see 151n.; on green, see 240n. Newton mentions several sorts of green, **Optics**, Bk. II, pp. 59, 90.

"mixt cause," i.e., composite cause, see 562. Berkeley is arguing that light being composite, our light sensations will be composite; he is using the term "cause" here in the popular sense.

506. Speaking of the Society's original meetings at Oxford, Sprat says that they furnished a race of young men with "minds receiving from them their first impressions of sober and

generous knowledge..." -- <u>The History of the Royal Society of London for the improving of Natural Knowledge</u> (by Thos. Sprat, 1667), p. 53.

507. Berkeley does not give a formal definition of idea; but he comes near doing so in 808 where he writes, "yt I think on wtever it be, I call Idea"; in <u>Princ</u>. 39 he says, "Since therefore the objects of sense exist only in the mind, and are withal thoughtless and inactive, I chose to mark them by the word idea, which implies those properties." On definition, see 44n.

508. "Second Book," i.e., <u>Principles</u>, Part II, which was lost in Italy. Berkeley refers to it in the Preface to the <u>Three Dialogues</u>, in his draft letter to Le Clerc (<u>Works</u> VIII 48), and in his letter to Johnson dated November 25, 1729 (<u>Works</u> II 282). It dealt with moral philosophy. The <u>Principles</u> in 1710 came out as Part I; the "Part I" was omitted from the title-page, though retained at the beginning of the text, in the second edition.

Berkeley originally planned three Books or Parts, besides the <u>Theory of Vision</u>; he mentions the first book in 571, 792, the second book again in 807, 878, and the third book (on natural philosophy) in 583, 853; he refers to his literary plans and intensions in 139, 212, 378a, 401, 513, 543, 562, 679, 680, 719, 736, 817, 858; see also 676n. On God, see 107n.; on moral freedom, see 149n.

509. On geometry, see 117n.; on practice versus speculation, see 434n.

510. 511. For the related problems of squaring and rectifying

the circle, see 245n. This proposition of Archimedes has to do with squaring the circle; it is distinct, apparently, from the proposition of Archimedes referred to in 462, where see note; the latter deals with rectifying the circle. On inequality discerned by the microscope, see 360n.; on Barrow, see 75n.; on minimal points see 59n.

512. Locke (II xxiii 2-4) distinguishes between substance in general and our ideas of particular substances, which are collections of several simple ideas. Berkeley clearly has this distinction in mind, but he is in the main giving his own doctrine here; viz., that things are "collections of ideas" (Princ. I), i.e., are the sensible qualities which we see and sense; that there is no non-spiritual substance; that there is no abstract or general idea of body or matter.

"or any thing else" an inexact term for "or any other unthinking thing"; Berkeley always affirmed spiritual substance. In Princ. 37 he distinguishes the philosophic sense of corporeal substance (denied) from the vulgar sense (affirmed); on substance, see 80n.

513. On words, see 178n.

514. 515. 516. The problem of equality is examined again in 525, 528-531, 778. Berkeley starts from the definition, "quae sibi mutuo congruunt...," which Sir H. Savile, Hobbes says, held to be "the foundation of all geometry." What is congruence? Berkeley asks; it cannot consist in superposition; for a curve cannot be superposed on a straight line; besides, superposition involves external distance (cf. TV 155), and directly contradicts the esse est percipi; for the "under triangle" is not perceived. Congruence cannot be judged by sight or by

touch (528), nor by imaginaton or pure intellect (531), and it must consist therefore in having the same number of sensible points (see 59n.). This answer is modified in 530a, where Berkeley says that those lines are equal between which no difference can be observed by the senses and which are therefore called by the same name, cf. 778. He uses the term "congruent" in 150. In 516 for "as many," Fraser and Johnston read "the same."

517. 517a. 518. Berkeley here considers the meaning of substance (see notes on 80 and 512), and argues that the surrender of material substance is not a surrender of reality (see 52n.); "<u>nec quid nec quantum</u>," etc., i.e., matter, see 22n.

Edward Stillingfleet (1635-1699), Bishop of Worcester, author of <u>Origines Sacrae</u> (1662), is referred to in the opening words of the entry; for he styled Locke (see Locke, II xxiii note B), "one of the gentlemen of this new way of reasoning, that have almost discarded substance out of the reasonable part of the world!" Berkeley was anxious not to offend "the Stillingfleetians" (see 700), the English Church party who had lingering sympathies with the Scholastics.

519. 520. On curves, see 360n.; on points, see 59n.

521. For the metaphor cf. 742 and <u>Locke</u>, Ep. to the Reader, "Its searches after truth are a sort of hawking and hunting"; for truth in the mind, see 696 and <u>Locke</u>, <u>passim</u>; on the nature of truth, see 554n.

My reading "afoot" seems to me certain; Fraser and Johnston read "a fool." Berkeley does not cross his "t's"; the "l" in fool in 542 is looped, but there is no loop here.

Besides, "afoot" makes much better sense; it is in contrast with "on horseback" understood in "fleet," as "clumsey" is in contrast with "dexterous."

522. 523. This Lockian principle, accepted in 312, placed at the head of his "demonstration" of the Principle in 378, but denied in 730, is here set down for examination, not in approval; for it confronts Berkeley with delimma, either there is no self-knowledge, or there is an idea of an active being (on which, see 490n.); on person, see 25n.

524. On general ideas, see notes on 318 and 401.

525. On equality, see 514n.

526. Locke (IV ii 10, 11) makes this distinction between quantitative simple ideas (number and extension) and other simple ideas, and gives it as a reason why demonstration is thought to be limited to mathematics. Berkeley considers that simple ideas do not admit of modes or degrees (see 53n. and 134), and turns to his experiments in colour composition (see 151n.) in proof that so-called simple ideas are -- some of them -- complex.

527. On curves, see 360n.; on curves treated as polygons, see 481n., <u>Anal</u>. 21.

528. 529. 530. 530a. 531. Further studies in the nature of equality; see 150n. and 515n.; on points, see 59n.

The last word or two in 529 are almost illegible, but I prefer "difficulties" to "difficulty truly" (Fraser and Johnston).

The reference to the threefold division of our cognitive faculties, sense, imagination, pure intellect (prominent in Malebranche's <u>Recherche</u>) should be noted, cf. 472, 828, and especially 775, where Berkeley first wrote "any sensible or imaginable or intelligible thing."

The imagination holds an important place in Berkeley's philosophy, partly for its own sake as being the first evidence of the mind's activity (<u>Princ</u>. 28), and partly because its ideas form a foil to ideas of sense (<u>Princ</u>. 29ff.); the imagination is often mentioned, and is sometimes considered, in the <u>PC</u>; see 31, 36, 294, 321, 415, 417-418, 472-473, 582, 609, 657a, 792, 818, 823, 830, 886. Berkeley's main contentions are that ideas of the imagination are copies of ideas of sense, and that the Principle (<u>esse est percipi</u>) extends to the imagination; cf. "they both [sense data and <u>imaginata</u>] equally exist in the mind, and in that sense are alike <u>ideas</u>" (<u>Princ</u>. 34).

Pure intellect is mentioned once more in the <u>PC</u>, viz., in 810, "Pure Intellect I understand not." It is not mentioned in the <u>Principles</u>, but it appears in the <u>Three Dialogues</u> (<u>Works</u> II 193), accepted with reserve as a faculty by which we apprehend "spiritual objects, as virtue, reason, God,..." but under suspicion of being a pseudo-faculty of abstract ideas; so also <u>Mot</u>. 53. In <u>Alc</u>. VII 6 (1st ed.) the term occurs in the mouth of Alciphron for the alleged faculty of abstract ideas. Berkeley's hesitation about pure intellect was due to his desire to affirm a rational faculty of spiritual apprehension without leaving a loophole for false abstraction. In this entry he argues that if there be such a faculty, it could not be concerned with lines and angles, which are not operations of the mind, and therefore not spiritual objects.

532. An expansion of 468; on demonstration and certainty, see 163n.

["jnjure" is obviously intended for "injure." -- Editor]

533. On the corpuscularian essences, see 234n. Locke (IV iii 11-14) is arguing that we know very little of the inner constitution of things, that the connection between primary and secondary qualities is undiscoverable, and that the connection between primary qualities themselves is, for the most part, known to us only by experience; but he grants that in a few cases the connection is seen to be necessary, and he instances the dependence of figure on extension and motion on solidity. Berkeley denies that motion (see 262n. and cf. 864, 876) pre-supposes solidity (see 78n.).

534. A quotation from Locke, duplicate of 76, where see note.

535. The first of the Objections to immaterialism, stated and answered in Princ. 34 along the lines of this entry; on the reality of body, see 52n.; on ens rationis and ens reale, see 474n.

536. On real and nominal essences, see 234n.

537. One of the few entries without index letter or sign. On the abuse of words, see 178n. The use of words without clear and distinct ideas is, for Locke (III x 2), "the first and most palpable abuse." For "clear and distinct ideas" -- a slogan of the Enlightenment -- Locke in his fourth edition (see Ep. to the Reader) substituted in most places "determinate" or "determined." Berkeley here, as in 591 and 636, combines the terms.

538. 539. These should be read together; otherwise 538 might give the impression that Berkeley is doubting the life beyond. His point is that Locke's system undermines faith in the supersensible, while his own confirms it.

Locke speaks of the intellectual world (loc. cit.) as "a greater, certainly, and more beautiful world than the material," adding that it is almost entirely concealed from us "in an impenetrable obscurity." The scepticism or agnosticism latent in that position was clear to Berkeley; such a heaven draws no response from the will and has no influence upon conduct. Locke's distinction is therefore "vain," and his scepticism is rooted, Berkeley implies, in his distrust of the senses. Our higher faculties, Berkeley holds, are linked up with sense; if therefore we trust our senses and have a reasoned belief in the sensible (not material) world, we can rise to a conception of the supersensible more "agreeable to our present nature." The startling "Sensual Pleasure is the Summum Bonum" (769) should be understood in the light of this elevated conception of the senses (see 317n.), and of earthly pleasure as a pointer to heavenly bliss. See his sermon on Life and Immortality (Works VII 9ff.), which belongs to the same period as the PC, being dated January 11, 1708. "Introversion," sc. introspection; the term was a favourite with the mystics in the seventeenth century (see Oxford English Dictionary). The illegible word after "all" may be "kinds," and for the blank in the line above, perhaps read "for them."

540. This remarkable entry is evidence (if any were needed) of the maturity of Berkeley's mind and the breadth of his outlook in his early manhood. Commentators have remarked on his comparative silence about relations in his early books, and have considered it a mark of immaturity. This entry helps

to explain that silence, showing that he had considered relations and their nature, but regarded the _relata_ as more instructive than the _relation_ in the earlier stages of speculation. This view was, no doubt, a phase of his feeling for the concrete as against the abstract. Relations are mentioned also in 134, 461, 503, 545, 677, 733, 739, 853, but no systematic treatement of them is given. Relation for Locke is the largest field of our knowledge (IV iii 18); but for Berkeley it was an "Obscure ambiguous term" (733), associated especially with mathematics, yielding merely nominal knowledge. This judgement is corrected to some extent in later editions of his books, e.g., _Princ._ 89 (2nd ed.) and _Alc._ VII 12, 14 (3rd ed.), and indeed some relations such as cause and effect are discussed in the first editions.

541. 542. The notions of profit and pleasure meet in that of interest (cf. "advantage," _Princ._ 100). Berkeley teaches that pleasure is objectively determined, and that there is no state of hedonic indifference, 143-144, 833; that perception and desire are conditioned by pleasure and pain, 321, 692; that sensual pleasure "rightly understood" is the _summum bonum_, 769; that qua pleasure it is good and desirable, 773; that both happiness and good are relative, 569; that there are qualitative distinctions between pleasures, pure and impure, present and future, 787, 851, 852.

This frank hedonism startles those who associate hedonism with naturalism; but Berkeley was without question a hedonist, who attached importance, as did Butler, to the pleasures of the senses, seeing in them a pointer to the pleasures of heaven and "celestial joys" -- see 539n. There is nothing, however, in his published works corresponding to the extreme statement on "sensual pleasure" in 769, which ought not to be taken literally. Berkeley's hedonism was opposed to Epicureanism and Hobbesism (17, Princ. 93), was not exclusive or egoistic, and recognized qualities of pleasure, recommending the higher and purer pleasures; and therefore when he speaks of "sensual pleasure" as the summum bonum, he is not referring to pleasures of appetite; probably "sensual pleasure" means the sense of pleasure or perceived pleasure as opposed to abstract ideas thereof; Berkeley contended for reality in ethics, as he did in metaphysics, and he appealed from abstract ideas of happiness and goodness to pleasure actually felt, and goodness actually willed (see Princ. 100).

If his Part II of the Principles had been published, we should be in a position, no doubt, to clear up this difficulty and to judge his ethical system as a whole; but as it is, we have very little material on which to base a judgement, merely these few notes of his in the PC, Princ. 100, Passive Obedience, and casual references in his sermons and other writings. In 542 for "understanding," perhaps read "considering."

543. No statement of this type appears in the Preface of the Principles -- a book not wanting either in modesty or in decision. The statement of 532 is a better expression, I think, of Berkeley's attitude.

544. On the metaphorical use of sensible terms for operations of the mind, see 176n. On the imperfections of language, see 178n.; Berkeley himself uses his technical terms (e.g., "idea," "external") "in some Latitude." On the understanding which is carefully studied in the latter part of the PC, see 362a n.

545. "That I have any such idea answering the word unity I do not find," Princ. 13, cf. TV 109. Number, for Berkeley, "consists

in Relations," and is therefore "entirely the creature of the mind," Princ. 12; on relations, see 540n.; on unity, see 75n.; on simple ideas, see 53n.

546. 546a. On the same contradiction between recto and verso, see 474n.; 546 is scarcely consistent with 535; 546a has been missed by other editors; "words" is not certain; on the reality of body, see 52n.

547. Johnston reads "no" for "an," a blunder that may have serious consequences in Berkeleian exegesis. Berkeley is no solipsist, nor problematical idealist; for he knows the existence of "other things besides our selves," and this knowledge, for him, is logically prior to self-knowledge.

Intuitive knowledge of other things is asserted again in 563 (cf. 813 for the denial that we have an intuition of God); intuitive, for Berkeley, does not mean mystical, but direct and immediate. Johnston's statements in his note on 568 (my 563) that Berkeley in his published works never admits the possibility of intuitive knowledge and maintains that it is a broken reed are unfounded. Indeed Berkeley's main doctrines, existence in the mind and the esse est percipi, can be apprehended, he says, by "an intuitive knowledge," Princ. 3.

For Locke (IV ii) intuitive knowledge "is the clearest and most certain that human frailty is capable of" and is to be distinguished from demonstrative and sensitive knowledge. The entries 79-80 and 563 show that Berkeley has Locke's doctrine definitely in view, and is promoting our knowledge of the sensible world from the third rank ("an assurance that deserves the name of knowledge," Locke IV xi 3) to the first rank.

548. Malebranche (VI ii 3) writes, "There is no necessary connexion betwixt the will we may have of moving our arm, for instance, and the motion of the same arm. It moves indeed whenever we will it, and we may be called in that sense the natural cause of motion of our arm; yet natural causes are not true, but only occasional." Berkeley is glancing at this famous passage; he intends to allow more efficacy to the human spirit than the Oratorian does; but whether he succeeded in doing so may be doubted, see 107n., Princ. 53, 147, Siris 257. In justice to Malebranche (see 230n.) it should be remembered that he too held that "tis we that will their movement"; his point is that we cannot and do not give effect to our will to move the arm.

549. 549a. 550. The transition from the reality of knowledge to the reality of things is well illustrated by Locke's question in the passage here cited, "How shall the mind, when it perceives nothing but its own ideas, know that they agree with things themselves?" On reality, see 52n.

551. For this (to us) extraordinary emphasis on demonstration, see 163n.; on likeness as part of the argument for immaterialism, see 46n.; informal definitions of likeness are contained in 378, 13-19; on colour composition, see 151n.; on simple ideas, see 53n.

552. Showing the connection between Berkeley's New Principle on the nature of existence (see 408n.) and his doctrine of abstract ideas (see 318n.); "never thought of by the Vulgar," see 405n., 703, Princ. Introd. 10.

553. On Berkeley's study of words, see 178n.; "settle the Meaning of their words" -- cf. 544 and _Locke_ III ii 7.

554. 555. On truth. Locke (IV v 2) says that truth signifies "nothing but the joining or separating of signs, as the things signified by them do agree or disagree one with another." In the next chapter he argues that general truths require to be expressed in verbal propositions, and he proceeds to infer that, since general propositions about substances are never certain, we can attain general knowledge only by "the contemplation of our own abstract ideas." This argument "makes for" Berkeley by supporting his contention (_Princ_. Introd. 18ff.) that language is the source of mistaken claims for abstract ideas, see notes on 318 and 401.

Berkeley does not treat of truth systematically either in the _PC_ or in his publications; but we may glean the following observations: truth is what philosophy in its three branches, natural, mathematical, and moral, seeks, 676; Locke's account of truth is apparently commended, 376; truth is in our own understanding, 521, 696; to distinguish thing from idea destroys truth, 606; truth may be merely an abstract idea, 873; signs are not necessary to the finding of truth, 883. The last three of these observations are criticisms of Locke's account of truth. Locke, being a representationist, distinguishes idea, as sign, from the thing signified, and he can escape confessed scepticism only by his artificial doctrine of abstract ideas.

Berkeley himself believes in signs, but in signs that present and do not represent; his ideas of sense are signs, real signs, signs which do not differ in kind from the thing signified, and therefore a knowledge of nature, for him, is a knowledge of the connection between God-given ideas, i.e., a knowledge of signs by signs, see TV 140-148, Princ. 44, 65-66, 108; Alc. IV 7, VII 11, Siris 258, 261, 266.

556. The advance of science, Berkeley thought, had been purchased at the cost of neglecting the elementary principle of relativity to mind; hence his curious metaphor of traveling backward; on his Principle, see 285n.

557. 558. Berkeley raises this question in 86 and again in 445 (where see notes). On points, see 59n.

559. "Forasmuch as" occurs in 586, but in his books Berkeley avoids stilted phrases; on his literary style, see 209n.

560. Throughout his life Berkeley was interested in politics and public affairs; see his letters, Passive Obedience, the Querist, and several minor publications.

561. Here Berkeley reaches his full and final doctrine of abstract (general) ideas, see 318n. He distinguishes them from concrete universals or genera, traces their origin to a mistaken theory of words, finds them self-contradictory, and illustrates the contradiction by referring to Locke's "absurd triangle" (IV vii 9) -- all this exactly as he does in the Introduction to the Principles. The passage from Locke is referred to again in 687, Alc. VII 5 (1st ed.), Def. 45ff.

562. An a priori proof, based on Newton's Optics, of the composite character of colours (cf. 551); Berkeley claimed to have reached the same result by experiment (see 151n.). "my Treatise," i.e., the Principles. On "mixt cause," see

504n.; on simple ideas, see 53n.; on demonstration, see 163n.; on definition, see 44n.

563. Berkeley is concerned to refute the charge of scepticism (see 79n.), and he appeals to his intuitive knowledge (see 547n.) of sensible things, which, according to Locke, are known only by sensitive knowledge, i.e., opinion.

564. 565. 566. A group of entries dealing with words as the source of abstract ideas (see notes on 178, 318, 401). The reading "Bacon" for "Barrow" (Fraser and Johnston) is quite certain. This is the only mention of Bacon in the PC. The reference is probably to the Idols of the Marketplace (Nov. Org. Bk. I, 59-60) which are imposed by words on the understanding, and spring "out of a faulty and unskilful abstraction."

For Locke on recording and communicating ideas, see 495n.

566. This entry contains the first mention of the Solitary Man -- an experimental conceit doing for words and ideas what the blind man of the Molyneux Problem had done for sight and touch; it is applied to abstract ideas again in 727, to the esse est percipi in 588, to identical propositions in 592, to the recording of ideas in 600, 607, to number in 648, to complex ideas in 727a. The supposition is given in extenso in the Draft Introduction (Works II 141-142) and the next section (prima manu) begins, "I shall therefore endeavour, so far as I am able, to put myself in the posture of the solitary philosopher," and Berkeley proceeds to detail the consequences. The Solitary Man does not appear in the Principles as published, but possibly the illustration of the men made to speak (Dials., Works II 247-248) is derived from it. The conceit is an attempt

to reach the pure data of experience, and is comparable to the Philosophus Autodidactus of the Arabian tale, and to Defoe's <u>Robinson Crusoe</u> (1719) and his <u>The Dumb Philosopher</u> (1719).

In his discussions of words Berkeley, like Locke, is unsatisfactory; they both have a wrong conception of the relation of thought and speech; they assume that thought is a self-contained process; they do not allow for inner speech and the effect of speech on thought; in consequence speech to them is simply the expression of thought, mere utterance.

567. The "mist" is "the Mist or veil of Words" (642). There are scores of references to Locke in the <u>PC</u>, but this entry with 467 and 688 are among the few that give any indication of Berkeley's personal feelings towards him.

568. In 192 (see note) Berkeley refuses to accept any other identity than perfect likeness in respect of inanimate things; presumably then he would call two peas identical if they are perfectly alike, i.e., indistinguishable; and such identity, being generic and taking no account of the place and time of the object, would be that identity which he here calls "excluding Identity of Circumstances."

What then, for him, is the identity <u>including</u> identity of circumstances? And does he mean by the words "may be taken" that he himself would take identity in both senses? Identity <u>including</u> identity of circumstances could only be the momentary (numerical) self-identity which we ascribe, for instance, to this pea <u>hic et nunc</u>. Such identity is described in <u>Locke</u> II xxvii 1; it involves no likeness, and therefore Berkeley would be averse, it would seem, to using the term "identity" in such a case.

The erased verso comment 192a speaks of "difference

intrinsecal or extrinsecal," a reference, no doubt, to these two types of identity.

569. Berkeley denies that happiness and good are absolute, holding that a man's happiness is relative to that of his social group, and a man's good relative to the end in view, cf. 852. Thus ignorance of the relativity of happiness and of the relativity of good would be his "2 Causes of mistake"; on his hedonism, see 541n.; "much," no doubt a slip for "must."

The *personalia* of this entry are of some interest. First, we may infer from Berkeley's words that he was a man of moderate means; this tallies with what we know of him from other sources; he went to a good school, Kilkenny College, and he moved in good Dublin society; yet he could not have been a wealthy man; for he was an Erasmus Smith Exhibitioner.

Who were French and Madden? Clearly they were college friends and probably members with Berkeley of his society for discussing the New Philosophy, but we cannot identify them precisely. The names occur frequently in the Trinity College books of the period, and we can read the three names together, French, Berkeley, and Madden, in a contemporary document (a list of debts to Trinity College!). This document is part of a series of notes by Matthew French, senior, recently edited with comments by Dr. Alton in "Some Fragments of College History," *Hermathena*, Vols. LVII, LVIII (1941). There are four names to be considered: John Madden, Samuel Madden, Matthew French, senior, and Matthew French, junior, all men of distinction and in college about Berkeley's time. Two of them were Fellows, viz., John Madden (elected 1710, resigned 1724, Vicar of St. Anne's and Dean of Kilmore, died 1751) and Matthew French, senior (elected 1699, died 1714). The two non-Fellows were Samuel Madden (1686-1765 --

see <u>Dict</u>. <u>Nat</u>. <u>Biog</u>.) and Matthew French, junior, who won Scholarship of the House in 1701, and was therefore but one year senior to Berkeley. Samuel Madden, cousin of the above John Madden, was known as "Premium Madden" because of his advocacy of prizes for learning; he matriculated in 1700 (Berkeley's year), graduated B.A. in 1705 and D.D. in 1723; he was a noted philanthropist, and he wrote various works including the play <u>Themistocles</u>. He acted for Berkeley as "editor" of the <u>Querist</u>.

570. Locke (III iv 7) says that names of simple ideas (see 53n.) are indefinable because they contain no reference to other ideas. Berkeley here suggests another reason, viz., insufficiency of names. He does not discuss simple and complex ideas in his published works.

571. The word before "to use" is almost illegible; it is not "sensation"; it might be "reflection," but more probably it is "those."

"the 1st Book," i.e., <u>Principles</u>, Part I, see 508n.; a mention of sensation and reflection (cf. 585, 656, 670) at the beginning would suggest a treatise of Lockian lines. The <u>Principles</u> opens with a survey of the objects of human knowledge, but does not mention reflection, Locke's ideas of reflection being in a measure covered by Berkeley's objects "perceived by attending to the passions and operations of the mind." Berkeley had two objections to Locke's primary division of ideas, (1) It involves the absurdity of passive ideas of active operations, (2) It separates perception from objects of perception, see 585, 609.

572. A pointer to the tense discussion of mind, soul, and

ideas in 576-582.

573. The reference is, I think, to <u>Locke</u> IV x 10, where the supposition of matter and motion before thought is used to prove the existence of God. On "includes a manifest Contradiction," see 299n.

574. A repetition of 492, where see note.

575. Euclid's definition, What has no parts is a point, appears to favour the geometry of indivisibles, which Berkeley supported, see notes on 59 and 353; on curves, see 360n.

576. 576a. 577. 578. 579. 580. 581. 582. A remarkable group of entries on mind, soul, and ideas, which has given many readers the impression that at this stage Berkeley was a sceptic about the soul. Certainly if Berkeley had <u>published</u> statements like his, "The very existence of Ideas constitutes the soul.... Mind is a congeries of Perceptions," he would deserve to rank with Hume; but there is nothing of the sort in his books, where he always insists that "mind, spirit, soul, or my self" denotes "the perceiving, active being," a thing entirely distinct from ideas. How then are these entries to be explained? They are the result, I think, of an earlier technique, later discarded. Berkeley always from his earliest days of systematic thought believed in the active being; but he called it "person" when he was writing the first part of the <u>PC</u> (see 24). The person or active being stands in the background of these remarks, and by "mind" and "soul" he did not mean at the time what we mean by those terms and what he himself later came to mean by them. When the

-273-

active being to him was the person, then "mind" and "soul" were used by him as collective terms for the passive contents of thought and will; and they are still frequently used so in everyday speech, e.g., "I changed my mind." But as he worked on at his technique and filled the later pages of the second notebook (A), the active-passive distinction dominated his mind, and he began to see reasons, including theological reasons (713) for discarding the term "person." He gave up "person," and then he had to ask himself where he stood with regard to the active being, and whether he could still continue to treat mind and soul as passive and as identical with their contents. He decided against his earlier usage, and in his publications he speaks indifferently of mind, spirit, soul, or myself as active, and as the equivalent of what he had formerly called "person." On knowledge of the soul, see 154n. and 478n.; on the understanding, see 362a n.; on consciousness, see 200n.; on the imagination, see 531n; on "thing wch perceives," see 115n.

583. On empty space, see notes on 96 and 135. On "the 3d Book," see 508n.

584. Berkeley accepted the principle of demonstration (see 163n.), and he here considers it in relation to religion, natural and revealed. He allows proofs in natural religion, such as Clarke's <u>Demonstration</u> <u>of</u> <u>the</u> <u>Being</u> <u>and</u> <u>Attributes</u> <u>of</u> <u>God</u> (1705-1706); but he refuses to allow demonstrations with regard to the key doctrines of revealed religion, such as the Trinity (see 350n.). He would have these doctrines accepted by implicit faith (see 720, cf. <u>Maleb</u>. I iii) along with matters of institutional religion, such as episcopacy, deduced or demonstrated therefrom.

585. A criticism of Locke's distinction between ideas of reflection and ideas of sensation (see 571n.).

Hecht notes that the text is illegible; that is true only of the three words or so after "white." Up to that point the reading, as given, including the fullstop, is certain. Of the illegible words the first begins with "Men..." or "Mea..."

586. For demonstration in the Introduction as originally planned, see notes on 163 and 212. "It is the contemplation of our own abstract ideas that alone is able to afford us general knowledge," Locke IV vi 16. On abstract ideas, see 318n.

587. Berkeley is considering the double question as to how the understanding and the will, respectively, are related to their contents. At this stage of his thinking he would agree with Malebranche (I i) in calling the understanding "that passive faculty of the soul," and therefore he identifies it, more or less, with its ideas; but he did not for long remain at that stage, and in the end the understanding became for him active, distinct from its contents or ideas, and a synonym for cognitive mind, see 362a n. A somewhat similar development took place with regard to the will; here he is thinking of identifying it with the passions or things willed, which he often calls volitions; but later it stands out in contrast over against its contents or objects, and, joined to the understanding, forms "The Concrete of the Will & understanding," called mind (713).

588. 589. Applications of the New Principle (see 285n.); on the Solitary Man, see 566n. "There was an odour, that

is, it was smelt"; an instance of the <u>esse est percipi</u> given in <u>Princ</u>. 3. Note "it was smelt," <u>not</u> simply "there was a smelling"; Berkeley keeps the sensible object distinct from mind, though in relation to it.

590. Berkeley's attitude to apparent interruptions of conscious life is discussed in the note on 83. The intervals are "nothing," because time (see 4n.) is regarded as an unbroken sequence of ideas. On the privacy of time, see 9n.

591. On words as the source of abstract (general) ideas, see notes on 178, 318, 401; on "clear & determin'd," see 537n.

592. Berkeley is using trifling propositions as proof, against Locke, that words can be used without ideas; see 354n. and cf. 728. Locke (IV vii 10) quotes "the whole is equal to all its parts" as an instance of a scholastic "maxim" which, on analysis, proves to be a trifling proposition. On the Solitary Man, see 566n.

593. On the New Principle as the meaning of existence, see 408n., <u>Princ</u>. 3.

594. Locke (II xi 10-11) places the "proper" and the "perfect" difference between man and beast in the power of abstraction (see 318n.). Berkeley touches on the question lightly in <u>Princ</u>. Introd. 11; in this entry he suggests that besides the sharp differences, language and shape, there are graded differences, "Degrees of more & less." By these last he means, no doubt, such qualities as intelligence, which is found in the animal world, but is more highly developed in man. In 753 he suggests as a <u>differentia</u> "Composition of Ideas,"

i.e., the imagination.

595. On inferences in words, see Locke IV xvii 18, and 178n.

596. On the imperfection of language, see 178n.

597. This variety of the hypothesis of matter, perhaps the materia prima or subtilis referred to by Locke (II xxiii 23 and III x 15), is dealt with by Berkeley as an "unknown support of unknown qualities" in Princ. 77. On substance, see 80n.; on existence, see 408n.

598. Locke (II xxi 28-34) protests against the common confusion between will and desire; he describes will as "a power in the mind to direct the operative faculties of a man to motion or rest," and desire as "an uneasiness of the mind for want of some absent good." Thus, he says, I may try to persuade a man, at the same time not desiring to prevail. Berkeley does not make the point of his criticism very clear. For his objection to the doctrine of uneasiness, see 145n.; on will, see 131n.

599. Berkeley refers again to the spontaneity of the imagination in 707, where Locke's doctrine of uneasiness is also in view. He considers Locke's theory deterministic, and is using the imagination as an argument for freedom, as in Princ. 28, "This making and unmaking of ideas doth very properly denominate the mind active."

600. These very words occur in the Draft Introduction (Works II 142) as the third advantage to be gained from adopting "the posture of the solitary philosopher" -- see 566n. Locke

(IV v 4) said that many "would perhaps have little left in their thoughts and meditations" if they were to "lay by" cant words; on words, see 178n.

601. See 724 where the argument is expanded, and cf. Princ. 136 "we want a sense...proper to know substances withal." This confirms my reading "withal" (Fraser and Johnston read "with"). Locke discusses our inability to apprehend substance in II xxiii 8ff., and Berkeley seems to be referring to sect. 12, where Locke speculates on the consequences of an alteration in our senses permitting us to see the inner constitution of sensible things. It is "incongruous" to suppose substance an object of sense and at the same time define it as an unknown substratum.

602. "Genera and species are in order to naming," Locke III vi 39, cf. II xxxii 6-8; on abstract ideas and their source in language, see 318n.

603. By taking attention away from the internal marks such as faintness and confusion; on optic angles, see 73n.; for the effect of the invention of "glasses," see 63n.

604. On existence, see 408n.

605. Locke is writing on "Doubtful propositions taken for principles." Berkeley holds (Princ. 118) that in the mathematicians' "principles there lurks some secret error" common to them with the rest of mankind, viz., abstract ideas, and the existence of objects without the mind.

606. The view that things are ideas and ideas things is

essential to Berkeley's immaterialsm. Representationism, he holds, leads to scepticism (see 79n.), because it postulates reality out of range of our ideas; on truth, see 554n.

607. 608. Further studies of words, see note on 178; in 495 Berkeley calls it absurd to use words for recording thoughts; on the Solitary Man, see 566n.

609. Because it involves distinguishing between esse and percipi, see 571n., 585; on substance, see 80n.

610. 611. 611a. 612. 613. Arguments against Locke's doctrine of uneasiness (see 145n.) from the conception of the supernatural will (as in 357) and from the nature of the human will (see 131n.). For Locke's "proofs," see Essay II xxi 33ff. On God, see 107n.

614. 614a. 615. 615a. Studies in will, understanding, and their objects, see 362a n. The reading "alter'd" is certain; Fraser and Johnston read "allow'd." Berkeley's altered opinion on the point is expressed in 848.

616. Cf. 879. Similarly Locke (II xxi 25) says it is an absurd question "whether a man be at liberty to will which of the two he pleases, motion or rest?" On the freedom of the will, see notes on 131 and 149.

617. Abstract principles adopted by physicists to explain change. The list corresponds with that of Cheyne (Philos. Principles of Nat. Rel. p. 3) "That there is no such thing as an Universal Soul animating this vast system according to Plato, nor any substantial Forms according to Aristotle,

nor any omniscient radical heat according to Hippocrates, nor any plastick virtue according to Scaliger, nor any hylarchic principle according to Henry More, is evident...." The list is, in part, incorporated into the Three Dialogues, Works II 258. On anima mundi, see Siris 276-284, 322. On Hippocrates, see Siris 204; on substantial forms, see Mot. 8ff; on hylarchic principle, see ib. 20.

618. Duplicate of 361, where see note.

619. Berkeley considers that the weight of a stone may be equally well, or equally badly, explained in terms of its inertia as in terms of the earth's attraction; physical force, for him, signifies nothing "besides the effect itself," Princ. 103. My reading "attractrix" is confirmed by Berkeley's "vim lunae attractricem," De Aestu Aeris, Works IV 210.

620. Berkeley expresses his doctrines in Princ. 1-33, 85-156, and states and answers Objections ib. 34-84.

621. Locke (II xxi 5, 15) distinguishes between will and volition; he defines will as the mind's power of ordering the consideration (or otherwise) of an idea, or of preferring a motion to rest (or vice versa); he defines voliton as "the actual exercise of that power." Berkeley accepts the distinction (see 699), but, as in 635, he questions the definitions accompanying it; he regards them as circular; on power, see 41n.; on will, see 131n.

622. "Extension is a different thing from thought," Maleb. I x. The Cartesians regarded the soul as unextended, but united to the extended body, and extension as existing in

material substance. In the latter portion of the PC (e.g., 878), and in the Principles Berkeley, while denying, as in this entry, unthinking substance (see 80n.), makes extended ideas distinct from mind (see 14n.); but here evidently he is prepared to regard extension, not only as dependent on the mind, but as a mode of mind; see next entry.

623. Fraser and Johnston read "thinking good actions"; this reading means nothing; the comma and the "not" are certain, and the "action" is highly probable. I take the entry to be a comment on the previous entry, being in effect an attempt to justify his refusal to distinguish extension from thought. Berkeley is emerging from his early panpsychism (see 24n.); he is awaking to the danger of making extension a mode of mind; but he has not yet reached the position of the Principles, according to which thinking things and unthinking things are the two mutually exclusive heads of reality, and here, as in 286, he uses the distinction between active and passive mind in an unsuccessful attempt to ease the difficulty.

624. Further argument against Locke's doctrine of uneasiness, see 145n. and Locke II xxi 39ff. Hecht says the text is corrupt; but that is a mistake. The text and its meaning are clear. The argument is an enthymeme, the conclusion, "Therefore the greatest uneasiness does not determine the will," being left to the imagination. On will, see 131n.

625. Berkeley would have to recognize that many theists accept the existence of matter, and in the Principles he is content to argue that atheism finds support in matter (e.g., sect. 35); but this entry represents, I think, his true view, viz., that when matter is exactly defined, it becomes an anti-God,

and that therefore the thinker must choose between God and matter, and cannot have both.

626. 627. 628. 629. 630. 631. Further studies in the freedom of the will (see notes on 131, 149, Alc. vii 16ff.); difficulties are traced to the ambiguity of words, see 178n.; Locke's doctrine of uneasiness (see 145n.) is rejected in favour of "complacency," i.e., a prior state of hedonic indifference, which would allow scope for a spontaneous act of will. Finally (631) Berkeley glances at the objection that his own doctrine does not allow true freedom. He certainly conceived spirit as a free activity; but (not having his "Part II," on ethics, see 508n.) we do not know how he would work out the conception in the sphere of human action.

632. Marked N (natural philosophy) the entry is concerned with the nature of physical contact, and may form part of a discussion of solidity (cf. 78 and Locke II iv) or of action at a distance. Distance for the immaterialist being perceived distance, contact must be for him perceived contact, contact relative to the visual faculty of the observer. Thus what the physicist would call "absolute contact" is ruled out.

633. 634. Berkeley's more controversial works, Alciphron, the Analyst, and the Defence of Free-Thinking, employ with effect the weapon of satire; his early works use it rarely, if at all. For his resolve not to give offence, see 209n. On Nihilarians, see 337n.; this term does not occur in the PC after this entry, nor in the publications. The term forms part of my argument against Johnston's transposition of the text.

635. A reference to Locke's distinction (II xxi 5) between will and volition, the will being a power to begin or end actions "barely by a thought or preference of the mind ordering...," and the volition "the actual exercise of that power" -- see 621n.; on will, see 131n.

636. On the fault of language, see 178n.; on "clear & determinate," see 537n.

637. The existence of thinking substance, finite as well as the infinite, is an integral part of the Berkeleian philosophy (*Princ*. 36 *et* **passim**). Why then does Berkeley hesitate about it here? Because his psychology was still in a fluid state, see 14n.; he had not yet decided finally to make the soul active, and he felt the difficulty about unknown substance (see 80n.) which he discusses in *Dials*., Works II 231ff., viz., If unknown spiritual substance be granted, why not grant also unknown material substance?

638. 639. Locke's "infallible rule" (IV viii 13), viz., no words without distinct **ideas**, is here set forth with great emphasis, see 356n.; "substance" is probably the word in view, as in the previous entry. Berkeley then notices Locke's companion principle, "no knowledge without ideas," and applies it to the imagination. Soon after this he abandons both principles, largely because of the need to find room for knowledge of the soul without idea.

"banters," cf. "abused" (579) and Draft Introduction (Works II 124) where Berkeley says there was a time when he himself was "banter'd and abus'd by words."

640. 641. Locke (II ii 3) **and Malebranche** (I vi) also use

the comparison of the worm. Berkeley is considering our knowledge of God in the light of Locke's two principles (see 638-639). Later on (782) he decides for knowledge of God without idea; for God being active and idea passive, there can be no idea of Him; but here he speaks as if God were unknown or known only by anology. He is, however, not satisfied with that position, and reminds himself that he is "embrangled" (cf. Princ. 98 for the term) in words. The terms "difference," "number," and "known" are explained by the context; for Berkeley is reflecting on the difference between the number of ideas known to God and to man; the term "old" comes in strangely; it must be an echo of Locke II xxvi 4, where it is used as an illustration of a relative term. On God, see 107n.

642. Cf. "having remov'd the veil of words," Draft Introduction (Works II 142), where the metaphor appears frequently. "Mist," cf. ib. p. 380 and PC 567. On "Scholemen & Mathematicians," see notes on 327, 492.

643. The contrast between active and passive leads Berkeley to deny an idea of the will, but he has not yet reached his final doctrine of will and understanding, see 362a n.

644. On thing and idea, see 369n.; "much wt...the Same," i.e., much the same, cf. Locke II xii 1, "man's power... much-what the same in the material and intellectual worlds."

645. 646. On volition and perception, see notes on 131 and 362a; on existence, see 408n.

647. Berkeley is arguing that the succession of ideas which

is time (see 4n.) is more marked in hearing, smell and taste, because their data are apprehended successively, and not simultaneously as are those of sight and touch. On the comparative distinctness of the data of the various senses, see 240n. For the "diversity" of sensations and volitions, cf. "actions and ideas that diversifie the day" (Princ. 97).

648. On the Solitary Man, see 566n.; on number, see 104n.

649. The only mention of innate ideas in the PC. For the curious phrase "Ideas created with us" cf. Maleb. III ii 4, where the opinion is refuted, "That all ideas are created with us."

It would be unsafe to argue from this entry that Berkeley differed seriously from Locke on the native endowment of the mind, even though Berkeley asserts innate ideas which Locke denied; for the two thinkers mean different things by the term "idea."

Berkeley does not deal with the question in his earlier works; but in Alc. I 14 he discusses natural endowment, and accepts native dispositions to know, see also Siris 308-309. Both these passages have left their mark on the fine account of our "inbred dispositions" in his sermon on the will of God, preached shortly before his death. Here is an extract, "That there are appetites and aversions, satisfactions and uneasinesses, inclinations and instincts originally interwoven in our nature, must be allowed by all impartial and considerate men" (Works VII 130). I have shown, by comparison with the draft sermon published by Wild, that Berkeley had Locke's doctrine of innate ideas in view.

650. 651. 652. Three entries dealing with Locke's doctrine that "thinking is the action, not essence, of the soul"

(II xix 4), and that "the soul thinks not always" (II i 10). These views conflict with the _esse_ _est_ _percipere_, and Berkeley maintains, "The soul always thinks. And in truth whoever shall go about to divide in his thoughts or abstract the existence of a spirit from its cogitation, will, I believe, find it no easy task" (_Princ_. 98). With regard to sleep and trances which appear to support Locke's view, Berkeley teaches that these are not gaps in the consciouness of an existing mind, because mindless time-intervals or gaps in time do not exist; for if there is no succession of ideas there is no time, see 4n. This teaching agrees with the cryptic statements of 83; but, as I have shown in the note there, it is doubtful whether he held for long the paradox of repeated annihilation.

653. 654. On Locke's doctrine of uneasiness, see 145n.; on the freedom of the will, see notes on 131 and 149; on "determine," see 627.

655. Molyneux, _Dioptrics_, p. 199, says that Romer from observing Jupiter's satellites has proved that light takes a second to travel 9,000 miles, and that Newton asserts that light takes about 10 minutes to come from the sun to the earth. Berkeley regards such statements as involving unperceived time, motion, and existence, and therefore as absurd; on time, see 4n.

656. The entry is obscurely phrased; but it is clear that Berkeley is equating, as he ofted does, unperceived existence, duplicated existence, and external existence. The marginal letter S (Soul or Spirit) makes it probable that he is on a point of psychology, rather than metaphysics,

and I think he is really using his new conception of existence to explode Locke's distinction between ideas of reflection and ideas of sensation; he is arguing that the notion of external or unperceived existence leads men to the untenable (in his view) distinction between the perception and the thing perceived, just as in <u>Princ</u>. 3 he argues that there is not difference between "there was an odour" and "it was smelt"; see 571n. and <u>Dials</u>., <u>Works</u> II 194-195. On the "act of the mind perceiving," see 808n.

657. 657a. 658. 659. 660. 661. 661a. 663. 665. On idea and will. An idea, for Berkeley, is passive, the will active; therefore an idea cannot be or be like the will; or, as in 643, the will cannot be the object of thought; see notes on 131, 154, 478. Berkeley returns repeatedly to this question in the later part of the <u>PC</u>, showing the importance he attached to it and the difficulty he found in it.

Note in 657a the recognition, as in <u>Princ</u>. 33, that the term "idea" is more proper to the imagination (see 531n.). Berkeley opposes the representative idea of sense; for his idea of sense <u>is</u> the thing, never the copy; but his idea of the imagination is representative, a copy of reality. On idea and thing, and "idea of," see 115n. and 369n.; on "thing" and "is" as general, i.e., abstract, terms, see notes on 318, 401.

In 659 the first part of the consequent is Berkeley's usual teaching, but how are we to understand the second part, Nothing which does perceive wills? It seems inconsistent with the teaching of the <u>Principles</u> that the will is one aspect of the "simple, undivided, active being" which perceives ideas and operates about them (sect. 27). The explanation is that when he penned this entry, he was still at the transition period, and was disposed to take perceiving mind as passive and identical with its contents.

In 661 Berkeley again examines (see 178n.) Locke's principle, which he at first accepted but later rejected, "All significant words stand for ideas"; as instances of words that do not stand for ideas, he takes words that denote activity, e.g., will, and particles. Locke has a short chapter on particles (III vii), meant to lessen the rigidity of his doctrine of ideas and words; but Berkeley finds it inconsistent with that doctrine, and draws support for his own view from Locke's statement that particles are "all marks of some action or intimation of the mind." On "any other Intelligence," see 410n.

662. 664. On Berkeley's studies in colour composition, see 151n.; on simple ideas, see 53n.; for the two sorts of compound, mechanical and chemical, see 721, and Locke's note appended to Essay II xv.

The old idiom "being" for "seeing that" occurs again in 833 (as corrected); Hecht, not understanding this archaism, marks a lacuna in the text.

666. 668. Locke (III iii) begins his study of general terms from the principle that all things that exist are particulars; in IV vi 2 he recognizes knowledge of particular truths and knowledge of general truths, and goes on to say that our knowledge begins in particulars and spreads by degrees to generals; but in the passage here under consideration (note the use of the same syllogism) viz., IV xvii 8, Locke writes, "Every man's reasoning and knowledge is only about the ideas existing in his own mind, which are truly, every one of them, particular existences."

Berkeley accepts the particularity of all ideas, and uses it as an argument against general ideas here and in 318 and 497. In Princ. Introd. 15 he outlines his conception of universality accruing to things, names, or notions which are "in their own nature particular." For further criticisms of universals in syllogisms, see 698 and 728-729; on abstract ideas, see 318n.

667. On particles and ideas, see 661n.; note the reading "on't" (i.e., "of it"); Fraser and Johnston read "really."

669. Having no ideas of will, we have no ideas of its operations, and therefore no ideas of moral actions. Thus his argument brings Berkeley into conflict with Locke's theory of ethics (IV iii 18), which lays down that morality is capable of demonstration, and that "from self-evident propositions, by necessary consequences, as incontestable as those in mathematics, the measures of right and wrong might be made out." Locke instances, "where there is no property, there is no injustice," and "no government allows absolute liberty," and says that if you establish the ideas property, injustice, government, and liberty, you may reach mathematical certainty of the truth of these propositions.

Berkeley accepts this theory, or assumes it, in the early part of the PC, see 162-163, 239, 336; but here and in 683 he questions it on the ground that the ideas on which it depends are non-existent. What his final conclusion is, is doubtful. In 776 he speaks of "my Doctrine of Certainty," and from 690, 705, 729, 730, 731, 732, 734, we may gather that his doctrine was one of verbal certainty, i.e., certainty as to the use of words, as distinct from Locke's certainty about ideas. But this limited doctrine does not seem to have satisfied Berkeley for long, and in 731a he asserts that real certainty is of sensible ideas, and that "I may be certain without affirmation or negation." In 755 he writes that morality might be demonstrated as "mixt Mathematics," i.e., that ethics has as much claim to mathematical precision as, e.g., dioptrics, no less and no more. In the <u>Principles</u> (100) he denies abstract ideas of justice and virtue, but he does not deal directly with the question of demonstration in ethics. On demonstration, see 163n.

670. 671. Existence for Locke (II vii 7) is a simple idea (see 53n.) conveyed by all the ways of sensation and reflection. Berkeley denies that he has the idea, and simple ideas being indefinable in words (<u>Locke</u> III iv 11) he denies that others can convey the idea to him, see 746; on ideas of reflection, see 571n.; on existence, see 408n. Note the correct reading "such" in 671.

672. 672a. 673. 674. Again, as in 612-615 and 644-646, Berkeley is trying to clear up the relation between "the unknown substratum" (see 80n.), or will, and its volitions and ideas. He distinguishes sharply between active beings and passive, i.e., spirits and ideas; he takes note of the active element in perception, using the illustration of opening the eyes, as in <u>Princ</u>. 29, and he finds volition and existence inseparable from perception. For a general note on the faculties in Berkeley's tentative psychology, see 362a n.; on the will, see 131n. "their existence" (674), i.e., the existence of the two-fold "things" (673).

675. The problem of the divine experience becomes acute for Berkeley, especially in respect of pain; for pain involves

change and imperfection. The problem is not touched in the <u>Principles</u>; but in the <u>Three Dialogues</u>, <u>Works</u> II 240-241, he deals with it, contrasting infinite spirit with finite, asserting that God knows our pain and sometimes causes it, but denying that He himself suffers pain. On God, see 107n.

676. 677. These two entries are combined and made more explicit in 853. The three recognized branches of philosophy were, (1) natural philosophy, or physics, (2) pure mathematics, (3) moral philosophy, including ethics, politics, and metaphysics. Berkeley's plans for his books were connected with this division; he seems to have intended to cover much, if not all, of the field (see 508n.); it is certain that he planned a work on ethics and wrote a good deal of it (his lost Part II); he speaks of a third book in 583 and 853, which was to deal with natural philosophy; but whether a work on mathematics was originally designed (probably, see <u>Princ</u>. 125), and whether the <u>Principles</u> was intended as an introduction to the whole <u>corpus</u> we cannot say for certain.

The marginal signs of 676 and 853 should be compared, and it will be seen that the sign X prefixed to over three hundred entries marks the entries that deal in some way with mathematics, or that at any rate do <u>not</u> deal with the other heads, morality (Mo.) and natural philosophy (N).

There is clearly a reference to Locke's section (IV i 3ff.) on the fourfold agreement of ideas, where relation is associated with mathematics and coexistence with physics. On relation, see 540n.; on coexistence, see 403n.; on "Including," see 690n. and <u>Princ</u>. Introd. 22.

678. In spite of his acknowledged debt to the <u>Essay</u> and his esteem for its author (see 567n.) Berkeley regards Locke as his

main antagonist. There is a similar entry in another MS. (39304) in the Berkeley Papers in the British Museum, which uses the metaphor of mountain and molehill. Fraser prints it at the end of the PC in his (1901) edition of the Works, Vol. I, p. 92. The "I" after "acknowleg'd" probably means "Introduction."

679. Echoed in Princ. Introd. 4. The Introduction is prominent in this part of the PC.

680. The same request is made in TV 120, and in the Prefaces to the Principles and the Three Dialogues.

681. Locke (II xxvii 19) writes, "Personal identity consists, not in the identity of substance, but, as I have said, in the identity of consciousness; wherein if Socrates and the present mayor of Queenborough agree, they are the same person." Locke (ib. 13) thinks it theoretically possible that "the consciousness of past actions can be tranferred from one thinking substance to another," and thus that a man could be conscious of what he had never done. These anomalies are avoided, Berkeley thinks, by placing personal identity in the active spirit, whether viewed as will (cf. 194a) or as understanding (mind, see 192n.); on will and understanding, see 362a n.; on consciousness, see 200n.; for "etc" Fraser and Johnston read "surely."

682. Cf. "what a number of very great and extraordinary men have gone before me..." (Princ. Introd. 5) and the corresponding section of the Draft Introduction (Works II 122) which adds prima manu "and miscarry'd."

683. 684. On ideas of moral actions, see 669n. Locke's

theory, there outlined, has resulted, Berkeley here suggests, in unnecessary difficulties about demonstration. At this stage he himself believed in verbal certainty.

685. Berkeley explains his choice of the term "idea" in Princ. 39, not in the Introduction, see 369n.

686. 686a. On Malebranche's influence, see 230n.; 686 is an epitome of Malebranche's "Illustration" (excursus) on, Tis very difficult to prove the Existence of Bodies (for an analysis, see my Berkeley and Malebranche, pp. 58-61), which is referred to again in 800, 801, 818, and perhaps in 265. This Illustration is a curious piece of reasoning; its general trend is towards proving the nonexistence of bodies, but it advances the three proofs of their existence which Berkeley here mentions, and with which he deals as follows: (1) the proof from Scripture, in Princ. 82, (2) from "that poor possibility," in Princ. 75, and (3) from the propension, in Princ. 54-57. Berkeley's erased remark on this alleged propension should be noted. He erased the words, no doubt, when he came to recognise knowledge without ideas, i.e., knowledge of spirits.

The verso addition 686a probably records a development of Berkeley's thought; for he here says in so many words that he had second thoughts about the existence of bodies, cf. 517; at first he thought they did not exist, and that all was mind (see 24n.); later, as in this entry, he explicitly takes up the position of the Principles, viz., that there are bodies, distinct from mind, though dependent on mind, and that these bodies are not material, but sensible.

687. 688. For Berkeley's attack on abstract ideas, see 318n.; "the killing blow" is the criticsm of Locke's "absurd triangle" (IV vii 9), contained in TV 125 and Princ. Introd. 13-16, where it comes "at the last." In Geometry No Friend to Infidelity (1734) Philalethes (Dr. Jurin) argued that Berkeley had misrepresented Locke's argument here; Berkeley replied vigorously in his Defence of Free-Thinking, 45-48. On Locke's candour, see 567n.; "see with my own eyes," cf. Locke I iv 23.

689. If by "thing" be meant a passive object willed or perceived by God or man, Berkeley accepts the term, and he calls objects of sense ideas and things indifferently. But if by "thing" be meant a material archetype of our ideas, he rejects it and all that it stands for. On thing and idea, see 369n.

Archetypes are mentioned in the PC only here and in 823; in the Principles they are mentioned in sections 9, 45, 90, 99; and in the Three Dialogues, Works II 204, 206, 213, 214, 223, 239, 248, 254. They are probably referred to in the Principles sections 53, 70, 74, 76, 91, 148, and in the Three Dialogues, Works II 229, 233, 258. I have analysed these passages in my article "The Philosophical Correspondence between Berkeley and Johnson," Hermathena, LVI (1940), 99-105, concluding that Berkeley invariably denies material archetypes, nowhere denies immaterial archetypes but nowhere explicitly affirms them, that a few passages accept them as a legitimate hypothesis, and that a few passages can hardly be reconciled with a serious belief in archetypes. Johnson had asked some pertinent questions about archetypes, to which Berkeley replied briefly.

690. 691. On demonstrating morality and Locke's instances, see 699n. The dictionary of ethical terms was, no doubt, suggested to Berkeley by Locke's section (III xi 25) on a

dictionary of natural history terms. Berkeley hoped that
such a dictionary would fix the meanings of ethical terms and
enable them to be used with precision. He illustrates his
meaning with the proposition (705), "God Ought to be worship'd."
"Inclusion" is mentioned again in 677 and 853 as part of the
method of demonstration; presumably the definitions in the
dictionary would be such that, for instance, the comprehension
of "free" could be compared at a glance with that of "man."
There is a good discussion of demonstration and inclusion in
G. A. Johnston, Development of Berkeley's Philosophy, pp. 292ff.

692. Read "aversion" and "Spirit" for "exertion" and "spirit"
(Fraser and Johnston). As the marginal letter shows, Berkeley
is on the distinction between primary and secondary qualities,
and is asking why thinkers are ready to internalize the latter
while externalizing the former; he replies that some qualities,
e.g., heat and cold, tastes, etc., directly affect volition
through our sense of pleasure and pain, and are therefore felt
as within the mind; cf. TV 59 for a similar argument with regard
to visible and tangible figure and magnitude.

693. Berkeley had hopes at this period of eliminating error
(see 816n.) by aid of wordless thought, see 178n. and 719.

Locke's doctrine of certainty is under discussion. Locke
(IV ii) teaches that the greatest certainty is intuitive, the
immediate perception of the agreement or disagreement of ideas;
next in rank comes demonstrative certainty, which depends at
every step on intuition, but is liable to err, especially in
long deductions, owing to the defects of memory when dealing
with intermediate ideas. Lastly there is sensitive knowledge,
which yields no certainty of external existence, but only of
our own feelings of pleasure and pain.

Berkeley became critical of this account (see 669n.), and rejected it, reversing the verdict on the senses; in 740 he places certainty in the senses; but he keeps clear of sensationalism; for we can be certain of what is not actually perceived, such as the future judgement, 776-777, and the existence of God, 813. For the change of view on demonstration, see 163n.

694. Apparently the "cure for Pride" is the doctrine of man's "absolute and entire dependence" on God, see Princ. 149.

695. On the infinity of space, see 135n. and Locke II xvii 4ff.; on eternity and infinite space, see Locke II xvii 20; on the possibility of matter's thinking, see 573n. and Locke IV iii 6. The dangers attending these doctrines are dealt with in Princ. 117, 133; but Locke is not specifically mentioned.

696. Reappears with modifications in Princ. Introd. 25; on the fallacy of words, see 178n.; on truth in the mind, see 554n. "Gibberish, Jargon," cf. Draft Introduction, Works II 140.

697. 698. Studies in Locke's doctrine of certainty by intermediate ideas; see 693n. Locke speaks of algebra in IV iii 18, 20, and IV xii 15; for Berkeley on algebra, see 382n.; on sagacity, see Locke IV ii 3; on demonstration, see 163n.

699. For Locke's distinction between power (i.e., the will) and volition, see 621n.

700. 701. Locke (II xxiii 30) says that the substance of

spirit and of body are equally unknown to us; hence Stillingfleet (see 517n.) charged him with almost discarding "substance out of the reasonable part of the world." For Berkeley, there is no substance (see 80n.) other than spirit; and so when, as here and in 512, he affirms the substance of body, he is using the term "substance" in the non-technical sense, expounded in 724; thus the substance body means simply the sensible ideas that compose the body. The second part of 701 is at variance with Berkeley's full official teaching, viz., that we know spirit, but not by idea. With "purus actus" cf. 788, 828, 870.

702. On words, see 178n.

703. On abstract ideas, see 318n.; on "The Vulgar," see 405n.

704. Locke (II i 10) says that it is not "any more necessary for the soul always to think, than for the body always to move." Berkeley holds that the soul always thinks (see 83n.), and he here rejects Locke's comparison between soul and body.

705. Locke (I iv 7) analyses this principle in order to show that though of first importance it is not innate; Berkeley takes it as an instance of an ethical principle suitable for demonstration -- see notes on 163 and 690.

706. 707. 708. 709. A return to the much debated questions of will and understanding and idea (see notes on 131 and 362a); Berkeley insists again that there can be no idea of will, and that the will is spontaneous, and is not determined by uneasiness (see 145n.). Locke is more guarded than would

appear from the statement in 706; he writes (II ix 1), "In bare, naked perception, the mind is, for the most part, only passive."

Philippe van Limborch (1633-1712), Arminian theologian of Amsterdam, was an advocate of religious toleration and a friend and correspondent of Locke. Their correspondence forms more than half of <u>Some Familiar Letters between Mr Locke and several of his Friends</u>. The book was "printed and published in London in Easter and Trinity term [<u>i.e.</u>, May/June] 1708" (Edward Arber, <u>The Term Catalogue</u>, III 1697-1709). Therefore, as Prof. Aaron has pointed out, this entry helps to date this portion of the <u>PC</u>.

The quotation is from Locke's letter (p. 479) dated May 21, 1701; Locke is arguing that will and desire are widely different, but are commonly confused, because will rarely acts except at the impulse of desire.

710. It might be objected to Berkeley's doctrine of the heterogeneity (see 28n.) of sight and touch that visible and tangible <u>minima</u> (see 59n.), being <u>minima</u>, are indistinguishable. He here tries to meet the objection.

711. Cf. 878 where extension (see 18n.) is stated to be "no Property of the Mind." "sensible" is added to cover both visible and tangible extension.

712. 713. 714. Here Berkeley's psychology reaches its final form, and, as in the <u>Principles</u> (1, 2, 27 <u>et passim</u>), the perceiving active being, viz., "mind, spirit, soul, or my self," is set over against passive being, viz., the ideas. Will (see 131n.) and understanding (see 362a n.) become abstract aspects of the active being. The term "person"

(see 25n.) is not used in the **Principles**. Berkeley uses it freely in the early part of the **PC**, but he decides to avoid it owing to its use in the Trinitarian and Christological formulae. The idea-things are effects of the will of God, see 403n.; on God, see 107n.; on unity, see 75n.

715. 716. The doctrinal difficulties connected with the term "person" remind Berkeley of the need to conciliate ecclesiastical opinion (see 517n.). He does not, in point of fact, speak favourably of the Schoolmen, though he shows restraint in criticizing them, see **Princ**. Introd. 17, 20. These cautious resolves receive point from the fact that shortly after his ordination as priest Berkeley was prosecuted by Archbishop King in his ecclesiastical court on the charge of receiving irregular ordination. Berkeley's dignified letter of explanation, dated April 18, 1710, is extant in the **King Papers** in the Trinity College library (printed by Sir C. S. King in **A Great Archbishop of Dublin**, 1906, p. 121 and in **Works** VIII 33).

717. Note the corrected reading; "2d & 4th" (Fraser and Johnston) admits no explanation, and is certainly not in the MS. I have compared the "1st" with the same figure in 571; they correspond exactly.

Berkeley was not sympathetic towards Locke's attack on innate ideas in Book I, and he objected strongly to Locke's doctrine of words (as signs of abstract ideas), of which (in whole or part) Locke himself says, "it is one I thought not of when I began to write" (III v 16). Berkeley may have had these actual words in mind; in any case it is clear from the marginal sign I, crossed out and restored, that Berkeley is on abstract ideas; he is urging that had Locke begun with a study of words, as in Book III, and had he studied them to better purpose, he would not have been led into his doctrine of abstraction; note in particular Locke's argument in III iii 6, attacked in Princ. Introd. 11.

718. My reading "beards" is certain; Fraser reads "weeds," Johnston "words," Hecht, apparently, "wands." Berkeley is alluding to Locke's instances (IV x 9) of material things, "the clippings of our beards and parings of our nails."

719. On certainty and laying aside words, see 693n.; on demonstration, see 163n.

720. This entry well illustrates the theological distinction between implicit and explicit faith, and forms a complete refutation of the charge of deism recently brought against Berkeley. It should be read in connection with Toland's Christianity not Mysterious (1696). Toland's visit to Dublin was long remembered there. On scripture and revealed religion, see notes on 281 and 584; on transubstantiation, see 350 and Princ. 124. For "fact" (Fraser and Johnston) read "Text," i.e., text of scripture.

721. On colour composition, see 664n. The twofold "Complexation" refers apparently to the two sorts of composition discussed in 664.

722. On length without breadth, see 21n.; any general figure, for Berkeley, is a particular figure with its particularities disregarded; this principle is part of his explanation of "abstract ideas."

723. One of his alternative theories of the prehuman period of the Mosaic week, see 60n. and <u>Dials</u>., <u>Works</u> II 252; on intelligences, see 410n.

724. For Locke on substance, see 601n.; for Berkeley's uses of the term, see 80n.

725. Probably a note on 724 explaining why material substance, as distinct from sensible things, is supposed to have existence (see 408n.), and tracing the error to the doctrine of abstract ideas; see 318n.

726. Distance and magnitude are the subjects, respectively, of the first two divisions of the <u>Theory of Vision</u>; Berkeley tries to show that writers on optics (cf. 207) pay too much attention to angles, etc., too little to confusion, etc., and neglect the heterogeneity of sight and touch.

727. 727a. Berkeley concedes that the Solitary Man (see 566n.) on acquiring speech would learn new sounds and new complex ideas, but denies that he would acquire abstract ideas, see 318n.

728. 729. 730. 730a. 731. 731a. 732. A further examination of Locke's doctrine of certainty by intermediate ideas; see notes on 163 and 693. On identical propositions, see 592n.; on knowledge without ideas, see 312n. and cf. <u>Maleb</u>. III ii 7, "There are things we see without ideas."

Fraser omits 731a; Johnston omits from it the words "pro hic & nunc," which add point to Berkeley's insistence upon sensible certainty. Note the alternation in the marginal signs, transferring this group from the Introduction to Part II.

-301-

733. Berkeley is considering Locke's views on relation, see 540n.

734. Berkeley's views on demonstration (see 163n.) altered towards the end of the PC; he seems here to be contrasting the verbal demonstrations of ethics (see 669n.) with the false demonstrations of physics. In ethics, he held, you can demonstrate if you can define your terms, but in physics, not so, for there the laws of nature are concerned; and they are the ways in which God usually (but not necessarily) acts; see 144n.

735. The veritates aeternae are mentioned again in 831, in connection with Spinoza; they were a commonplace of the Platonic tradition. Norris, Theory of the Ideal World (1701) Part I vi sect. 2, discusses them, and shows how they result from the divine Ideas.

But Berkeley is probably considering Locke's account of them; for this entry is echoed in the Draft Introduction (Works II 132), "What becomes of those general maxims, those first principles of knowledge...all wch are supposed to be about abstract and universal Ideas?" Locke (IV xi 14) explains the veritates aeternae as general propositions which having been once made out about abstract ideas "must needs be eternal verities." They "vanish," for Berkeley, because the abstract ideas, on which Locke makes them depend, vanish.

736. 737. On words, see 178n.; 737 is an echo of Locke IV xvii 4, and appears verbatim in the Draft Introduction (Works II 142), where the notion of words as "dress," "veil," etc., is very common.

738. On Berkeley's principle (*esse est percipere*), Descartes' "*cogito ergo sum*" becomes *cogito ergo cognito*.

739. 740. A criticism of Locke's doctrine of certainty (see 693n.) and of his four sorts of agreement of ideas (IV i 3ff.). Identity, diversity, and real existence, if taken for anything over and above the perceived idea, are, for Berkeley, abstract ideas, and therefore the knowledge founded on them "vanisheth." Relation (see 540n.) is, for him, an "Obscure ambiguous term" (733) yielding only nominal knowledge, as in mathematics; but coexistence is a true and a large field of knowledge, a knowledge of the properties of things resting on the customary connection of sign and thing signified. If a certain yellowness, for instance, coexists with that collection of sensible ideas called gold, on seeing the yellowness I expect "the power to remain in the fire unconsumed"; and that is the meaning of saying we *know* that gold is fixed. On the senses, see 317n.; on the term "mob," see 405n.

741. If this entry has any relevance to Berkeley's books, must it not refer to the fulsome Dedication of the *Theory of Vision* to Sir John Percival -- which must have made his young friend "wonder"?

742. "overtake Truth," see 521n.; "my shortsightedness," no doubt metaphorical, cf. 774; the metaphor is reproduced in *Princ.* Introd. 5.

743. 744. 745. A discussion of free will (see 149n.) based on the Locke-Limborch correspondence (see 709n.). Free will is the main topic of this correspondence from p. 474 to the end of the volume, and "in this place" probably refers to p. 512,

where Locke reduces his views to ten theses, beginning "<u>Homo est agens liberum</u>"; on judgement and volition, see 362a n.; on indifference and uneasiness, see 143n. and 145n.

In 744 for "Both" (Fraser and Johnston) read "Res," i.e., <u>Respondeo</u>, for which Berkeley has several abbreviations in his <u>Arithmetica</u>, e.g., <u>Resp</u>., <u>Respon</u>. "My," the capital letter stresses the spontaneity of the active spirit in thought and will.

746. An argument against Locke's account (II vii 7) of these simple ideas (see 53n.); on unity, see 75n.; on existence, see 408n. and 671n.

747. An attack on what Berkeley calls "the excuse" (see 292n.), i.e., the finiteness of our faculties. This entry is followed closely in the <u>Draft Introduction</u> to the <u>Principles</u> (<u>Works</u> II 121), and has left its mark on the Introduction as printed, sect. 2.

748. In criticism of Locke's doctrine (IV vi 13) that general knowledge "consists barely in the contemplation of our own abstract ideas." The entry is followed closely in the <u>Draft Introduction</u> (<u>Works</u> II 133-134). "sheaves & bundles," based on <u>Locke</u> IV xii 12, "In the knowledge of bodies, we must be content to glean what we can from particular experiments; since we cannot, from a discovery of their real essences, grasp at a time whole sheaves, and in bundles comprehend the nature and properties of whole species together."

749. A speculation on the faculties of superior spirits (see 410n.), as in 835 and <u>TV</u> 84. Read "spheres" not "systems" (Fraser and Johnston); On the visual sphere, see 97n.; on

the m.v., see 59n.; on the enlargement of sight, see 175n.

750. Berkeley's study of words (see 178n.) had made him aware of their misuse; now as in Princ. Introd. 21, he shows himself aware also of their "excellent use."

751. "banishing Metaphisics," the phrase should be read in the light of 207; Berkeley was against the arid metaphysics of the Schools,; but of course he recognized speculative metaphysics (e.g., 162-163, 239). His own philosophy is a metaphysic; but he claims, not without reason, that it is a philosophy of commonsense; see Princ. 88, also the Three Dialogues, which literally begins and ends with an appeal to commonsense.

752. This is the only reference in the PC to our knowledge of other minds; the problem in dealt with briefly in Princ. 145; cf. Dials., Works II 233.

753. Locke makes abstraction the differentia of man (see 594n.); Berkeley would substitute the imagination or "Composition of Ideas"; see 531n., and cf. "compounding and dividing them," Princ. Introd. 10.

754. On cause and coexistence, see 403n.; on occasion, see 499n.

755. On demonstration in ethics, see 669n.; "mixt" is "applied," as opposed to "pure" mathematics. Geometry is assigned to mixed mathematics in 770.

756. On "Idea of Volition," see 643n.; on perception as

passive, see 301n.

757. On thing and idea, see 369n.

758-768. 770. A series of observations on the nature of numbers, and on the mathematical disciplines. They should be read in conjunction with Princ. 118-122, though that passage deals almost exclusively with Arithmetic. (Berkeley discusses geometry, ib. 123-131, and in TV 149ff.; but he does not deal with Algebra, see 382n.).

Berkeley's chief points are that number is a creature of the mind (see 104n.), that numbers in themselves are nothing but names (e.g., the figure 2), and that the sciences which rest on them are of practical utility, but do not yield speculative truth.

In his technical langauge numbers are signs of ideas, but not ideas; conventional symbols would thus form the subject matter of arthmetic (767-768); 761 and 763 should be taken together as illustrations of this teaching. Berkeley is arguing that the sight (idea) of a multitude of objects conveys little or nothing to the mind, but that the "name," the specialized symbol, sets the mind on its proper task of computing and reckoning. This teaching is part of the exposure of the claim that arithmetic has for its object abstract ideas of number (see Princ. 118-119).

Note the distinction between arithmetical figures and algebraical signs (758), and that between numbers (names) and words (763).

"Imaginary roots," i.e., $\sqrt{-1}$, would be, for Berkeley, simply one of the "hard knots" of speculative mathematics (868) without basis in reality. He does not directly "unravel that Mystery" in his published works. For "Mixt Mathematics," see

755n.; on arithmetic and geometry, see 458; on points, see 59n.

[In 763 the correct reading "meer" rather than "never" implies that numbers are words, and is consistant with other entries, e.g., 762, 750. -- Editor]

769. This challenging statement on "sensual pleasure" as the summum bonum is discussed above in my note on 541; the "rightly understood" shows that Berkeley knew that his statement was open to misunderstanding (cf. 773). Of the word "Gospels" not a letter is legible; the word is covered by a blot, apparently made by a reagent. Presumably it was legible in Fraser's time, or he would have marked it as doubtful. If the reading be sound, Berkeley must be considering the pursuit of pleasure in mundane matters as an earnest of eternal happiness, which is the sanction of the Gospel precepts; cf. 776 and Maleb. I xvii, "God being infinitely above all other things, the pleasure of those who shall enjoy Him, will certainly exceed all other pleausres."

771. Locke discusses Trifling Propositions in IV viii; Berkeley seems to have been interested in the chapter because of Locke's discussion of those identical propositions that are the supposed foundation of demonstration and certainty -- see 669n.

772. On abstract ideas, see 318n. and 55n.; on existence, see 408n.; on extension, see 18n.; for the appeal to the vulgar, see 405n.

773. An important comment on Berkeley's statement (769) that "sensual pleaure" is the summum bonum, recognizing that some so-called "sensual pleasure" is "contemptible." On his

hedonism, see 541n.; cf. <u>Maleb</u>. IV x. "Pleasure is always a good and pain always an evil...."

774. He is developing the metaphor, forcibly expressed in <u>Princ</u>. Introd. 5.

775. These are the two types of idea recognized in <u>Princ</u>. 33; note the erased "or intelligible thing," and for the three faculties, sense, imagination, and intellect, see 531n.

776. 777. Berkeley has a good deal in common with pragmatism, and he here shows a firm grasp of the connection between belief and action; on his doctrine of certainty, see notes on 163, 669, and 693; on his hedonism, see 541n.; he did not hold with disinterested religion or with disinterested virtue, and just as pleasure was, for him at this period, the goal of action here, so eternal happiness was, for him, the goal of action hereafter.

778. On the problem of equality, see 514n.

779. Hecht in his note on the entry expresses surprise at Berkeley's approval of this "<u>sensualistische</u>" proposition, and tries to explain it away or tone it down. But this proposition, reasonably understood, is by no means sensualist, and acceptance of it is quite compatible with belief in spirit. Berkeleianism is a philosophy of sense and spirit, and not of spirit alone. Berkeley always makes sense the basis of the cognitive process (see 317n.), and here, in effect, he traces the doctrine of abstraction to neglect of the evidence of sense. On abstract ideas, see 318n. The Schoolmen are

styled "those great masters of abstraction" in Princ. Introd. 17.

780. This "old known axiom" is used in the Three Dialogues (Works II 236 apparat. crit.) to prove that matter does not cause our perceptions; here, as the marginal letter G shows, he is thinking of it in connection with Deity. There Berkeley assumes its truth; here he denies it. The next group of entries are on Descartes, and he may be thinking of the use Descartes makes of the axion in the third Meditation. If the axiom be used against creative causality, Berkeley is bound to oppose it, but quite consistently he can make use of it against material causality (see 403n.). In the third edition of the Three Dialogues the reference to the axiom is dropped.

781. 782. 783. 784. 785. 786. A group dealing with Descartes' views. The Cartesians are named in 281, 424a, 453, 801, 811, and here Berkeley pays close attention to the Mediatations, reading them, it would seem in Molyneux's translation (1680), to which Hobbes's "Objections" and Descartes' "Replies" are appended.

Berkeley objects to Descartes' use of scholastic terms and arguments; he points out inconsistencies in Descartes' terminology; he criticizes Descartes' proof of the existence of God; he rejects problematical idealism, and tries to vindicate the senses against Descartes' attack on them -- see 790, 794-798, 805-806, 818-819, 845.

Berkeley denies the idea of God on the ground that ideas, being in their nature passive, cannot represent active spirit; but he had to guard his denial from misunderstanding, as he does in Princ. 140, because atheists and agnostics denied it too, see sermon by J. Harris, F.R.S., preached in St. Paul's

Cathedral, February 7, 1698, entitled, "The atheist's objection that we can have no idea of God Refuted." Malebranche sometimes affirms the idea of God, sometimes denies it. On God, see 107n.; on substance, see 80n.

787. Berkeley recognizes distinctions of quality in pleasures, including the distinction between "pure" (i.e., free from attendant pain) and "impure" pleasures, and thus he avoids many of the objectionable features of hedonism; see 541n.

788. His doctrine of soul (see 14n.) and will (see 131n.), long debated, has reached its final stage, and he here recognizes, as in the <u>Priniciples</u>, (a) the active principle under various names, and (b) the passive effects of ideas.

789. Cf. 608. Locke (III xi 7) deprecates party spirit, and there is little or no trace of it in Berkeley's writings; cf. "I have always thought and judged for myself" (<u>Def</u>. 19). Both he and Locke are thinking of the emotive power of words in the formation of parties.

790. Locke (IV xi 5) writes, "If I turn my eyes at noon towards the sun, I cannot avoid the ideas which the light or sun then produces in me"; and Descartes (<u>Med</u>. VI), "These ideas...presented themselves...without my consent being required...." The former passage is echoed in Berkeley's section (<u>Princ</u>. 29) on the causal arguments for the existence of God.

    A line is drawn in ink across the recto page beween 790 and 791. There is no indication of its meaning.

791. Berkeley conceives the will as a continuous activity,

see notes on 131 and 590.

792. The principle <u>esse</u> <u>est</u> <u>percipi</u> (see 408n.) is extended to objects of the imagination (see 531n.). The will, not being an idea (see 131n.), cannot be imagined, on "the first Book," see 508n.

793. 793a. Locke (IV v 2) divides propositions into mental and verbal, corresponding, respectively, to the truth of thought and the truth of words. In IV viii 13 he gives "gold is a metal" as an instance of verbal proposition; Berkeley is correct in doing likewise; but Berkeley's other two examples of verbal (nominal) propositions, the perceptual quality and the scientific property, are not convincing. He is apparently speaking in criticism of Locke; for Locke (IV i 6) gives "gold is fixed" as an instance of coexistence, which, with non-coexistence, constitutes his third type of knowledge.

794. 795. 796. 797. 798. 799. A second series dealing with Descartes (for the first, see 781n.) and especially with Hobbes's objections appended to Molyneux's translation of the <u>Mediations</u>.

In the last few paragraphs of the sixth Meditation Descartes takes the pain in the foot as an instance of the fallibility of the senses. Berkeley decides to "vindicate the senses" (see 317n.); he does so by urging that thought misleads us, not the senses; for thought makes us attribute the connection between pain and the bruised foot to nature instead of to God. On God and nature, see 485n., <u>Princ</u>. 150; for the denial of necessary connection, see 181n.

Hobbes's second objection (795-796) was directed against the <u>cogito</u> <u>ergo</u> <u>sum</u>; he says the <u>sum</u> is not validly inferred; for we only know the <u>cognito</u>, because "we cannot conceive any act without its subject, as dancing without a dancer." Locke (II xxi 17) uses a similar illustration. Descartes replies in effect: "That is true; but it applies to any substance; we do not know it directly, but only as the subject of various acts."

In his third objection (797-798) Hobbes argues that if Descartes identifies himself with his understanding, "we shall fall into the scholastic expression -- the understanding understands, the sight sees, the will wills," and that then "the walking shall walk." Descartes replied, "I do not deny that I who think am distinct from my thought, as a thing is distinguished from its <u>modus</u> or manner."

Berkeley dreaded Hobbes's materialism, and traces it to the separation of <u>esse</u> from <u>percipi</u> (799); but the two thinkers had points in common; for instance, they both rejected the "idea of God," and they had similar views on the mathematical problems and on general terms.

800. 801. 802. An important trio of entries containing Berkeley's final position about the reality of bodies and his theory of powers; see notes on 41 and 52. At the opening of the <u>PC</u> (24) he wrote, "Nothing properly but persons i.e. conscious things do exist," and bodies at that stage of his thought were not actual, but were simply powers in God to cause sensations in us. He became dissatisfied with that position; he saw its sceptical tendency; the contrast between active and passive began to dominate his thought; he saw the radical distinction between the mind of God and the mind of man, and by means of that distinction he reconciled the <u>esse est percipi</u> with the reality of the perceivable. Here he accepts sensible things as independent of Our (note the capital for emphasis as in 477a) mind, and yet dependent on the mind of

God, and that is his official teaching; see 838 and Princ. 48, 90. The "powers" theory is not mentioned in the Principles, but it comes up for brief discussion in Dials., Works II 240.

The unperceived perceivable is "still with relation to perception," because God actually does perceive it and man may do so. Things are "effects," because caused by God, see 433n.

On Malebranche, see 230n. I have given an account of his "Illustration" in my note on 686. Johnston, ignoring the capital letter, misunderstands the term; he takes it of a casual illustration employed by Malebranche (I 19), whereas it refers to the most important of the many excursuses appended to the Recherche. "Illustration" was the recognized English translation of Malebranche's term Eclaircissment (see T. Taylor's translation, London, 1700, 2nd ed.)

803. The point is developed in Princ. 121-122; "Indian," i.e., Arabic figures; "Signs not Ideas," see 766-767.

804. Locke (IV xvii) makes reasoning ancillary to demonstration, see notes on 163 and 817, and cf. 734. "I question, no matter, etc."; these must be instances of the formulae of reasoning.

805. Descartes, towards the end of the third Meditation, argues that the idea of God is innate; "for it is not in my power to diminish it or to add anything to it." Berkeley denies that we have an idea of God (782), but here he is content to argue that Descartes' argument for its innateness is unsound, because all ideas, both of sense and imagination, could be proved innate by the same argument. For Berkeley's criticism of Descartes, see 781n.

806. Hobbes in his Objections (see 781n.) has failed to distinguish between will and idea, and thus he has confused active and passive, and has, in consequence, been led to a denial of spirit.

807. From his own day to ours Berkeley's philosophy has been misconceived in this way, and he treats this misconception as the First Objection, and answers it in Princ. 34-36; on the reality of body, see 52n.; on the reasons for preferring "idea" to "thing," see 369n.; on the "Second Book," see 508n.

808. "Subject" is here non-technical, a synonym for "object," i.e., "yt I think on," or "idea," here sharply distinguished, as in the Principles, from the thinking, the act of volition or will (see 131n.). This teaching is not at variance with that, e.g., of 656, where the distinction between "perception" (not the act of perceiving) and "the Idea perceived" is in effect denied; for there the "act of the mind perceiving" is not identified with its object. For this definition of "idea" cf. "the immediate object of sense, or understanding," TV 45. For Berkeley's earlier use of "thought" as the equivalent of "idea," see 153n.

809. Locke (IV v 4) says that in the case of complex ideas, like fortitude, we think more readily about the name than the idea, but that in the case of the simpler ideas, like white or black, we can and do frame the idea without reflecting upon the name. It is not complexity that makes the difference, replies Berkeley, but abstraction, see 318n.

810. "Pure Intellect" is the title of Book III of Malebranche's

Recherche; for Berkeley's hesitation about the faculty, see 531n.

811. This entry has no marginal sign, and perhaps it is not a considered judgement. Certainly there are difficulties in both parts of it. Is it true that where Locke differs from the Cartesians, Berkeley takes side with Locke? (Of the Cartesians Malebranche is, no doubt, principally in view, see 265n.) It is true, with regard to general approach to philosophy and the empirical method; in some few respects it is true of Locke's teaching on solidity. It is not true with regard to many, if not most, of the other points of difference. On matter Locke and Malebranche are both far from Berkeley, but Locke is the further. On innate ideas, the imagination, causation, and the immanence of God, Berkeley is closer to Malebranche than to Locke. Berkeley apparently does not regard abstract ideas as a point of difference; but he specifically attacks Locke's doctrine, and while the Cartesians do use abstract ideas, they have nothing corresponding to Locke's doctrine.

The second half of the entry is hardly consistent with the first; for if Locke is right, and the Cartesians are wrong, how could fidelity to their own principles make them "allow of his opinions"? Perhaps Berkeley simply meant that Locke and the Cartesians have a good deal of common ground about abstract ideas. On existence see 408n.; on abstract ideas, see notes on 318 and 552.

[Note the correct reading "cant." Fraser and Johnston read "causes" and Luce read "cause." -- Editor]

812. "The propertys..." This proposition occurs in Latin in 177a (see note) as a quotation from Le Clerc. "Blind agent"

-315-

is a contradiction, for Berkeley, because he regards will and understanding as necessarily conjoined; cf. "blind unthinking deputy," Princ. 150.

813. On certainty, see notes on 163, 669, and 693; on God, see 107n.; on intuition, see 547n.

814. At first when he was experimenting in terminology Berkeley was disposed to question the immortality of the "soul" (see notes on 14 and 478), but here, as in Princ. 93 and 141, he treats it as immortal and incorruptible.

815. 816. On will and perception, see 131n.; on will and understanding, see 362a n. Error, mentioned in 737 and 783, is not discussed elsewhere in the PC or in the Principles. Berkeley here agrees with Descartes (Med. IV) and Malebranche (I iv) that will is the real cause of error. That perception is inerrant is stated also in 693; cf. Princ. 87, "Colour, figure, motion, extension, and the like, considered only as so many sensations in the mind, are perfectly known: there being nothing in them which is not perceived."

817. "Tell a country gentlewoman that the wind is south-west, and the weather louring and like to rain, and she will easily understand it is not safe for her to go abroad thin clad in such a day, after a fever." Locke (IV xvii 4) thus illustrates the distinction between reasoning and demonstration; see 804n.

818. Descartes (Med. VI) and Malebranche, "Illustration" on Bodies (see 686n.) speak of the supposed inclination to believe in the existence of bodies. They did not examine,

Berkeley argues, the meaning of "existence" (see 408n.), and consequently they have to suppose the existence of matter as "something we know not what." For ideas of the imagination as copies of ideas of sense, see Princ. 33.

819. Descartes (see 781n.) deals with the nature of ideas in his Discourse on Method, Part IV. In answer to Hobbes's 5th objection, viz., that we have no image or idea of God, and on that account are forbidden to worship Him under an image, he replies that Hobbes is identifying idea with image, but "I take the name idea for whatever is immediately perceived by the mind" (Molyneux's translation, p. 131). See also Meditation III for idea and "objective reality."

820. 821. On will and understanding, see 362a n.

822. Berkeley, probably with Hobbes in mind, refers to the "belief, that the mind of man is as a ball in motion," Princ. 144, cf. PC 193; on will, see 131n.

823. A distinction fundamental in Berkeley's philosophy. He holds the reality of the sensible world, and distinguishes it carefully from the world of the imagination, see Princ 28-33; on archetypes, see 689n.

824. 825. 826. 827. A study of Spinoza (1632-1677) begins here and is continued in 830-831 and 844-845; these entries contain references to the materializing tendency of Spinozism, to the doctrine of space as an attribute of God, to transcendental and general terms, to immanent causality, to eternal truths, to extension conceived in and through itself, and to the definition of God.

Berkeley mentions the Opera Posthuma (1677) which contains

the Ethics, Tractatus Politicus, De Emendatione Intellectus, and 74 letters including those to Oldenburgh. Its Preface quotes for the 21st letter to Oldenburgh Spainoza's statement, "Deum omnium rerum causam immanentem, ut aiunt, non vero transeuntem statuo. Omnia, inquam, in Deo esse, et in Deo moveri, cum Paulo affirmo."

Berkeley, as did many thinkers in his day, viewed Spinoza as an atheist and a materialist, and shows no consciousness of the resemblance between his own doctrines and those of Spinoza, alleged by Clayton, Essay on Spirit (1750), p. 1, and in the review of the Three Dialogues in the Acta Eruditorum (1727), pp. 380-383.

On Epicurus, see 17n.; on extended Deity, see 107n.; on causality, see 403n.; on Raphson, see 298n. St. Paul's text, "In Him we live..." (Acts XVII 28), the closing words of Malebranche's famous chapter (III ii 6) on "That we see all things in God," became a great favourite with Berkeley. He quotes it in Princ. 149, in Dials., Works II 214, 236, in Alc. IV 14, and on the title page of TVV.

828. 829. For "purus actus" and the denial of the idea of the will, see notes on 131 and 701; on substance, see 80n.; on the three faculties, sense, imagination, and pure intellect, see 531n.

830. 831. Creation de nihilo is explained by Berkeley as the causal production of ideas by God, and is here illustrated by man's power of productive imagination (see 60n.); on the imagination, see 531n., Princ. 28; on Spinoza, see 824n.; on eternal truths, see 735n.; on cause, see 403n.; on God, see 107n.

832. In the <u>Principles</u> Berkeley denies absolute existence (sect. 24) and absolute time, space, and motion (sect. 110-117); but here (the marginal letter P suggests it) he has in view Locke's distinction between primary and secondary qualities, the former supposed to exist absolutely, the latter only in relation to us.

833. For "seeing" (Fraser and Jonston) read "being," an old idiom on which see 662n. Berkeley regards conation as the seat of personal being, arguing here that a state of comparative indifference is willed in preference in annihilation, just as he argues in 791 that acquiescence in being is willing. On will and perception, see 131n. and 362a n.; on pleasure and pain, see 541n.; on uneasiness, see 145n.

834. Thos. Hobbes (1588-1679), author of <u>Leviathan</u> (1651), <u>De Corpore</u> (1655), and many other works, claimed to have solved the traditional problems of Euclidean geometry. His claim gave rise to the famous controversy here referred to, bringing under discussion many of the mathematical problems discussed in the <u>PC</u>, e.g., the quadrature of the circle, the angle of contact, and the definitions of point, line, and angle.

Prof. Seth Ward attacked Hobbes in <u>Vindiciae Academiarum</u> (1654), and Wallis continued the attack in his <u>Elenchus Geometriae Hobbianae</u> (1669), and in <u>Thomae Hobbes Quadratura... Confutata</u>, and denuo <u>Confutata</u> (1669). Hobbes wrote several replies, including <u>Six Lessons to the Savilian Professors</u> (1656), <u>Examinatio et Emendatio Mathematicae Hodiernae</u> (1660), and <u>Quadratura Circuli Cubatio spherae, Duplicatio Cubi, breviter demonstrata</u> (1669). On Wallis, see 482n.

835. On superior spirits, see 410n.; on their enlarged sight,

see 749n., TV 84 and 153ff.

836. This seems to have formed part of a projected indirect argument against matter (cf. 68n.); viz., if there be matter, how are the beauty and proportion of things to be explained, which, like the sorts or species, are the workmanship of the mind? Cf. Locke III iii 13.

837. For the Hobbes-Wallis controversy, see 834n.

838. This is Berkeley's main proof of the existence of God (see 107n.), formally stated in Princ. 29-30. On the laws of nature, see 144n.

Here, as in Princ. 90, he admits that sensible things are outside our minds in respect of their origin; they are in our minds when we perceive or think them; but they do not originate in our minds; they may pass out of our minds into other minds, but they remain permanently in the mind of God who gave them. "independent of my Will," cf. 477a, 801.

839. The marginal sign shows that ethics is under discussion. No doubt Berkeley is criticizing the hedonism which takes account only of the pleasure of the moment. His own hedonism takes account of the future and the supernatural, see 541n. and 851.

840. A jeu d'esprit connecting literal solidity (see 78n.) with Sergeant's Solid Philosophy Asserted, Against the Fancies of the Ideists (1697).

John Sergeant (or Sargent, 1622-1707), Roman Catholic controversialist and critic of Locke, wrote also The Method to Science (1696); for an account of his philosophy, see G.

A. Jonnston, Development of Berkeley's Philosophy, pp. 383ff.

841. 842. On will and understanding and their contents, see 362a n.

843. The distinction between "idea" and "ideatum," common in Spinoza, and assumed by all representationists, disappears, for Berkeley, in the case of the idea of sense; there he admits no "idea of," see 115n.; the distinction remains, however, in the case of the idea of the imagination, as explicitly stated in Princ. 33. On the laws of nature, see 144n.

844. 845. Both entries arise from the one passage in a letter of Spinoza (see 824n.) to Oldenburgh, dealing with space (see 18n.) and Deity (see 107n.).

Oldenburgh (1626?-1678), of Bremen, philosopher and man of letters, corresponded with Milton and Cromwell, and afterwards settled in London, becoming the first secretary and foreign correspondent of the Royal Society. In August 1661 he wrote to Spinoza and inquired his views on God, extension, and the Cartesian philosophy. Spinoza replied, "De Deo... quem definio esse Ens, constans infinitis attributis, quorum unumquodque est infinitum, sive summe perfectum in suo genere. Ubi notandum me per attributum intelligere omne id quod concipitur per se et in se...ut, ex. gr. extensio per se et in se concipitur" (Spinoza, Opera Post, p. 397).

Descartes in his enumeration of the divine attributes (Med. 3) more than once uses the term "sovereignly perfect."

Berkeley has not given a formal definition (see 44n.) of God, but the lines it would have taken may be gathered from his statements in 838 and Princ. 146 and Dials, Works II 257. In the last of these passages Berkeley speaks of "God, in the strict and proper sense of the word. A being whose spirituality, omnipresence, providence, omniscience, infinite power and goodness, are as conspicuous as the existence of sensible things...."

846. "Nothing...does more contribute to blend and confound them together, than the strict and close connexion they have with each other," TV 145; see 28n.

847. 848. 849. In 848 note "not" (which Johnston omits) before "mention."

The "Grand Mistake," for Berkeley, lies in thinking we know our active nature as we know ideas. His terminology and teaching here are those of the Principles, viz., that will and understanding (see notes on 131 and 362a) are aspects of the active spirit, and are therefore distinct from their contents, the objects willed and perceived.

850. Spirit is the only true cause, for Berkeley, but he concedes the name "cause" to ideas in the sense of sign, see 403n. "many absurditys," e.g., causes that do nothing, see 856.

851. 852. On present good, see 839n., and on Berkeley's hedonism and the two sorts of pleasure, see 541n.

853. For the three branches of philosphy, see 676n.; on coexistence, see 403n.; on relation, see 540n.; on definition see 44n.; on inclusion, see 690n.; on Berkeley's projected books, see 508n. Here only is the work on natural philosophy named; it is represented to some extent by the De Motu, as the projected work on mathematics is represented by the Analyst.

854. Will, thought, and feeling, as elements in the active being, are one; they are differentiated by their contents or objects, see 362a n.

855. 856. Cf. 850; on cause, see 403n.; on occasion, see 499n.

857. "The motive for continuing in the same state or action is only the present satisfaction in it; the motive to change is alwasy some uneasiness," Locke II xxi 29. Berkeley regards the statement as a *reductio ad absurdum* of the doctrine of uneasiness, see 145n.; on sleep and trance, see 651n.

858. On demonstration, see 163n., and for Berkeley's original intention to deal with demonstration in the Introduction, see 212.

"I must Cancell all passages..." Passages from what? Not from the PC; for then the entry would be rather pointless, and in point of fact its passages on demonstration are not cancelled; nor from (what we now call) the Draft Introduction, for it does not deal at all with demonstration. It remains that a good deal of the work referred to, perhaps a draft of the Draft Introduction, must have been written before he finished the PC. This supports my view that the PC was originally rather a commentary on an actual composition than notes on his reading. I have pointed out in my note on 212 that some 27 entries originally had the marginal letter I (Introduction), the letter being subsequently stroked out owing to changes in the design of the Introduction. Berkeley may well have written a draft composition, covering both Introduction and the body of the work, subsequently cancelling in it the extreme passages on demonstration, and erasing the marginal letter of the corresponding passages in the PC.

859. 860. Read "covet" and "Discovery" for "cavil" and "diseases" (Fraser and Johnston).

Berkeley is trying to explode the "excuse" (see 292n.) -- "the natural weakness and imperfection of our understandings." Princ. Introd. 2, 3. Our faculties are not at fault, he urges, but our principles. "We have first rais'd a dust, and then complain, we cannot see." Were our faculties naturally defective, he here argues, we ought not to philosophize at all.

861. 862. Against the representationist theory which regards the idea as the likeness of matter, see 46n. and Locke II viii 15.

863. Berkeley's views on the existence of bodies underwent important modifications while he was writing the PC (see 52n.). This entry shows his thought at the final stage. On the distinctness of the mind, see 14n. "without the Mind," cf. Princ. 90.

864. 865. Contrasting visible motion, which depends on diversity of colours (see 533), with the abstract idea of motion; see 318n., TV 137, Princ. Introd. 9, 10.

866. Berkeley is thinking, probably, of those consequences of the belief in matter which he mentions in Princ. 92-96. Matter "involves a contradiction" (ib. 54), because it is not a possible object of sense, and yet one is supposed to see and touch it.

867. "The Concrete of the Will and understanding" (713) is fully real, for Berkeley, but its elements when taken separately and divorced from actual experience become abstract ideas, see 318n. and 871. On the vulgar and the learned, see 405n. and 703.

868. "Some of the more intricate and subtile parts of <u>speculative mathematics</u> may be pared off without any prejudice to truth"; <u>Princ</u>. 131; cf. 207n. and 434.

869. If the objects of sight and touch are in fact heterogeneous (see 28n.) how comes it that we are commonly supposed to see and touch the same thing? Berkeley gives a broad answer to this question in <u>TV</u> 144-145, and deals with it more narrowly in terms of minimal points (see 59n.) in this entry and also in 70, 710, and <u>TV</u> 62.

"it might have been otherwise," a reference to Berkeley's doctrine that the connection between ideas is customary and not necessary; see 181n.

Notebook B deals, for the most part, with vision, and notebook A with metaphysics, and therefore the occurrence of this stray entry on vision, marked with the marginal sign for all three divisions of the <u>Theory of Vision</u>, and actually represented in each of those divisions (49, 54, 144), on the last page but one of notebook A is remarkable. This page was probably filled in the late summer of 1708, and the <u>Theory of Vision</u> (published in May/June 1709) must have been at an advanced stage by that time; these facts confirm my view that Berkeley wrote the <u>PC</u> rather as a commentary on a draft work of his, already written, than as a preliminary study.

870. On "pure act," see 701n.; on "Soul or Mind," see notes on 14, 154, 576.

871. 873. Time and again Berkeley returns to the problem of will and understanding, see notes on 362a and 867; on truth, see 554n.; his doctrine of abstract ideas (see 318n.) now dominates his thought. "ratione," i.e., in conception.

-325-

872. Spirits are thinking things, for Berkeley, and ideas are unthinking things; he uses "thing" and "idea" convertibly with regard to the latter type of reality; but if he were to do so with regard to the former type, he would in effect be calling spirits "ideas," making active things passive, thus involving the notion of spirit in contradiction, see 369n.

874. He is thinking of Locke and Malebranche and other "moderns" who, accepting the distinction between primary and secondary qualities, "prove certain sensible qualities to have no existence in matter, or without the mind" (Princ. 14). Holding that the primary and the secondary are inseparable, he argues that those who internalize the secondary qualities are in effect also internalizing the primary. If he intends the term "Sort" to be taken technically, he is referring to Locke's proof that the sorts are the work of the mind, see 836n.; on the reality of body, see notes on 41 and 52.

875. Will (see 131n.) here might be the will of God, or the will of man, but the marginal sign S.G. suggests that Berkeley is chiefly thinking of the former, and is asking whether man can know the will of God with regard to the present or the future. A similar question *mutatis mutandis* could be raised of the human will, and Berkeley's broad answer (see Princ. 135ff.) is that the will, as an aspect of spirit, is not to be know as ideas are known, but yet is know.

876. Motion, for Berkeley, being relative, postulates at least two bodies, see Princ. 112, Mot. 58. He may be thinking of Malebranche's (VI ii 9), "I imagine here only God, myself, and one ball." For motion apprehended by variety of colour, see 533n.

877. The infinite divisibility (see 11n.) has scarcely been mentioned since the opening pages of notebook A. Berkeley argues that if the given space be infinitely divisible, so also must be the sensible qualities inseparable from that apace -- a reductio ad absurdum, he thinks, of the doctrine.

878. Extension (see 18n.) is in the mind, says Berkeley in Princ. 49, only by way of idea, and not by way of mode or attribute; an application of this important principle is given in 886 (cf. 882). This principle distinguishes Berkeley's philosophy from Spinoza's, and corrects the first impression left by his doctrine of existence in the mind. On "Book 2," see 508n.; on the soul, see 14n.

879. Locke II xxi 22ff., says that this question "is what is meant, when it is disputed whether the will be free," and his answer to it is "that in most cases a man is not at liberty whether he will will or no." Berkeley regards the question as absurd because free activity is implied in the notion of the will (see 131n. and 616).

880. On algebra, see 382n. In his De Ludo Algebraico Berkeley uses the term "quaestio" for the forming and solving of algebraical equations; but what "the Rule" is does not appear.

881. In 761-768 Berkeley argues that numbers are names, not ideas, that they yield no speculative knowledge, though they are of practical use; on numbers, see 104n.

882. He admits here, as again in Princ. 90, that things are external to the mind in the senses specified; see notes on 79, 863, and 878; on extension, see 18n.; on mind, see 14n.

883. If the defects of memory and imagination, which give rise to the need for signs, especially verbal signs, could be cured, the need for signs would disappear, Berkeley here suggests. His later doctrine of signs, best expressed in Alc. VII 11-14, gives them an essential place in human knowledge.

884. The laws of nature depend on the will of God, Princ. 32; there is therefore no necessary connection between our ideas, ib. 31, and "there is nothing necessary or essential in the case," ib. 106; cf. 181n. and 794.

885. Read "simple" for "single" (Johnston: Fraser omits the entry); cf. 484n. and 496. The second sentence should be read as a satirical comment on Locke's doctrine, "Ideas of primary qualities are resemblances." Visible extension and material extension differ fundamentally. The one is "in the mind"; the other (ex hypothesi) is not. Therefore the one cannot resemble the other. On simple ideas, see 53n.; on resemblance, see 46n.

886. Against the doctrine of space as a mode of mind, see 878n.

887. 888. The text is doubtful, and the meaning of these two references to de Vries is not clear. Fraser reads "we know the mind agrees with things not by idea but sense or conscientia"; Johnston reads, "we know the mind as we do Hunger not by idea but sensation conscientia."

Johnston's reading in the main is strongly supported by De Vries' words on p. 66 (two pages after the page mentioned in the previous entry) of his Diatribe de ideis rerum innatis, appended to the New Edition (1695) of his Exercitationes rationales de deo divinisque perfectionibus (1685), "In nos descendere si voluerimus, plurimarum rerum quarum immediate nobis sumus conscii, sensum magis & conscientiam in nobis deprehendemus, quam ullum earundem per ideam repraesentamen. In quarum numerum fames, sitis, dolor...." The manner of our knowledge of spiritual objects was keenly debated between de Vries, Roell, Wagardus, and others.

Gerard de Vries, Professor of Theology at Utrecht (not to be confused with Simon de Vries, Spinoza's friend and correspondent) was a copious writer on moral and natural philosophy. Besides the works mentioned above he wrote, De fictis innatarum idearum mysteriis (1688-1692) and De natura dei et humanae mentis (1690).

Berkeley's doctrine of self-knowledge (see Princ. 135ff.), Dials., Works II 231 ff., is very like that of Malebranche, viz., that we know our own minds, not by idea, but immediately by an act of reflection -- "conscience" as Malebranche calls it; and therefore the phrase in De Motu 21, "conscientia quadam interna" may well derive from Malebranche, and be reflected in these entries; since the reading is uncertain, it is useless to speculate as to the point on which Berkeley differs from De Vries and Malebranche. On Malebranche, see 230n.

Folio 95. After "Adventure of the" there is a word of five or six letters printed as "shirt" by other editors.
I have not been able to identify "Clov."
The small sum is, I think, in Berkeley's handwriting.

INDEX

<u>Editor's note</u>. The index is exclusively for Berkeley's text, and not for my introduction or Professor Luce's notes. The introduction is primarily historical rather than interpretive, and thus in my mind does not require indexing. The interpretation of Berkeley's text in Professor Luce's notes can be located by checking his table of "key doctrinal notes" on pages 118-119 and the notes for particular entries listed in the index. Therefore, <u>the numbers in the index are entry numbers, not page numbers</u>.

A

"A.B." See King, Abp. Wm.
Ability, natural, 694
Abscisse, 329
Absolute existence, 832
Abstract
  color, 85, 253, 494
  extension. See Length, abstract
  ideas. See Ideas, abstract
  in animals and man, 594
  length. See Length, abstract
  Locke on. See Locke, abstract ideas
  magnitude, 132
  point, 394
  space, 96, 452
  succession, 53a
Abstraction, 203, 238, 318, 328, 365a, 440, 564, 687
Absurdity. See Contradiction
Accuracy, mathematical, 251, 313, 330, 383-383a, 414
Act, 378:11, 611-611a, 621, 635, 795, 808, 848, 850, 854
Action, 37a, 157, 160, 166, 598, 644, 669, 683-684, 804, 808, 821, 857
Active, 41, 52, 131, 155, 286, 362a, 712, 848, 850, 870
Activity, 437a, 777
Actual, 200, 293a
Actus purus, 701, 828, 870
Acute senses, 82, 91, 97
Adam, 17
Affirmation, 731-731a
Agent, 143, 166, 627, 745, 812, 850
Agreement, 677, 739
Air, rays of, 152
Algebra, 382, 697, 758, 767-768, 770, 880
Analogy, 532
Ancient philosophers, 682, 781
Angels, 410, 610, 723, 749, 835
Angle, 85, 227, 432
  infinite divisibility of, 393
  of congruence, 528
  of contact, 168, 309, 381
  mathematicians on, 381, 393
  optic, 73, 94, 140, 150, 174-175, 182, 191, 195-198, 205-206, 210, 213, 215, 218, 229, 233, 302, 603

Anima mundi, 617
Animals, and man, 594
Annihilation, 83, 135, 590, 833
A posteriori, 379-380
A priori, 379-380
Arch, of a circle, 250, 309
Archetype, 689, 823
Archimedes, 462, 510
Arguings, my first, 265
Arguments, a posteriori and a priori, 379-380
Aristotle, 413, 425
Arithmetic, 458, 766-768, 770, 803
Assemblage, of simple ideas, 280
Assent, 777
Association of ideas, 225
Astrology, 702
Astronomy, 434
Attractive power, 486, 619
Aunt, Deering's, 201
Authority, 532
Axiom, 117, 354, 356, 779, 831
Axis, optic, 262, 400, 443

B

Bacon, 564
Banter, 89, 386, 639, 867
Barrovian case, the, 147, 170, 501
Barrow, 75, 263, 334, 362, 384, 462, 510
Bayle, 358, 424
Beauty. See Mind, work of
Being
  abstract idea of, 552
  formal, 781
  objective, 781
  of God, 41, 52
  of soul, 44
Belief. See Faith
Billiard balls, 146
Billys, the, 389
Blind man, the. See Molyneux Problem
Body
  cohesion of, 71
  contact between, 632
  definition of, 228, 282, 293
  essence of, 234, 533
  existence of, 32, 52, 79-80, 96, 135, 228, 282, 293a, 305, 312, 391, 424-424a, 437, 477-477a, 563, 686-686a, 800-801, 818, 863, 874
  extension of, 55, 61, 63, 78, 512, 878
  general, 512

-331-

Body (continued)
  ideas constitute, 427-427a, 512, 585, 589, 606, 609
  ideas from, 818
  ideas not in, 280
  mind distinct from, 863
  motion of, 45, 262, 704
  number not in, 110
  particular, 512
  powers, 228, 293-293a
  reflect light, 151
  shape of, 112, 512
  size of, 103
Book, Berkeley's projected
  first, the, 571, 792
  my, 696, 736
  publication style of, 858
  second, the, 508, 807, 878
  third, the, 583, 853
Brain, 74, 435
Breadth, 21, 82, 85, 105, 108, 254, 722. See Length, without breadth
Bulk, 283, 476, 517

C

Calculus, differential, 333
Cartesians, 281, 424a, 453, 477-477a, 801, 811
Catoptrics, 501
Cause
  and effect, 461, 499, 504, 562, 780
  coexisting ideas, 403, 461, 754
  definition of, 562, 856
  God only, 433, 485, 499, 827
  materialists' view, 486
  mixed, 562
  moving our legs, 548
  necessary connection, 181, 195, 206, 227, 233, 246, 256, 794, 884
  occasion, 228, 499, 754, 856
  of ideas, 228, 282, 499
  physical, 855
  power, 228, 282, 493
  second causes, 433, 485
  spiritual only, 109, 850, 855
  traditional view, 850
  types of, 855
  will only, 131, 155, 499
Cavallerius, 346
Certainty
  about God, 813
  about words, 731
  by ideas, 729
  in ethics. See Demonstration in morality

Certainty (continued)
  in geometry. See Demonstration in mathematics
  in metaphysics. See Demonstration in metaphysics
  in perception, 693, 731-731a, 739-740
  in senses, 740
  of ideas, 731-731a, 739
  of Berkeley's own philosophy, 532
  of what not perceived, 777
  meaning of, 813
  "my doctrine of," 776
  without words, 719, 730
Change, 262
Cheyne, 367, 387, 459
Church, 608, 715
Church-men, 715
Chymical principles, 664
Chymistry, 702
Circle
  abstract, 258
  arch of, 250
  circumference of, 249, 340, 457, 462, 481-482, 510
  concentric, 122, 315
  diameter of, 249, 340, 457, 481-482
  idea of, 445-446
  not a polygon, 481
  perfect, 235
  points of, 462, 510
  squaring of, 245, 249-251, 395, 457-458, 510-511
  tangible, 251
  visible, 250
Circumference. See Circle, circumference of
Clarity of vision. See Sight, confusion of
Clericus. See Le Clerc
Clock, pendulum, 487
Co-existence, 132-133, 165, 287, 403, 677, 739, 754, 793a, 853
Cogito ergo sum, 738
Cohension, 71
Cold, 136, 226
Collection of ideas. See Ideas, collection of
Colour
  abstract, 85, 253, 494
  applied to tangible qualities, 42, 114
  basis of visible motion, 135, 533, 864, 876
  blind see, 294
  Cartesian view of, 281, 453
  compared only to colour, 861-862
  complex (compound), 153, 242, 489, 504, 526, 551, 562, 721

-332-

Colour (continued)
   composition of, 242, 502-505, 662, 664, 721
   definition of, 153
   existence of, 185-185a, 222, 253, 362a, 363, 801
   extension is, 165
   heterogeneous, 138, 151
   idea of, 253, 662
   in bodies, 222, 265
   in *minimum visibile*, 442, 489
   in subtle matter, 388
   mixed, 151, 242, 489, 502-504
   Newton on, 388, 453, 505, 562
   not abstract, 318, 362, 494
   of space, 454
   only one, 93
   only thing we see, 136, 226-227
   only two simple, 662
   rays of light, 152
   sensation, 111
   simple idea, 134, 151, 153, 222, 662, 664
   without extension, 85, 253, 494
   without the mind, 121, 185-185a, 222, 362a, 376, 882
Commensurable, 258, 263-264
Common sense, 368, 405, 751
Comparison, 47, 51, 192-192a, 280, 299, 378
Complacency, 630
Complex ideas. See Ideas, complex
Composition, 242, 502-505, 662, 664, 721, 753
Concave, 183, 187
Concrete, 75, 713
Conformation, 218
Confusion. See Vision, confusion of
Congeries, 580
Congruence, 150, 514, 528-531
Conics, 335
Connexion, necessary, 181, 195, 206, 227, 233, 246, 256, 794, 884
Conscientia, 888
Consciousness, 24, 200, 202, 578, 681, 744
Consequences, 157, 542, 564, 595, 694, 788, 799, 838, 843, 866
Conservation, 402
Considering, 104, 110, 166, 217, 223, 254, 284, 318,

Considering (continued), 440, 460, 527, 540, 588, 697, 722, 832
Contact
   angle of. See Angle, of contact
   between bodies, 632
Contemplation, 539, 606, 626, 643, 748
Continuity, 78-78a
Contradiction, 21, 37, 49, 90, 123, 249, 299, 308, 312, 337, 347, 350a, 411, 417, 419, 464, 475, 561, 575, 576a, 579, 652, 655, 663, 679, 812, 866
Convex, 183, 187-188, 190, 199, 210, 232, 296
Cooperation, 402
Copernicus, 404
Corpuscularians, 234, 533
Count, German, 42, 114
Creation
   act of will, 831
   before man, 60, 436, 723
   by God, 60, 830
   by man, 830
   causation, 831
   explanation of, 293
   imagination like, 830
   nothing before, 339
   of earth, 60, 723
   out of nothing, 830-831
   related to perception, 60, 436, 723
   scriptural account considered, 60, 436, 723
Crystalline. See Eye, ball
Cube, 32, 82, 306
Curve, 251, 309, 511, 515, 520, 527, 575

D

Death, 83, 390, 590
Deduction, 693
Deering, Mr., 127, 201
Definition
   of angle, 432
   of cause, 562
   of colour, 153
   of equality, 515, 525
   of existence, 408
   of extension, 178, 320
   of God, 845
   of idea, 507
   of likeness, 551
   of motion, 451
   of person, 713
   of points, 575
   of soul, 44, 154, 178
   knowledge of, 853
   understanding without, 178

Deity. See God
Demonstration
   avoid in publication, 858
   by intermediate ideas, 729
   in Locke, 586, 691
   in mathematics, 160-163, 239, 261, 336, 426, 466, 697, 750, 755, 778, 804
   in metaphysics, 162-163, 239, 336
   in morality (ethics), 158, 162-163, 239, 336, 669, 683, 690-691, 697-698, 729, 755, 769, 804
   in natural philosophy, 383, 583, 804
   in Newton, 374, 383
   in theology, 584, 705
   nature of, 212, 586
   of contradictions, 312
   of existence of bodies, 80
   of existence of God, 41, 838
   of heterogeneity of distance, 49
   of infinite divisibility, 21
   of nature of imagination, 639
   of non-existence of matter, 597
   of primary and secondary ideas, 20, 265, 363, 551
   of the Principle, 291, 363, 378-379, 407, 588
   promised for all of Berkeley's doctrines, 586, 719
   refused, 532
   verbal, 551, 562, 690, 705, 719, 730-732, 734, 750, 778, 804
Denomination, 758, 766
Depth, 106, 108
Descartes, 738, 784-785, 790, 794-795, 798, 805, 818-819, 845
Desire, 158-159, 166, 598, 692, 854
Determined, 166, 627
DeVries, 887-888
Diagonal
   incommensurability with side, 29, 263-264, 469, 500
   of square, 258-259
Diameter, 210, 249, 311, 340, 457
Dictionary, 690
Diminishing the size of images, 182-183, 189, 191, 199, 210, 255, 271

Dioptricks, 94
Disposition, 777
Distance
   abstract, 253, 259-260, 447
   and optics, 726
   auditory, 108
   between man and God, 640
   existence of, 253
   idea of, 253, 447
   not perceived by sight, 196, 603
   points in, 253, 447
   tangible, 49, 58, 95-96, 174
   visible, 49, 62, 95, 132, 169-170, 174, 182, 191, 215, 220a, 231, 233, 296, 302-302a, 307, 311, 603, 774
Distinctness, 206, 208, 240-243, 283, 296a, 400, 460, 647, 834
Diversity, 739
Divines, 406, 642
Divinity. See God
Dreams, 39, 823, 843
Duration, 5, 7-8, 12, 118

E

Effect, 461, 499, 504, 562, 699, 712, 780, 788, 802, 808, 843
Enlargement of sight, 175, 296, 749, 835
Enquiring, 166
Ens, rationis and reale, 474-474a, 535, 546-546a
Epicurism, 17
Epicurus, 824
Equality
   of circles, 122
   of inches, 49, 558
   of lines, 150, 267, 360, 511, 514-516, 525, 528-531, 778
   of points, 169, 267, 276, 322, 530, 558
   of spheres of vision, 169
   of triangles, 528-531
   See Congruence
Errour, 274, 603, 693, 719, 737, 783, 794, 816, 846
Essence, 34, 44, 177, 234, 533, 536, 622, 630
Eternal, 92, 290, 735, 776
Eternity, 1, 2, 14, 695
Ethics. See Morality
Euclid, 425, 575
Evanescency, 480
Excuse, the, 292, 323, 350-350a

Existence
- absolute, 185, 832
- abstract idea, 552, 725, 772
- created (idea) by Schoolmen, 725
- duration and, 5
- idea of, 670-671, 746
- in different languages, 412-413
- independent of mind, 801
- knowledge of, 547, 563, 739, 746
- meaning of, 408, 429-429a, 437, 473, 491, 593, 604, 646
- nature of, 491, 588
- of active and inactive things, 673
- of bodies, 52, 78-80, 96, 135, 228, 282, 293a, 305, 312, 391, 424-424a, 437, 477-477a, 563, 686-686a, 800-801, 818, 863, 874
- of colours, 185-185a, 222, 253, 362a-363, 801
- of extension, 26, 33, 37, 55, 57, 63, 65, 74, 121, 288-288a, 801
- of figure, 288
- of God, 41, 782, 838
- of ideas or thoughts, 228, 280, 359, 377, 656
- of imagined objects, 792
- of invisibles, 464
- of lines, 117, 253
- of material cube, 82
- of matter, 128, 131, 359, 597, 686-686a, 718
- of objects, 790, 792, 832
- of persons, 24, 185, 791
- of primary and secondary ideas, 20, 262a-263, 265, 477a
- of self, 791
- of soul, 154, 479, 563
- of sounds, 363
- of space, 135
- of spirit, 437
- of will, 792
- related to perception, 185a, 280, 588, 646, 670, 799, 802
- related to idea, 408, 639, 791, 842
- relative, 832
- subsistence and, 109
- unperceived (and intermittent), 98, 185-185a, 194, 280, 282, 293a, 362a-363, 377, 408, 429, 472, 597, 639, 656, 802, 874

Existence (continued)
- willing and, 791
- within the mind, 235, 440, 474-474a
- without the mind, 95, 235-236, 359, 362a-363, 874

Experience, 174, 203, 227, 262, 368, 638

Extension
- abstract, 55, 85, 111a, 328, 342, 362, 365-365a, 440, 772
- a sensation, 18, 34-35, 37, 100, 111, 392, 440, 711
- definition of, 178, 287, 320
- existence of, 26, 33, 37, 55, 57, 63, 65, 74, 121, 288-288a, 801
- idea of, 81, 86, 105, 181
- inertness of, 57
- infinite divisibility of (and infinitely great), 11, 21, 26, 67, 72-73, 81, 86, 247, 263, 314, 342, 353, 364, 381, 420, 475
- knowledge of, 34-35, 59, 74, 78, 100, 174, 181, 540
- mathematics and, 56, 460
- meaning of, 100, 105, 164, 167
- nature of, 100, 105, 540
- of body, 55, 61, 63, 78, 512, 878
- of colour, 165, 242, 262
- of matter, 40, 65, 81, 265, 269-270, 289, 325
- of space, 78, 96, 105
- passive mode of thought, 623
- perceived at once and confused, in succession and clearly, 400, 460
- points in, 325, 353, 365, 475-475a
- proportion, 365
- related to mind, 270, 287-290, 299, 342, 440, 622, 878, 882, 886
- relation to essence of soul, 622
- relation to thought, 622
- relation to visible and tangible qualities, 288a
- simple or compound, 86, 134, 164-165, 167
- smelled, 137, 241

-335-

Extension (continued)
  tangible, 28, 54-55, 61, 70, 78-78a, 91, 100-101, 103, 138, 181, 203, 240, 243, 256, 287, 295, 328, 441, 711
  tasted, 137, 241
  visible, 28, 32, 54-55, 61, 63, 65, 70, 73, 78a, 87, 91, 100-101, 103, 121, 138, 140, 165, 181, 203, 205-206, 215-216, 220, 240, 242-243, 249, 283, 287, 294-295, 297, 318, 328, 400, 441, 443, 460, 526, 711
External existence, 26, 45
Eye
  ball, 210, 255, 296
  center of concentric circles, 122
  conformation of, 218
  convexity of, 210, 296
  crystallines. See ball
  fund of, 211, 275, 296, 302a
  images in, 102
  magnifiers or diminishers, 271
  microscopic, 97, 116
  naked, 236
  object behind, 501
  objects viewed near, 256
  straining of, 206, 210
  within and without, 58

F

Fact, matters of, 693
Faculties, 44, 159, 478, 747, 753, 848, 871
  operative, 149, 156, 166
Faintness of vision, 206, 244, 256, 302
Faith, 584, 720
Fardella, 79
Fathers, the, 413
Ficinus, Marselius, 390
Field of vision. See Visual sphere
Figure
  existence of, 288
  general, 483
  infinite, 419
  infinite divisibility of, 248
  of body, 112, 512
  of matter, 40, 81, 288, 478
  relations of, 540
  sensible, 173, 466
  tangible, 28, 91, 101

Figure (continued)
  visible, 28, 91, 101, 231
  without the mind, 222
Finiteness, 145, 292, 350a
Flats, 124
Flint, 78
Fluxions, 168, 333
Fly, age of, 48
Focus, 366
Foot (length)
  idea of, 86, 557
  magnified, 324
  points in, 469, 475, 588
  tangible, 49, 203, 297
  visible, 49, 203, 297, 311
Force, 99, 456. See Vis
Foresight, 145-146, 875
Freedom, 146, 149, 156-159, 508, 626-627, 631, 745, 879, 884
French (the person), 569
Fund (of the eye), 211, 275, 296, 302a

G

Genera, 561, 566, 703
General
  figure, 483
  ideas. See Ideas, general
Genius, 371
Geometers, 276, 292, 320, 432, 515
Geometry
  demonstration in, 239, 778
  improved by Berkeley, 384, 428
  infinite divisibility in, 247-248, 261, 263
  metaphysics and, 207
  minima and, 441a
  mixed mathematics, 770
  object of, 101, 443
  of nothings, 384
  presupposes existence without the mind, 117
  squaring the circle in, 458
  useful, 384, 509
German Count, 42, 114
Glasses
  concave, 183, 187
  convex, 183, 187-188, 190, 199, 210, 232, 296
  diminishing, 191, 198
  focus of, 366
  ignorance of, 63, 237
  inverting, 148, 190, 278
  magnifying, 191, 197-198, 229, 236-237, 249, 324
Globules, 453
God
  agent, 812
  a thinking thing, 109
  being of, 508, 838

God (continued)
  cause, 485, 499, 713, 827
  certainty about, 813
  creation by, 60, 830
  demonstration of, 41, 838
  Descartes on, 845
  distinct from nature, 485
  essence of, 177
  existence of, 782
  extended, 825
  freedom of, 794
  idea of, 177, 433, 782, 805
  ideas in, 641, 675
  knowledge of, 640
  laws of nature and, 794, 838
  material, 625
  nature of, 838
  no sensations in, 675
  not extended, 290, 298, 310, 391
  not intuited, 813
  not perceived, 813
  power, 107, 298, 640
  powers in, 52, 433
  properties of all things in, 177a, 348, 812, 827
  Spinoza on, 845
  time and, 3, 15, 92
  understanding in, 812
  will of, 610, 713, 794, 812
  worship of, 705
Good, 157-158, 166, 569, 773, 851
Gospels, 769
Gravity, 361, 618-619
Greatness. See Magnitude

H

Halley, 448
Happiness, 539, 569, 776
Harangue, 361, 393, 396, 574
Hard, 135, 226
Harris, 432
Hayes, 308
Hearing, 108, 152, 240
Heat, 222
  omniscient radical, 617
Heaven, 160, 357, 423, 539
Heterogeneity, 28, 38, 42-43, 49, 54-55, 57, 59, 61, 69-70, 91, 95, 100-101, 103, 106, 108, 136-138, 148, 150, 173-174, 181, 183, 224-227, 240-241, 243, 246, 256, 295, 647
Hexagon, 462
Hobbes, 795-799, 806, 822, 824-825, 827, 834, 837
Hobbism, 17

Homoeomeries, 60, 64
Homogeneal, 164
Homogeneous, 60, 64, 277, 393
Homonymy, 643
Hot, 226
Huygens, 487
Hylarchic principle, 617
Hyps, 431

I

Idea
  absolute, 119
  abstract, 53a, 55, 96, 111a, 134, 139, 174, 238, 494, 496-497, 513, 552, 561, 564, 586, 602, 703, 727, 748, 772, 779, 809, 865, 867, 873
  abstract and general, 561, 566, 688, 725
  adequate, 221
  agreement of, 739
  association of, 225
  beyond our control, 805
  cause of, 228, 282, 499
  certainty by, 729
  certainty of, 731-731a, 739
  certainty without, 719, 730
  clear and distinct, 688
  collection of, 179, 282, 512
  compareson of, 484, 496, 861-862
  compleat, 638
  compose the understanding, 579, 587, 614, 681, 841
  compose things, 369, 606, 807-808
  consequences of (effects of), 595, 712
  constitute the soul or mind, 577, 580-581
  contemplation only of, 606
  coexistence of (as cause), 133, 403, 739, 754
  Descartes' definition, 819
  definition of, 507, 570, 657a, 665, 775, 808
  determined, 248
  eternity and, 14
  existence of, 228, 280, 359, 377, 656
  from senses, 539
  from within, 378
  from without, 318, 378, 539, 656, 670, 838
  general, 318, 401, 497, 524, 555, 591, 666, 784
  heterogeneity of, 28, 95, 103, 174, 181, 225, 240-241, 243, 256, 647

Idea (continued)
  "idea" (the word), 685, 757, 807-808
  "idea of" cause of mistakes, 660
  identity of, 568
  images, 818
  impotent, 712
  inert, 230, 684
  infinite, 475
  infinite divisibility of, 75
  in God, 641, 675
  innate, 649
  intermediate, 447, 697-698, 729
  intermittency of, 280
  in the mind, 641
  intromitted, 95, 241, 287, 454, 496, 670
  knowledge consists of, 312, 378, 522, 606
  knowledge of, 312, 378, 522, 606, 739
  knowledge without, 730
  likeness of, 47, 51, 280, 299, 378, 484, 551, 657, 861-862, 884-885
  necessary connexion between, 195, 206, 227, 233, 246, 256, 794, 884
  necessary for thought, 547
  nice (precise), 330
  no one essential to existence, 842
  no words without, 354a, 356, 378, 422, 494
  not in unperceiving things, 378-379
  of actions, 683-684, 808
  of circle, 445-446
  of distance, 253, 447
  of existence, 670-671, 746
  of extension, 81, 86, 105, 181
  of figure, 81, 248
  of God, 177, 433, 782, 805
  of infinitesimals, 354
  of length, 85-88, 105
  of line, 253, 445-447
  of matter, 573
  of mind or spirit, 176a-177, 490, 663, 808, 829, 849, 887-888
  of minima, 272
  of motion, 45, 135, 167, 184, 222, 450-450a, 573, 865
  of number, 167, 526, 760-762, 766, 803
  of operations of the mind, 490, 663, 808
  of quantities, 448

Idea (continued)
  of reflection, 585, 656, 670
  of sensation, 571, 585, 656, 670, 724, 746, 818
  of sense, 818, 823
  of sensible only, 490
  of sight, 28, 95, 103, 135, 138, 181, 206, 240, 243, 246, 256, 846
  of smell, 138, 241
  of substance, 597, 700, 724
  of taste, 138, 240-241, 497
  of touch, 28, 95, 103, 114, 138, 181, 240, 243, 246, 256, 846
  of unity, 545, 746
  only in the mind, 301, 692
  particular, 318, 497
  passive, 643
  perceive only, 50, 74
  primary and secondary, 20, 41, 76, 112, 265, 362-363, 392, 477a, 534
  pure, 151, 153
  reasoning about, 804, 817
  relation to body, 280, 427-427a, 512, 585, 589, 606, 609, 818
  relation to creation, 831
  relation to *ideatum*, 843
  relation to imagination, 582, 639, 657a, 753, 818, 823
  relation to mind, 490, 579-581, 637, 650-652, 663, 760, 808, 847, 849, 887-888
  relation to names, 153, 761
  relation to numbers, 167, 526, 762, 766, 803
  relation to perception, 50, 74, 378, 522, 572, 578, 580-582, 589, 609, 656, 756
  relation to pleasure and pain, 833
  relation to reality, 807
  relation to self or person, 523, 791, 847
  relation to signs, 803
  relation to soul, 183, 185, 194, 230, 478-478a, 576-577, 704, 842
  relation to spirit, 829, 849, 872, 887
  relation to thing and word "thing," 369, 644, 657a, 689, 757, 807-808, 872
  relation to will, 611a-613, 624, 643-644, 791, 806, 831, 833, 841-842

Idea (continued)
  relation to words, 551-552, 561, 565-566, 570, 584, 591, 595, 600, 602, 607, 626, 638, 641, 667, 671, 719, 727, 730a-731, 736
  relative, 119
  same as consciousness and perception, 578, 580-581, 656, 756
  sensations, 378
  simple and complex, 53, 86-87, 104-105, 133-134, 139, 151, 153-154, 167, 177, 179, 184, 222, 280, 378, 450, 461, 484, 493, 496, 526, 545, 551, 562, 570, 662, 664, 671, 721, 727a, 760, 809, 885
  simultaneous, 647
  sources of, 818
  subject of arethmetic, 803
  succession of, 3, 4, 12, 16, 39, 53-53a, 92, 99, 132-133, 167, 262, 460, 629, 647
  time a succession of, 3-4, 6, 12, 15-16, 39, 92, 460, 590, 647
  uniform, 378
  unperceived, 377, 656
  without the mind, 359, 692
  without words, 223, 354a, 356, 378, 422, 494-495, 513, 600, 693, 719, 727
Ideatum, 843
Identity, 192-194a, 200, 568, 681, 739, 744
Idolatry, 17, 411
Ignorance, 63, 157, 285, 642
Images, 81, 102, 280, 411, 684, 706, 818, 823
  retinal. See Retinal images
Imagination, 31, 36, 98, 135, 253-254, 294, 472-473, 494, 531, 582, 599, 639, 657a, 753, 777, 792, 818, 823, 843, 883
Immaterial, 19, 24, 71
Immorality, 411
Immortality, 14, 127
Immutable, 290, 452
Implicit faith. See Faith
Impressions, 74
Inch
  idea of, 86-87, 341-341a, 445, 475, 557
  in a circle, 445
  in a line, 445, 570
  infinite, 475

Inch (continued)
  infinite divisibility of, 247, 260-261, 341-341a
  not a determined idea, 87, 203, 261
  points in, 324, 445, 469-470, 475, 558
  relation to foot, 86, 558
  relation to mile, 260
  square, 445, 469-470
  tangible, 49, 69, 203, 297
  visible, 49, 69, 203, 297
Inclusion, 153, 512, 677, 690, 853
Incommensurability, of diagonal and side, 29, 263-264, 469, 500
Increate, 290
Indian numbers, 803
Indifference, 141, 143, 149, 158-159, 166, 743, 833
Indivisibles, 346, 374, 462-463, 510
Inequality, 215, 227, 511
Inference, 595
Infinite
  divisibility, 237
    arguments against, 463
    in Newton, 374
    makes a thing infinite, 352, 416
    of abstract length, 85
    of duration, 8
    of extension, 11, 21, 26, 67, 72-73, 81, 86, 247, 263, 314, 342, 353, 364, 381, 420, 475
    of figure, 248
    of idea, 75
    of inch, 247, 260-261, 341-341a
    of lines, 236, 261, 267, 393, 415, 462, 510
    of magnitude, 132-133, 247
    of matter, 17, 67, 81, 322
    of number, 342
    of time, 8, 10, 83
    of unity, 75, 263, 342
    relation to invisibility, 438-439, 465
    relation to smell, 877
  figure, 419
  idea, 475
  magnitude, 132, 448
  number, 123, 416, 481
  parts, 352
  regression, 161, 797
  space, 90, 135, 417, 675
Infinites, 72, 459
Infinitesimals, 308, 337, 351, 354-355, 415, 421, 459

Infinity, 72, 323
Inquiring, 166
Insensibles, 176, 439, 464
Inspection, 284
Integer, 351, 415
Intellect, 3, 531, 779, 810, 819
Intelligences, 9, 23, 145, 382, 410, 663, 723, 749
Interest (self), 542
Intermittency, 83, 98, 185-185a, 194, 280, 282, 293a, 362a-363, 377, 408, 429, 472, 639, 656, 704, 802, 874
Intervals, 590, 632
Introduction or Preface (to Principles), 212, 401, 513, 543, 586, 678-680, 682, 685, 688, 716, 719-720, 742, 747, 757, 817, 866
Intromitted, 95, 241, 287, 454, 496, 670
Intuition, 547, 563, 813
Inverted retinal image, 102, 126, 148, 172, 190, 224-225, 227, 278, 307
Inverting glasses, 148, 190, 278
Invisible(s), 21a, 176, 438-439, 464

J

Jargon, 517, 696, 716, 832
Judge, 174, 225, 296, 302a, 307, 528, 531, 603
Judging, 166, 222, 373, 569, 726
Judgement, 148, 532, 688, 743
future, 776

K

Keill, 308, 322, 364
King, Archbishop, 142, 159, 166
Knowledge
about ideas, 312, 378, 522, 606, 739
certain, 693
defects of, 223
demonstrative, 80, 698, 750
extended and clarified, by Berkeley, 679
foreknowledge, 145-146, 875
in mathematics, 750, 768
in the understanding, 521
intuitive, 547, 563, 813
Locke on, 522, 549-549a, 555, 666, 668, 739

Knowledge (continued)
of coexistence, 677, 739, 853
of definition, 853
of diversity, 739
of existence, 547, 563, 739, 746
of extension, 34-35, 59, 74, 78, 100, 174, 181, 540
of identity, 200, 739
of intellectual beings, 410
of matter, 74
of motion, 45
of particular ideas, 666, 668
of real existence, 739
of relation, 733, 739, 853
of self, 547
of soul or person, 25, 154, 576-576a
of will, 875
real, 549a, 739
relation to faith, 584, 720
relation to senses, 539, 748
relation to words, 607, 693, 750, 883
scope of, 640
sensitive, 80
speculative, 768
types of, 739, 853
without ideas, 730

L

Language
about ideas, 312
abuse of, 176, 564-565
correction of, 185
differentiates men and animals, 594
imperfection of, 178, 223, 596, 636
meaning of, 636
meaningless, 492, 574, 592
metaphorical. See Metaphor
necessary connexion with thoughts, 220
nice (precise), 209
relation to numbers, 762-763
same applied to heterogeneous qualities, 43
signifies complex ideas, 727a
simplicity of, 300
use of, 565
Lattice, orbicular, 180
Law, 702
Laws of nature, 144, 220-221, 312, 734, 794, 838, 843
Lawyers, 642

-340-

Learned, the, 405
Le Clerc (Clericus), 177a, 348
Leibniz, 333
Length
　abstract, 21, 85, 254, 260, 342, 365-365a, 483, 722
　by hearing, sight, and touch, 108
　infinite divisibility of, 342
　intangible, 365a
　invisible, 21a, 342a, 483
　mere proportion, 365
　relation to extension, 105, 365-365a
　relation to minima, 88
　without breadth, 21, 85, 254, 342, 365-365a, 483, 722
Lenses. See Glasses
Liberty. See Freedom
Life to come, the, 539
Light, 151-152, 226, 281, 376, 662
Likeness. See Ideas, likeness of, and Comparison
Limborch, 709, 743
Limbs, 49
Lines
　abstract, 253, 261, 447
　altered by position, 85, 120
　bisected, 276
　broad edges, 82
　congruent, 150, 528
　curved, 511, 515-516, 519
　demonstration about, 426, 466
　distance, mere, 259, 519
　equal, 150, 267, 276, 360, 515-516, 525, 528, 530a, 778
　existence of, 117, 253
　finite, 389
　for the 1/m of the Billys, 389
　idea of, 253, 445-447
　infinitely divisible, 236, 261, 267, 341-341a, 393, 415
　in geometry, 458
　insensible, 393, 466, 528
　magnified, 197, 236
　magnitude, 197, 417-418
　mathematical, 319, 341-341a, 393, 458, 519
　meaning of, 537
　oblique, 259
　parallel, 259
　perpendicular, 259
　points in, 132, 253, 261,

Lines (continued)
　points in (continued), 267, 445-447, 470, 516
　rectify, 457, 511
　right, 124, 360, 511, 515-516
　sensible, 466
　"strait," 180
　terminations of (ends of), 31, 119, 319
　unequal, 267, 778
　visible, 124, 341-341a, 389
　without the mind, 117
Locke, 326, 567, 605
　Berkeley compares himself to, 678, 688
　inconsistency of, 717
　on abstract ideas, 561, 586, 602, 687-688, 809, 811
　on algebra, 123, 697
　on body, 80, 112, 265, 704
　on certainty, 376
　on demonstration, 586, 691
　on duration, 118
　on existence, 80, 573, 790, 811
　on extension, 78, 265, 298, 533
　on general triangle, 687
　on God, 177, 298, 825, 827
　on infinite numbers, 123
　on intermediate ideas, 697-698
　on knowledge, 80, 522, 549-549a, 555, 563, 666, 668, 739
　on language (use of words), 492, 495, 554-555, 565, 570, 574, 595, 602, 700, 770, 809
　on liberty (freedom of will), 149, 879
　on matter, 89, 265, 573, 695, 718
　on mind, 112, 650, 796, 836
　on Molyneux Problem, 49
　on motion, 118, 451, 533, 573
　on operative faculties, 149
　on perception, 112, 706
　on power, 112
　on primary qualities, 76, 112, 534
　on reasoning, 817
　on simple and complex ideas, 53, 179, 526
　on solidity, 78, 533
　on soul, 704
　on space, 695
　on substance, 89, 179, 601, 700, 724
　on succession, 53

Locke (continued)
    on terminations of lines, 319
    on truth, 376, 554-555
    on will, 149, 598, 610, 709, 743, 857
    on worlds, intellectual and material, 538
    relation to Cartesians, 811

M

Madden, 569
Magnetical attractions, 403
Magnification, 94, 182-183, 189, 191, 197-198, 210, 229, 232, 236-237, 271, 296a, 324
Magnitude
    apparent, 182, 197, 213, 244
    defined as proportion, 203-204, 208, 213, 219, 269, 365
    determined, 132, 203, 211
    diminishing, 182-183, 189, 191, 198-199, 210, 255
    infinite, 132, 448
    magnifying, 182-183, 189, 191, 198, 210, 229, 296a
    of horizontal moon, 125, 140, 171, 233, 244, 302
    of matter, 40, 128
    of *minima*, 277, 480
    relation to angles, 73, 140, 150, 174-175, 182, 191, 195-198, 205-206, 210, 213, 215, 218, 229, 233, 302
    relation to coexistence, 132-133, 287
    relation to confused (and distinct) vision, 197, 206, 208, 232, 244, 256, 283-284, 296a, 303, 400, 835
    relation to distance, 174, 182, 191
    relation to succession, 132-133
    relation to successive vision, 283-284, 400, 443
    sameness, 257
    tangible, 49, 69-70, 91, 103, 174, 203, 213, 220, 256, 297
    to microscopical eyes, 116

Magnitude (continued)
    visible, 49, 69-70, 91, 103, 116, 125, 169, 174, 182-183, 189, 191, 195-196, 203-206, 208, 210-211, 213-216, 218-220, 229, 233, 244, 255-257, 275, 283-284, 297, 303, 307, 311
    work of the mind, 68-69, 325, 836
Malebranche, 230, 255, 257, 265, 269, 288, 358, 424, 548, 686-686a, 800, 818, 888
Man, 508, 594, 631, 640
Manners (modes) of existence, 24
Marsilius Ficinus, 390
Mass (ecclesiastical), 720
Materialism, 486
Materialists, 74, 399, 486
Material world, 476, 538
Mathematicians
    accuracy of, 251, 313, 330, 383-383a, 414
    banter of, 386
    certainty of, 468, 532
    compared to the Schoolmen, 327, 409, 449, 492, 642
    despise sense, 317, 373
    fools, 375
    hypothetical, 406
    insensibles, 391-392
    light and colour without the minds, 376
    meaningless language of, 574, 642
    method and arguments, 409, 449, 574
    Nihilarians, 372, 471
    not call them "Nihilarians," 633
    not to be admired, 368
    nothings of, 330, 384, 394, 449, 466
    on angles, 381, 528
    on curves, 527
    on equality (congruence), 525, 528
    on infinite divisibility, 341-342, 381, 393
    on lines, 393, 519, 525, 575
    on magnitude, 324
    on points, 394
    refute, 633
    subject matter of, 409
    treat with respect, 633
Mathematics
    accuracy of, 313, 330
    Berkeley will improve, 385, 414
    contradictions in, 334

-342-

Mathematics (continued)
  definitions in, 162
  demonstrations in, 163, 336, 466, 697, 750, 755
  extension in, 56
  intermediate ideas in, 697
  mixed, 755, 770
  motion in, 56
  practical, 471
  relation of ideas, 677, 853
  relation to general ideas, 401
  relation to perception, 400, 460, 466
  relation to succession, 400, 460
  relation to the scale, 329
  speculative, 868
Matter
  Berkeley's doctrine deprives philosophers of, 391
  existence of, 128, 131, 359, 597, 686-686a, 718
  extension of, 40, 57, 65, 67, 81, 128, 265, 269-270, 289, 325
  figure of, 81
  God and, 625
  homogeneous portions of, 64
  ideas not in, 20
  idea of, 573
  infinite divisibility of, 17, 67, 81, 322
  Locke on, 89, 265, 573, 695, 718
  relation to cause, 131
  relation to creation, 293
  relation to perception, 359
  relation to points, 325
  relation to thought, 573, 695
  source of doctrine of, 609
  source of evil, 17
  unnecessary, 476
  world consists of, 68
Meaning, 491, 535, 537, 553, 579, 581, 591-593, 631-632, 636, 638, 644, 696, 700, 818, 832
Meditation, 607
Memory 200, 435, 607, 707, 883
Metaphor, 176-176a
Metaphysics, 162-163, 207, 239, 336, 751
Method, 296, 308, 409, 449, 697
Microscope, 94, 360, 511
Microscopic eyes, 97, 116

Mile, 205, 260, 311, 341-341a
Mind
  abstracts, 85
  active, 286, 362a, 870
  composed of will and understanding, 713
  creates beauty, proportion (magnitude), and number, 68, 104, 110, 325, 836
  creates complex ideas, 760
  Descartes on, 798
  distinct from bodies, 863
  distinct from understanding, 362a
  existence independent of, 801
  finiteness of, 292, 350a
  Hobbes on, 796, 798
  identical with perceptions or ideas, 579-581, 651-652
  intermittent, 651-652
  "in the mind," 13, 58, 112, 165, 222, 235, 440, 474-474a, 641, 878, 886
  Locke on, 112, 650, 796, 836
  locus of truth, 696
  makes the sorts (species), 271, 288-289, 836, 874
  meaning of, 579, 581, 847
  no ideas of, 490, 663, 808, 888
  operations of, 176a, 286, 378, 490, 531, 544, 667
  passive, 286, 301, 378
  pure spirit, 870
  relation to colour, 121, 185-185a, 222, 362a, 376, 882
  relation to extension, 270, 287-290, 299, 342, 440, 622, 878, 882, 886
  relation to ideas, 490, 579-581, 637, 650-652, 663, 760, 808, 847, 849, 887-888
  relation to space, 96
  relation to time, 651
  relation to volitions, 849
  thinking substance, 637
  "without the mind," 18, 22-23, 26, 33, 41, 55, 58, 74, 79, 95, 97, 100, 104, 117, 121, 235, 270, 280, 359, 362a-363, 376, 477a, 863, 874, 878, 882, 886
Minima, 60, 64, 88, 261, 267, 287, 321, 365, 480
  sensibilia, 296, 343-345, 439, 441
  tangibilia, 59, 70, 78a, 273, 441-442, 710, 869

Minima (continued)
    visibilia, 65-66, 70, 78a,
        175, 218-219, 250, 256,
        258, 272-273, 277, 296,
        400, 441-442, 464, 489,
        710, 749, 869
Mist, 244, 567, 642
Mite, 364
Mob, 111a, 405, 740. See
    Vulgar, the
Mode, 176, 526, 623, 711,
    785, 798
Molyneux, 49, 197
Molyneux Problem, the, 27, 32,
    49, 58-59, 62, 95, 97, 100,
    121, 174, 183, 294, 307,
    454
Moment, 324, 333, 389
Moon, horizontal, 125, 140,
    171, 233, 244, 302
Morality
    definitions in, 162, 677,
        853
    demonstration in, 158,
        162-163, 239, 336, 669,
        683, 690-691, 697-698,
        729, 755, 569, 804
    principles of, 508
    relation to freedom of
        will, 146, 149, 156-
        159, 508, 626-627, 631,
        745, 879
    relation to uneasiness of
        the will, 166
    relative good in, 569
    responsibility, 694
    self-interest in, 542, 776
    sensual pleasure in, 541,
        769, 773
    signification and inclusion
        of ideas, 677
More, 298
Motion
    absolute and relative, 45,
        99, 129
    abstract idea, 135, 450a,
        865
    apparent, 45
    cause of, 461, 619
    denied, 491
    imagined, 36, 135
    in a vacuum, 36
    local, 193
    Locke on, 451
    mathematical propositions
        about, 56
    measure of, 456
    Newton on, 30, 451-452,
        456
    not in matter, 622
    of light, 655
    of spirit, 193
    relation to colour, 533,
        864, 876

Motion (continued)
    relation to duration, 118
    relation to soul, 622
    relation to thought, 573,
        622
    simple idea, 167, 184, 222,
        550
    space covered in a given
        time, 129
    tangible, 28, 38, 101, 135,
        262
    visible, 27-28, 38, 101,
        135, 262, 864, 876
    will is not, 822
    without the mind, 222
Mystery, 599, 764
Mysteries, holy, 720

N

Names, 153, 570, 602, 700,
    761, 763, 881, 883
Natural
    abilities, 694
    consciousness, 202
    philosophy, 754, 853
Nature
    coexistence of ideas in, 677
    course of, 305, 312, 330,
        535, 550
    distinct from God, 485
    effects of God's will, 734,
        794
    existence of, 305
    laws of, 144, 220-221, 312,
        794, 838, 843
    not yield accuracy, 330
Near-sighted, 170, 199, 742
Nec quid, nec quantum, nec
    quale, 22, 517
Necessary connexion, 181, 195,
    206, 227, 233, 246, 256
Necessity, 794
Negation, 731
Newton
    begs question, 407
    Berkeley will simplify, 383
    cave intellexeris finitas,
        331
    fluxions, 333
    on colour, 388, 453, 505,
        562
    on gravity, 361, 618
    on indivisibles, 374
    on motion, 30, 451-452, 456
    on number, 452
    on quantities, 455
    praised, 372
    Principia (scholium of 8th.
        definition), 316
Nihilarians, 372, 399, 471
Nominal, 793
Nothing, creation out of, 339,
    830-831

Nothings (mathematical points), 75, 263, 337-338, 345, 384, 394, 439, 449, 464, 466, 488
Notion, 96, 540
Number
   Indian, 803
   infinite, 123, 416, 481
   infinite divisibility of, 342
   in themselves, 540
   large, 77, 217
   motion of, 452
   nature of, 458, 759-763, 766
   rational, 482
   relation to denomination, 766
   relation to ideas, 167, 526, 762, 766, 803
   relation to infinitesimals, 354a
   relation to language (words), 762-763
   relation to names, 763, 881
   relation to senses, 762
   relation to succession, 6, 460
   relation to utility, 765-766
   relations, 540, 545
   Roman, 803
   signs, not ideas, 803
   simple and complex ideas, 167, 526
   Solitary Man and, 648

O

Objects
   absolute and relative, 832
   made pleasant by nature, 144
   magnified, 229
   of geometry, 27, 443
   of thought, 427a, 643, 665, 828
Objections, 60, 312, 354a, 414, 620, 795-798, 866
Occasion, 228, 499, 696, 754, 856
"Of & thing," 115
Oldenburgh, 844
Operations of the mind, 176a, 286, 378, 490, 531, 544, 667
Operative faculties, 149, 156, 166
Optic axis, 262, 400, 443
Optic angle, 73, 94, 140, 150, 174-175, 182, 191,

Optic angle (continued) 195-198, 205-206, 210, 213, 215, 218, 229, 233, 302, 603
Opticians, 603
Optics, 207, 366, 726
Orb, visual. See Visual sphere

P

"P" (Earl of Pembroke), 396
Pain, 7, 57, 136, 143, 444, 675, 692, 773, 794, 833
Parabola, 329
Paraboloid, 360
Pardies, 432
Particles
   homogeneous, 60, 293
   (parts of speech), 661, 567
Particulars, 76, 152, 318, 497, 534, 614, 666, 668, 784, 848
Parts, 54, 70, 96, 132, 134, 272, 276-277, 284, 322, 352, 416, 439, 460, 592
Passions, 587
Passive, 286, 301, 378, 623, 643, 777
Paul, St., 827
Pendulum clock, 487
Perception(s)
   active, 672a
   actual, 473, 777, 802
   basis of comparison, 51
   caused by God, 499
   certainty of (no error in), 693, 731, 777
   constant, 57a
   defined, 286, 301, 378
   God not, 813
   identical with object, 585, 589
   immediate and direct, 427-427a
   inactive, 673, 706, 756
   in dark, 294
   inseparable from person, 744
   of breadth, 108
   of colour, 242
   of depth, 106, 108
   of distance, 95, 97, 174, 196
   of extension, 28, 35, 37a, 100, 138, 174, 203, 242-243, 249, 287, 299, 400, 460
   of figure, 28, 112, 173, 466
   of length, 108
   of magnitude, 203, 208
   of motion, 28

Perception(s) (continued)
  of solidity, 106
  of texture, 173
  only of ideas, 50, 74
  passive reception of ideas,
    286, 301, 378, 756
  relation to creation, 60,
    436, 723
  relation to dreams, 843
  relation to existence,
    185a, 280, 588, 646,
    670, 799, 802
  relation to imagination,
    582, 777, 792, 843
  relation to sensation and
    reflexion, 571, 656
  relation to soul, 154, 478
  relation to understanding,
    614
  relation to volition, 645,
    659, 672a, 674, 706,
    756, 833
  relation to will, 659,
    674, 706, 744, 815,
    828, 833, 842
  same as consciousness or
    mind, 580-581
  same as ideas, 280, 478,
    572, 589, 609, 756
  same as ideas and cons-
    ciousness, 578
  smell, 138
  taste, 138
  understanding composed of,
    587, 614
  unperceived, 52, 74, 249,
    347, 472, 579, 656
Percipere (and percipi), 429
Perfection, 786, 835
Peripheries. See Circles,
  circumference of
Person, 14, 24-25, 36, 142,
  185, 192, 194a, 200, 523,
  590, 713
Personalia (Berkeley), 266,
  279, 300, 397-398, 465,
  634
Petitio principii, 263, 462
Phantasm, 807
Philosophy (philosophers)
  experimental, 406, 498
  lose matter, 391
  natural, 403, 406, 754,
    853
  on absolute and relative
    things, 832
  on limits of reason, 747,
    859-860
  the new, 781, 786
  the old, 491, 682, 781
Physiques, 430, 702
Picture (painting), 227

Pictures, retinal (retinal
  images), 204-205, 211, 256,
  268, 274-275, 302a
  inverted, 102, 126, 148,
    172, 190, 224-225, 227,
    278, 307
Plain (plane), 204, 283-284
Plastic virtue, 617
Platonic, 300
Pleasure
  as means and end, 852
  as recreation, 852
  determined by laws of
    nature, 144
  relation to profit, 541
  See Pleasure and pain
Pleasure and pain
  determined by laws of
    nature, 144
  felt, 136
  indifference to, 143
  of eye and ear, 787
  relation to extension, 57
  relation to minima, 321
  relation to perception, 833
  relation to time, 7
  relation to volition, 692
  sensual, 769, 773
Points
  absolute, 119
  abstract, 394
  abstract unity is, 75
  as terminations, 119
  basis of equality, 530
  in a foot (length), 469,
    475, 558
  mathematical, 345, 394, 770
  number of, 440
  of circle, 445-446, 462,
    510
  of curved line, 520, 575
  of distance, 253, 447
  of extension, 325, 353,
    365, 475-475a
  of intersection, 85
  of length, 365
  of line, 132, 253, 261,
    267, 445-447, 470, 516
  of matter, 325
  of square, 469
  of surface, 132
  sorts of, 440
  tangible, 78a, 295
  visible, 62, 78a, 97, 116,
    169, 295, 400, 835
  See Minima
Politics, 560
Polygon, 527
Position, 85, 87, 120, 132,
  148, 172
Possibility, 686
Potentia, 141-142, 159

Power (powers)
  combinations of rejected, 802
  existence of, 293a
  in active being, 52
  number of, 84
  of unperformed wills, 107
  one simple perfect, 282
  primary ideas are, 41
  relation to bodies, 80, 100, 112, 282
  relation to cause, 100, 228, 282, 293-293a, 433, 461
  relation to God, 41, 52, 433
  relation to will, 131, 155, 621, 699
  simple or complex idea, 134, 282, 461, 493
  state of unperceived bodies, 52, 282, 293a
  to perceive, 228
Preface. See Introduction
Prejudice, 163, 239, 465, 576, 583, 603
Prescience, 145-146, 875
Present (time), 839, 851
Preternatural consciousness, 202
Pride, 694
Primary and secondary ideas, 20, 41, 76, 112, 265, 362-363, 392, 477a, 534
Principle(s), 223, 288, 312, 383, 395, 508, 542, 584, 726, 734, 769, 788, 811, 874
Principle(s), my, 303, 305, 363, 407-408, 429
Principle, the, 285, 291, 304, 379-380, 402, 410-411, 429, 556
Profit, 541
Progression
  mathematical, 332
  of wills, 161
Proof. See Demonstration
Propension, 686
Properties, 177a, 348, 597, 812, 878
Proportion
  meer, 365
  of circumference and diameter of circles, 340, 457, 481-482
  of extensions, 269
  of gravity to gravity (Newton), 361
  of infinite quantities, 448
  of lines, 458, 470
  of magnitude and faint vision, 244

Proportion (continued)
  of parts of the visual sphere, 204, 219
  of pleasure and pain, 692
  of points, 470
  of space and velocity, 99, 130
  of visible and tangible extension, 54, 69, 203
  of visible and tangible magnitude, 208, 213
  of visible and tangible motion, 38
  work of the mind, 836
Propositions
  complex, 809
  identical, 728
  mathematical, 56, 117, 163
  meaning of, 720
  mental, 731, 738, 793, 809
  nominal, 793
  sorts of, 793-793a
  trifling, 771
Purblind, 170, 199, 742
Purpose (Berkeley's), 642, 679
Pythagorean theorem, 500

Q

Qualities
  Cartesians on, 424a, 477a
  in minimum tangibile, 442
  primary and secondary. See Ideas, primary and secondary
  sensible, 439-440, 517, 711
  tangible, 43, 288a, 363a, 442, 711
  visible, 43, 288a, 363a
Quantities, 448

R

Radius, 97, 169, 462
Raphson, 298, 827
Rays
  of air, 152
  of light, 152, 453, 662
Real, 823
Reality, 80, 550, 783, 807
Reason
  finite, 747
  in morality, 569
  limitation of, 747
  relation to faith (revelation), 584, 720
  relation to sensation, 373, 466
  relation to the Principle, 380, 411
Reasoning
  about ideas or things, 804, 817

Reasoning (continued)
  about infinitesimals, 354, 421
  errors in, 544
  pure, 638
  relation to ideas, 638, 804, 817
  relation to visual sphere, 204
  subject of, 804
  without words, 693, 719, 804, 883
Rectify. See Circle, squaring of
Reflection
  and sensation, 571, 656, 670, 724, 746
  ideas of, 585, 656, 670
  of light, 151-152, 662
Relations, 134, 461, 503, 540, 545, 677, 733, 739, 853
Relative, 119, 832
Religion, 298, 824
Representation, 260, 341
Rerum natura, 96, 305, 330, 550
Resemblances, See Ideas, likeness of and Comparison
Responsibility, moral, 694
Rest, 45
Resurrection, 127
Retina, 169, 186, 214
Retinal images, 204-205, 211, 256, 268, 274-275, 302a
  inverted, 102, 126, 148, 172, 190, 224-225, 227, 278, 307
Revelation, 720
Revolutions, 12
Roman numerals, 803
Roots, 764
Rough, 226
Royal Society, 506
Rules, 682, 688, 691, 880

S

Scale, 329, 332
Scaliger, 370
Scepticism, 80, 304, 411, 517a, 563, 606
  Berkeley's early, 266
Sceptics, 79, 491, 747
Schoolmen (scholastics)
  abstract ideas of, 779
  compared to mathematicians, 327, 409, 449, 492, 642
  confused by words, 642
  metaphysiques of 207
  on entia realia and entia rationis, 546
  on heaven, 539

Schoolmen (continued)
  on mind, 870
  on pure act, 870
  on substance, 724
  on will, 797
  speak favorably of, 716
  subtle style of, 300
Science, 379-380, 564, 702, 883
Scripture, 281, 404-405, 455, 686, 720
Secondary. See Ideas, primary and secondary
Self, 362a, 523, 547, 752, 847
Self-interest, 542
Sensation
  colour a, 111
  demonstrates God, 838
  extension a, 18, 34, 111, 299, 440
  ideas from without, 378
  insensible, 391
  judged by senses not by reason, 373
  like only a sensation, 46
  material world unnecessary for, 476
  mind passive in, 286
  motion a, 36
  particular ideas, 666
  reflection and, 571, 585, 656, 670, 724, 746, 818
  relation to magnitude, 197
  relation to laws of nature, 838
  relation to minds, 752
  relation to rays, 152
  shape a, 112
  time a, 13, 647
Senses
  acute, 82
  certainty in, 740
  common, 751
  compared, 647
  despised, 317, 539, 748
  heterogeneity of. See Heterogeneity
  ideas of, 818, 823
  judge sensations, 373, 466
  numbers and, 762
  source of all ideas, 539, 779
  trust, 539, 748, 794
  yield sensations, 378
Sensibile. See Minima, sensibilia
Sensual pleasure, 769, 773
Sergeant, 840
Shame, 193, 231
Sight
  acute, 250
  breadth by, 108
  bulk by, 283-284
  clearness of, 835

-348-

Sight (continued)
  colour only by, 136, 242
  confused, 147, 197, 206, 208, 232, 244, 256, 283-284, 296a, 303, 400, 835
  congruence of angles by, 140, 215, 528, 531
  depth by, 106
  distance by, 95, 169, 174, 196, 215, 220a, 231, 307, 603, 774
  distinctness of, 206, 208, 243, 283-284, 296a, 835
  dullness of, 250
  enlargement of, 175, 296, 749, 835
  extension by, 35, 87, 174, 215-216
  faintness of, 206, 244, 256, 302
  heterogeneous with other senses, 28, 38, 43, 49, 54-55, 57, 59, 61, 69-70, 91, 95, 100-101, 103, 106, 108, 136-138, 148, 173-174, 181, 183, 224-227, 240-241, 243, 246, 256, 295, 647
  ideas intromitted by, 95, 241, 287, 454, 496, 670
  length by, 108
  lines by, 124, 341-341a, 389
  magnitude by, 197, 203-204, 311
  motion by, 27-28, 38, 101, 135, 262, 864, 876
  near, 296
  perceives same ideas as touch, 647
  relation to man born blind (the Molyneux Problem), 27, 32, 49, 58-59, 62, 95, 97, 100, 121, 174, 183, 294, 307, 454
  solidity by, 106, 215
  space by, 135
  successive, 283-284, 400, 443
  surfaces by, 35, 283
  vigorousness of, 206
Signification, 286, 293, 544, 626, 677, 696, 727a, 831, 850
Signs, 554, 693, 732, 750, 767, 803, 883
Signum, 344
Similar, 309, 340, 481
Simple ideas. See Ideas, simple and complex
Singling, 139, 321

Situation, 302a, 307. See Position
Size. See Magnitude
Sleep, 651, 857
Slowness, 99
Smell, 137-138, 193, 241, 265, 589, 862, 877
Smooth, 226
Society, the Royal, 506
Soft, 136, 226
Solidity, 74, 78, 105-106, 114, 215, 512, 533, 840
Solitary Man, 566, 588, 592, 607, 648, 727-727a
Sorts, 288-289, 440
Sorting, 139
Soul
  being of, 44
  constituted by ideas, 478, 577, 704
  definition of, 44, 154, 178
  distinct from its ideas, 478-478a
  essence of, 44
  existence of, 479, 563, 577
  existence of during sleep, 479
  identical with the will, 478a, 814
  immortality of, 14, 814
  incorruptible, 814
  knowledge of, 25, 154, 576-576a
  no idea of, 230, 576-576a
Sounds, 152, 223, 240, 363, 497, 576, 710, 727, 834, 861
Space
  abstract, 96, 452
  Bayle on, 424
  between bodies, 632
  colour of, 454
  congruent, 529
  empty, 583
  equal, 529
  existence of, 135
  extension of, 78, 96, 105
  infinite, 90, 135, 415, 695
  Malebranche on, 424
  meaning of, 529
  motion of parts of, 452
  not eternal, 695
  not infinite, 695
  not simple idea, 105
  relation to motion, 99, 129, 452
  size of, 417-418
  tangible, 454
  visible, 454
Species, 271, 288, 561, 566, 703, 758, 836

Speculum, 182, 186-189, 191, 198-199
Speech. See Language
Sphere, 32, 419
  of retina, 214
  of vision, 97, 122, 169, 175, 204-205, 208, 213-214, 219, 256, 296, 475, 749, 774
Spinoza, 824-827, 831, 844-845
Spirit
  active, 437a, 829, 848, 850, 870-871
  agent, 850
  causes, 829, 850
  effects of, 788
  existence of, 437
  God is, 838
  only one, 788
  perfection of, 786
  purus actus, 701, 828
  relation to ideas, 829, 847, 849, 872, 887
  relation to thing, 872
  relation to understanding, 848, 871
  relation to will, 692, 788, 828-829, 848-849, 871
  substance, 701, 829
Spirits, superior, 610, 835
Sprat, 506
Square, 29, 258-259, 469, 500
Squaring the circle, 245, 249-251, 395, 457-458, 510-511
Stillingfleetians, 700
Stone, 107
Straight lines, 180
Straining, 206, 210
Style (Berkeley's), 300, 858
Subject, 76, 808
Subsist, 109
Substance
  collection of simple ideas, 179
  combinations of thoughts, 194
  consists of, 512
  Descartes on, 785, 795
  existence of, 597
  idea of, 597, 700, 724
  Locke on, 80, 601, 700, 724
  material, 17, 74, 89, 597, 609
  of body, 512, 517, 701
  of soul, 44
  of spirit, 701, 829
  of wood, 179
  philosophic and non-philosophic view of, 517
  Schoolmen's sense of, 724

Substance (continued)
  seen and felt, 724
  term used by Aristotle and Church Fathers, 413
  thinking, 637
  vulgar sense, 724
Substantial forms, 617
Substratum, 80, 672
Subtangent, 329
Subtle matter, 388
Succession, 6, 53-53a, 132-133, 167, 460
  of ideas, 3-4, 16, 39, 92, 262, 629, 651
Summum bonum, 769
Sun, 311
Surds, 306, 469, 482
Surface, 31, 35, 124, 132, 205, 213, 215, 259, 528
Swiftness, 15-16, 39, 99

T

Tangibile. See Minima, tangibilia
Taste, 137-138, 193, 240-241, 497
Tautology, 738
Termination (end), 31, 119, 319
Texture, 173
Theology, 584
Theorems, 532
Thief and paradise, 127
Thing
  active and inactive, 673
  conscious, 24
  definition of, 369
  existence of, 656, 673
  likeness of, 47
  perceived, 656, 673
  relation of the word "thing" to archetype, 689
  relation of the word "thing" to ideas, 369, 657a, 689
  relation of the word "thing" to volition and will, 644, 689, 807-808, 872
  relation of the word "thing" to the word "idea," 644, 757, 872
  subject of reasoning, 804
  thoughtless, 37-37a, 228
Thinking substance, 637
Thinking thing, 109
Thought (thoughts), 22, 33, 37a, 153, 164, 178, 220, 228, 280, 282, 286, 293, 378, 513, 600, 693, 752
  See Ideas
Time
  death and, 83, 127, 390, 651
  duration of, 5, 12, 83, 118

Time (continued)
  foretelling, 145
  God and, 3, 92
  infinite divisibility of, 8, 10, 83
  in pain and pleasure, 7
  intermittent, 83
  no common present, 9
  relation to motion, 129-130, 655
  relation to simple ideas, 167
  relative, 48
  seconds of, 488
  sensation, 13, 647
  succession of ideas, 3, 4, 6, 12, 15-16, 39, 92, 167, 460, 590
  without the mind, 222
Touch, 28, 42-43, 49, 54, 59, 61, 69-70, 78, 95, 100-101, 103, 108, 114, 135, 138, 224-227, 240, 243, 246, 287, 528, 531, 632, 647, 840
Train of ideas, 4, 629
Trances, 651
Transubstantiation, 350
Treatise, the, 378a, 396, 562, 719
Tree (trees), 98, 107
Triangle, 528-530, 687
Trinity, Holy, 310, 350, 584
Truth, 270, 279, 376, 379, 392, 396, 467, 532, 658
  abstract idea, 873
  available to less intelligent, 742
  discovery of 742
  eternal, 735
  general, 555
  method of presenting, 163, 185
  only in one's own mind, 521, 696
  real, 606
  relation to perception, 693
  relation to words, 555, 696
  sorts of, 676

U

Understanding
  an action, 821, 854
  as spirit, 871
  distinct from mind, 362a, 848
  included in spirit, 848
  in God, 812
  locus of truth and knowledge, 521
  mind is will and, 713

Understanding (continued)
  no error in, 816
  not a faculty, 848, 871
  relation to desire, 854
  relation to ideas, 579, 587, 614, 681, 848
  relation to meaning of words, 544
  relation to will, 614a, 641, 643, 681, 708, 713, 812, 820-821, 828, 841, 854, 871
Uneasiness, moves the will, 145a, 166, 357, 423, 598, 610-611a, 613, 624, 628, 630, 653, 707, 743, 833, 857
Uniform, 96, 242, 280, 378
Unit, 263
Unite (unity), 75, 104, 342, 545, 714, 746
Universals, 826
Upper, 148
Utility, 765-766

V

Vacuum, 36
Velocity, 130. See Motion, swiftness of
Veritas, 873. See Truth
Veritates aeternae, 735, 831
Vessels, 367, 387
Vice and virtue, 149, 193, 669
Vis
  attractrix, 619
  Impressa, 456
  Inertia, 619
Vision. See Sight
Visual orb. See Visual sphere
Visual sphere, 97, 122, 169, 175, 204-205, 208, 213-214, 219, 256, 296, 475, 749, 774
Volition
  abstract idea, 867
  an act, 621
  essence of, 630
  only one at once, 647
  relation to mind, 286, 629, 635
  without idea, 624
  without perception, 645
  without uneasiness, 624, 628, 630
  word not used by vulgar, 867
  See Will
Vries, de, 887-888
Vulgar, the, 405, 408, 544, 552, 643, 703, 724-725, 772, 867. See Mob

W

Wallis, 482, 834, 837
Warm, 136
Will
    abstract idea, 867, 871
    active, 131, 155, 643, 706, 777, 788, 828, 854, 857
    as a faculty, 871
    cause, the only, 131, 155, 499-499a
    distinct from idea or object, 612-613, 624, 643, 658, 706, 806, 847
    distinct from mind, 849
    distinct from spirit, 849
    effects of, 788
    essence of, 630
    existence of, 792
    freedom of, 149, 156-157, 627, 631, 879
    Hobbes on, 797
    infinite regression of, 160-161, 797
    in God, 812
    in heaven, 357, 423
    immortal, 814
    incorruptible, 814
    inseparable from ideas, 841-842
    knowledge of, 875
    locus of error, 816
    mind is understanding and, 713
    no idea of, 643, 657-661, 663, 665, 669, 672, 706, 756, 808, 828
    none without idea, 833, 842
    not distinct from particular ideas, 848
    not imaginable, 828
    not intelligible, 828
    not motion, 822
    objects of, 854
    only one, 788
    particles stand for, 667
    power, 131, 155, 621, 699
    principle of personal identity, 194a
    pure act, 828
    relation to desire, 597, 854
    relation to existence of self, 791
    relation to memory, 707
    relation to mind, 629, 635, 713, 849
    relation to morality, 669, 694
    relation to passions, 587

Will (continued)
    relation to perception, 659, 674, 706, 744, 815, 828, 833, 842
    relation to soul, 154, 478a, 788, 828
    relation to spirit, 692, 788, 828, 848-849
    relation to understanding, 614a, 643, 681, 708, 713, 820, 841, 854, 871
    relation to volitions, 615, 681
    relation to word "thing," 689
    Schoolmen on, 797
    uneasiness of, 145a, 166, 357, 423, 598, 610-611a, 613, 624, 628, 630, 653, 707, 743, 833, 857
    unity of, 714
    unperformed, 107
    word related to word "can," 616
Words
    abuse of, 178, 537, 544, 565, 579, 592, 608, 627, 639, 696, 702
    arbitrary, 732
    cause of ignorance and confusion, 642
    certainty about, 719, 730-731
    defects of, 223, 636
    demonstration using, 551, 562, 690, 705, 719, 730-732, 734, 750, 778, 804
    inadequate for abstract ideas, 513
    meaning of, 162, 178, 491, 535, 537, 544, 553, 579, 581, 591-593, 631-632, 636, 638, 641, 644, 696, 700, 720, 818, 832
    metaphorical, 176-176a
    mist of, 642
    relation to ideas, 220, 223, 551-552, 555, 561, 565-566, 584, 591, 595, 600, 602, 607, 626, 638, 641, 661, 667, 671, 693, 719, 727, 730a, 736, 750
    relation to knowledge, 607, 693, 750, 883
    relation to numbers, 763
    relation to truth, 696
    Schoolmen, mathematicians, lawyers, and divines on, 642

Words (continued)
    stand only for ideas, 312, 356, 378
    thought without, 600, 693, 719
    use of, 495, 544, 565, 608, 696
    veil of, 642
    without ideas, 223, 354a, 356, 378, 422, 494-495, 513, 600, 693, 719, 727
World, 22-23, 68, 257, 397, 476, 517, 538, 566, 588
Worm, 640
Worship, 705
Writing, preserves knowledge, 607